Science in Society

Also by Matthew David

*Social Research: The Basics* (with Carole D. Sutton)

*Knowledge Lost in Information* (with D. Zeitlyn and J. Bex)

# Science in Society

Matthew David

palgrave
macmillan

First published 2005 by
PALGRAVE MACMILLAN
Houndmills, Basingstoke, Hampshire RG21 6XS and
175 Fifth Avenue, New York, N.Y. 10010
Companies and representatives throughout the world

PALGRAVE MACMILLAN is the global academic imprint of the Palgrave Macmillan division of St. Martin's Press, LLC and of Palgrave Macmillan Ltd. Macmillan® is a registered trademark in the United States, United Kingdom and other countries. Palgrave is a registered trademark in the European Union and other countries.

ISBN-13:978–0–333–99347–7 hardback
ISBN-10:0–333–99347–0 hardback
ISBN-13:978–0–333–99348–4 paperback
ISBN-10:0–333–99348–9 paperback

This book is printed on paper suitable for recycling and made from fully managed and sustained forest sources.

A catalogue record for this book is available from the British Library.

A catalog record for this book is available from the Library of Congress.

10   9   8   7   6   5   4   3   2   1
14   13   12   11   10   09   08   07   06   05

Printed in China

*In memory of **Sam Nelson** 1965–2001*

# Contents

## PART TWO    THEORETICAL APPROACHES

# List of Tables

# Acknowledgements

This book has greatly benefited from the ideas and assistance of many people. Thanks then goes to: Alison Anderson, Barry Barnes, Jane Bex, David Brockington, Lea Campbell, Sue Child, Tracey Collett, Harry Collins, Elizabeth Ettorre, Peter Glasner, Catharine Gray, Claire Heristchi, Marta Herrero, Devorah Kalekin-Fishman, Barbara Katz Rothman, Sheree Keep, Lauren Langman, David Mason, Kevin Meethan, Steve Miles, Alan Petersen, Keith Povey, Chris Rootes, Hilary Rose, Emily Salz, Mike Sheaff, Bevereley Tarquini, Clare Wilkinson, Iain Wilkinson, Malcolm Williams, Sergei Yerofeyev, Steve Yearley, and David Zeitlyn. And a special thanks also to my family and friends outside academia from whom this book did not benefit but I did.

MATTHEW DAVID

# Introduction

The sociology of science (alongside the wider field of science and technology studies) asks a number of questions about science and the wider society. Note that science is seen as a part of society and not something 'outside' it. To say that science is a social activity should not be controversial, even if some of the questions that arise from this observation are highly contentious. Even Lewis Wolpert (1992), perhaps the keenest defender of science against sociological questioning, declares that science is 'unnatural'. By this he means that science requires its practitioners to suspend both 'common-sense' assumptions and immediate impressions. Such a suspension requires training and a community of practitioners interacting and regulating each other. Science is not simply an act of unmediated looking. This admission that science is a social activity, rather than something outside social life, does not in itself lead to the conclusion that science is simply 'ideology', or a practical tool of dominant social groups. However, such possibilities require investigation. So what are the questions which the sociology of science asks? I suggest there are two basic questions: (1) Can scientific knowledge claim to be universal knowledge? (2) Does science facilitate human emancipation? These questions can be posed in many different ways, and have been asked by a range of social researchers over the course of the twentieth century, and now beyond.

## Particularism or Universalism?

Can science claim to offer a method of knowledge generation that transcends the particularities of specific cultures and allows the production of knowledge that is 'true' by some universal standard? Alternatively, is all knowledge relative?

## Emancipation or Domination?

Has science fostered a culture of critical enquiry and material security or has it justified and assisted the dominance of an elite while at the same time undermining the lifeworld of all living things?

Truth (often equated with science) and freedom (personal choice and/or political liberty) represent *the* two dominant metanarratives of modernity (Lyotard 1986[1979]). Modernity is premised upon the positive association of these two objectives. Modern faith in 'progress' is the belief that more truth leads to more freedom and vice versa. The postmodern outlook is premised upon doubting the possibility of 'more truth', and/or 'more freedom', and/or doubting the link between them (Mills 1959:166). Can science deliver truth and will more truth/ science bring 'progress' in the sense of 'human freedom'?

In recent years a number of rich traditions of research have emerged or developed within the sociology of science. These offer insights into ongoing changes. Debates within this field have tended to be relatively self-contained within specific traditions, with reference to other traditions being very limited and stilted. Within the sociology of science field, feminist, Marxist, interests-theory and ethnographic/discursive accounts have become largely self-contained, with authors displaying relative indifference or hostility to researchers in other 'camps'.

The purpose of this book is to show that, while differences exist between the dominant perspectives within the sociology of science, these differences are often exaggerated in ways typical of career-building and academic advancement, but which stifle intellectual development. This book is unique in providing a balanced and comprehensive account of the range of alternative approaches, as well as in demonstrating the value of combining and/or critically contrasting approaches when researching specific scientific topics.

Part One of this book contains three chapters. Chapter 1 outlines the roots of the sociology of science from the nineteenth century to the end of the 1960s. This discussion highlights the divergent approaches to the two core questions outlined above, places these in historical context, and also demonstrates underlying continuities that were developed and challenged by the contemporary sociology of scientific knowledge that first emerged in the 1970s. Chapter 2 sets out the purpose of this book as well as its theoretical framework: reflexive epistemological diversity. Chapter 3 addresses the relationship between science and technology in contemporary society. The argument that science and technology can best be understood together is defended with reference to debates over *Risk* that have developed alongside the sociology of science and technology, again since the 1970s.

Part Two contains four chapters, each one outlining one of the dominant perspectives in today's sociology of scientific knowledge. Chapter 4 introduces what is sometimes called the 'strong programme' or the 'interests perspective' in the sociology of science. Chapter 5 addresses the 'ethnographic' and 'discursive' perspectives. Chapter 6 looks at Marxist approaches to the study of science and Chapter 7 looks at feminist perspectives.

Part Three presents three 'case-studies'. Chapters 8, 9 and 10 outline research from each of the four traditions discussed in Part Two in the fields of medical genetics, genetic accounts of human behaviour and genetically modified foods.

Part Four (Chapter 11) concludes with an overview of the value and the limits of sociological approaches to contemporary technoscience. The case for *reflexive epistemological diversity* is restated and clarified in the light of the preceding chapters.

# Part One

## Emergence and Innovation

# 1

# An Introduction to Issues and Forebears

## The Emergence of a Sociology of Science

The sociology of scientific knowledge today addresses questions that would have seemed entirely beyond the scope of sociology only a generation ago. The idea that science was itself something that could be studied sociologically took a long time to emerge, largely because sociology's founders preferred to emphasize the reverse: that society could be studied scientifically and sociology was the way to do just that. To have questioned science itself as a source or method of generating 'truth' would have undermined the project of establishing a 'social science'.

The existence today of a field of study within sociology addressing science, its social and institutional structure, its knowledge claims and its role, should not lead anyone to conclude that a consensus has emerged either within sociology or beyond as to the legitimacy of such an enterprise. Even within the sociology of science conflict rages as to just what it is that sociologists might be able to say about 'science'.

Outlined below is a brief history of ideas about science within the sociological tradition. This shows how tensions existed right from the birth of the discipline, over the social 'function' of science (for liberation or domination), and even over the nature of scientific knowledge (as truth or ideology), though this latter issue was always marginal.

## Early Sociological Approaches

Karl Marx was the quintessential Victorian believer in science. While his methods would not be recognized as scientific today he saw science and

3

materialism as the bedrock of human progress, both intellectually and socially. Marx and Engels always referred to themselves as materialists and scientific socialists (Marx and Engels 1970; Engels 1940). Their socialism, they believed, was 'grounded' in a the study of real social processes, their advocacy of revolution, the spur to objective social forces already at work in the world. Engels counterposed utopian and scientific socialism (1988). This was a reference to the belief, held by Marx and Engels (1971[1848]), that the forces governing social organization and social transformation were 'material' forces to be analysed by scientific methods. Utopians, from this position, were those who dreamt of better worlds but had no way of relating them to reality, or of bringing them into reality.

Marx sought to dedicate his text *Capital* to Charles Darwin (Woods and Grant 1995). However, Darwin never read past the first few pages of the copy sent to him (Rose and Rose 2000:111). Marx saw Darwin's materialism as being as radically anti-idealistic as his own. Yet it was Engels himself who first noted the potentially ideological residues that pervaded Darwin's account of 'natural' selection. It was no accident that Darwin's account of nature was 'simply the transference from society to organic nature of Hobbes' theory of the war of each against all' (Engels cited in Dickens 2000:26). Marx went on to write that 'it is remarkable how Darwin recognises in beasts and plants his English society with its divisions of labour, competition, opening up of new markets, "inventions" and the Malthusian "struggle for existence"' (cited in Dickens 2000:29). However, these reservations were not taken very far at the time. Marx observed that Newton's atomistic view of the universe coincided with the rise of a money-based economy in which everything is broken down and exchanged (a theme taken up and developed by the Marxist Gideon Freudenthal (1986)). Again, this was only an aside set against Marx's more general endorsement of science.

There is, then, a tension in Marx and Engels's own writing. On one side science is a material force dispelling illusions (part of the productive forces brought about by capitalism and which would help lay the foundations for a freer society in the future). On the other, science is an ideological superstructure of capitalism, a system keen to project its own social arrangements into the frame of natural inevitability. While these tensions were largely latent, the greater emphasis being placed on the former over the latter, they were to develop within Marxist accounts of science in future generations. Chapter 6 examines the development of Marxist theories of science in more detail.

Early German sociology was ambivalent about the consequences of modern science. In Weber's discussion of *Science as a Vocation* (1991b:129–56) modern science gives humanity in general an understanding of the physical world that far exceeds anything that could have been generated by premodern thinking. However, the state of knowledge held by any one individual is doubly impoverished; first by the impending inevitability of any knowledge being discredited in the future, and second by knowledge's fragmented nature. All scientific knowledge must one day be replaced by new knowledge. All certainties are certain to one day be rejected as misconceptions. What any one person can possibly know within a modern scientific division of intellectual labour is only ever one splinter within the tree of knowledge. Just as with bureaucratic rule, so the collective power affected by science renders the individuals who comprise these institutions increasingly dependent. Weber also felt the irony of a pursuit of truth that sought to rid us of our illusions only to leave us thereby disillusioned. 'The polar icy darkness in which no flower blooms' (1991a:128) is Weber's depiction of a world in which all sacredness is extracted, from both the physical and the social realm.

Early French sociology was more enthusiastic about creating a 'science of society'. Emile Durkheim's *The Rules of Sociological Method* (1982[1895]) attempted to give sociology a scientific basis. However, Durkheim's attempts to understand the systematic processes that underpinned individual thoughts and actions led him to a rather ambiguous position. If the way the world is seen by members of society is best understood with reference to the operations of the social systems those individuals are a part of, what then? To what extent are the modern understandings of the world (those produced within a scientific framework) also products of a particular set of social processes? While Durkheim's analysis of 'primitive' belief systems led him to suggest that such beliefs were best understood as functional expressions of social systems (1995[1912]), he held back from any such conclusions about the 'modern' beliefs provided by science. Durkheim could accept that Australian aboriginal myths of origin and knowing were useful both as practical know-how and as stories that bind communities together. He was less willing to accept fully that modern science might also be infused with this double-edged character, being a map of physical reality shaped by, and reinforcing, the social relationships in which it was created.

While Durkheim believed in the superiority of modern science over traditional world views, his account of functional belief, and of the social foundations of 'ways of seeing', were to prefigure subsequent developments in the 'sociology of science'. This new sociological field would at first (in the work of Robert Merton) seek primarily to address the question; what were the social conditions that enabled the rise of modern science? However, later writers (notably Barry Barnes), drawing upon Durkheim's account of functional belief, would come to question whether scientific knowledge was as much the product of the social relations in which it was formed as were other realms of belief.

Early sociological attention to science largely accepted that science was a method of acquiring 'true' knowledge. Doubts, where expressed, were largely put to the margins. Regarding the social role of science in promoting human liberation or domination, there was greater tension, though still the emphasis was largely on the former over the latter.

# Three World Wars

In the period between the First and Second World Wars, and in the early years of the cold war, new approaches developed that drew together elements of what had gone before, but in new and interesting ways. Karl Mannheim combined elements of Marx and Weber. J. D. Bernal developed the work of Karl Marx. Robert Merton combined elements of Weber and Durkheim in opposition to the work of Marxist writers. It will be pointed out in this section that despite ideological differences, the social and economic dynamics of the cold war period up until the late 1960s acted to incorporate all major approaches. Differences and challenges within and between different traditions were suppressed for a generation.

## *The Sociology of Knowledge*

Karl Mannheim's (1960[1928]) *Ideology and Utopia* sought to develop a general theory of ideology, or a sociology of knowledge. Mannheim set out three theories of ideology. The 'particular theory of ideology' (1960:57) refers to a common mode of everyday thinking as well as something characteristic of social and political debate and theory. To hold a particular theory of ideology is to hold the view that someone else or a group of people think a particular thing because of the social position they occupy. The 'total theory of ideology' (1960:59) is the name given by Mannheim to the view that a person or group's whole outlook is a manifestation of their social position. Mannheim suggests that Marx's theory of capitalist ideology is the most sophisticated manifestation of a total theory of ideology. However, Marx did not develop a full sociology of knowledge. Marx was an antagonist for what he saw as objective 'truth' against 'ideology'. Mannheim challenges this distinction in his development of a 'general theory of ideology' (1960:68). It is commonplace to see the whole of another's worldview as a manifestation of their 'ideology'. What would happen if you turned your critical reasoning upon yourself? To include your own outlook as equally the product of its social location would allow a general theory of ideology. Mannheim suggests that under normal conditions the possibility of holding a general theory of ideology are remote, and that only a relatively detached relation to the conflicts of everyday economic and political life would enable such an outlook. Mannheim suggested that a 'relatively class-less intelligentsia', made up of people from across the social spectrum, and occupying a relatively detached position in relation to wider social conflicts, would be best able to adopt such an 'end-of-ideology' outlook. Of course, Mannheim's advocacy of a 'third way' can be seen as just another ideological stance built upon the growth of a white-collar, educated class of non-owners and non-workers within twentieth-century capitalism. Such a belief in their own neutrality could be said to be serving the interests of that class (see Gouldner 1979). This of course would be to extend the logic of Mannheim's own 'sociology of knowledge' to itself. Mannheim rejects the claim that knowledge is 'simply' relative. To admit this would be to suggest that no knowledge is better than any other, only different. Mannheim does not want to say this and in fact argues that, in his theory, knowledge is 'relational' rather than 'relative' (1960:70–1). All knowledge has its roots in the social situation out of which it emerges, but that does not mean the knowledge produced is only the product of those roots. Some social situations are more conducive to clarity and open-minded enquiry than others. Mannheim believed that the existence of a relatively open intelligentsia, drawing in the best minds from all classes, would be the social situation best suited to generating knowledge. Within this relatively classless intelligentsia the natural sciences are seen as exemplary (1960:146–53). It is at this point that Mannheim points out that his theory of knowledge is really only a theory about social knowledge and beliefs. He effectively excludes knowledge of the natural world, or at least that ordered and obtained by modern scientific methods. In this way, Mannheim steps back from the radical possibilities of his own thinking. Only later would others take his insights further.

## The Social Function of Science

John Desmond Bernal's (1964[1939]) *The Social Function of Science* is a founding text in the social study of science and science policy. There was a near-universal, yet one-dimensional, application of elements of his work, by capitalist and Soviet socialist states alike, in the period after it was published. This, and significant limitations in Bernal's own questioning of science's objectivity, also make his legacy a point of critical (and often amnesic) departure for today's sociology of science and technology.

Bernal's work as a crystallographer laid the foundations for identifying the structure of DNA. His studies on the history and social relations of science reflected a Marxist politics forged in the inter-war economic depression and struggle against fascism. Bernal's vision was of a world beyond want, war and ignorance, where science was in the vanguard on all fronts, as the instrument of enlightenment against physical, social and psychological oppression. Eric Hobsbawm (1999:xi) characterizes Bernal as 'the most influential prophet of the unlimited potential of science for progress'. Brenda Swann (1999:xxv) adds that for Bernal 'The role of science should be to fulfil human needs'. To this end Bernal's *The Social Function of Science* set out to catalogue the achievements, condition and potential of science, alongside the fetters that restrain its potential.

Chris Freeman (1999) sums up the first side of this equation in four propositions put forward in Bernal's work. First, science is the greatest achievement of

.ian reason and action. Second, science is driven by the desire for truth and .ne satisfaction of human needs. Third, as science develops, so new forms of social and political organization are required to harness rather than to fetter such potential. Finally, there are no intrinsic limitations to human potential once we embrace reason and science over tradition and ignorance. Dispensing with God, man will reach the heavens through science, and will live forever. Rose and Rose (1999:135) suggest of Bernal: 'His science and his politics were integral to his enlightenment universalism. Science served Marxism, and Marxism served humanity, justice and freedom.'

But *The Social Function of Science* also sets out three obstacles in the way of such potential. First, reactionary governments, not grasping the potential of science, fail to invest in research. Bernal's monumental labour was to calculate the total research activity in Britain in 1936 to be around 4 million pounds, around 0.1 per cent of national income. This, he calculated, was 6 times less than in the United States and 8 times less than in the Soviet Union. While his calculations were crude, this work gave birth to a new field of research, now universal in the advanced economies of the world. Bernal asserted the need for a rapid and radical expansion in research funding, presenting an empirical case for the strong causal link between levels of research and levels of economic growth. The second constraint was the misallocation of what research money there was to unproductive fields, most particularly to military research and certain unnecessary consumer products. Bernal devoted much of his life to the campaign for peace and disarmament. Finally, there were inefficiencies within the research system itself, both in non-communication of developments within science and in insufficiently strong links between research and application to human need. Bernal's suggestions concerning a computerized scientific information system and for rational science planning, while things now taken for granted, at the time led him to be branded a dreamer, a proto-tyrant, or both.

Ironically, it was world war (1939–45) that saw Bernal's demand for a tenfold increase in British science funding fulfilled in less than a decade. Critics who had dismissed the idea of science planning could only retreat to highlighting its limits and difficulties, while accepting its overall value. Bernal's fiercest critic, Michael Polanyi (1957), argued that 'tacit knowledge' in science limits the ability of non-practitioners to evaluate (and therefore plan) scientific research priorities. While himself forced to accept the necessity of science planning, Polanyi's work has now been reappropriated by a new generation of sociologists of science (see Chapter 4). These researchers reassert the impossibility of total intellectual transparency between fields of research, but for other ends. Whether in state or corporate research, the case for research intensification and planning was won. While Bernal may have declared 'I am no Bernalist' (cited in Rose and Rose 1999:145), by the end of the Second World War all advanced industrial states had adopted 'Bernalism', or at least the one-dimensional version of it that Bernal wanted to avoid.

Bernal's research and policy work during the Second World War contributed to the victory of his argument and the defeat of fascism. Bernal's involvement in the Association of Scientific Workers in Britain, the Cambridge Scientists' Anti-War Group, the World Federation of Scientific Workers, the World Peace Council and UNESCO extended his influence in certain circles. However, his loyalty to the Soviet Union saw him marginalized within the major institutions of Western science. The version of Bernalism embraced (East and West) during the cold war arms and space race, and by technocrats in Britain's Labour Party, was a one-dimensional boosterism, servicing the needs of existing power, rather than liberating humanity from domination. The naming of a prize after him by the Society for the Social Study of Science, in the United States, at the height of the McCarthy anti-communist witch-hunts, gives testament to the appropriation of the name, but not the man.

The incorporation of Bernalism, and the exclusion of the man, was aided by Bernal's own tacit acceptance of the doctrine of 'scientific neutrality' (discussed below) in the aftermath of the Lysenko affair in Soviet science. This incident will receive greater attention in Chapter 6. Here it is sufficient to say the following. Bernal supported the Soviet Union and its claim to have disproved the 'bourgeois science' of genetics, and developed a 'proletarian science' of vernalization (stimulating the inheritance of acquired characteristics). Subsequent revelations about Lysenko's flawed empirical methods, and the 'liquidation' of his scientific rivals, damaged Bernal's reputation further. Bernal's support for Lysenko against the extremes of reductionism in genetics, and for the idea of a proletarian science, was rounded upon in the West. Criticism came not least from those geneticists whose condemnation of communist politicization of science had not stopped them embracing eugenics (a politicization of science far more odious, murderous and scientifically flawed even than vernalization).

In the aftermath of the Lysenko affair (from the mid-1950s on) Bernal distanced himself increasingly from the idea of a proletarian science, and of class struggle in scientific knowledge, focusing instead on promoting the growth and positive use of objective knowledge through science. By the mid-1960s, as Peter Mason (1999) points out, this view that more science, in the right hands, equals more good, was beginning to be questioned by a new generation of radicals and researchers. Nuclear energy, computers and biological sciences were coming increasingly under suspicion (see the last section of this chapter), even as Bernal continued to envisage a future transformed for the good by their development and application. As members of this new radical science movement of the late 1960s onward, Hilary Rose and Steven Rose (1999:144) write of Bernal: 'His enemy was too little science; we and our environment all too often suffer from too much capitalist science.'

Bernal's answers to the two questions at the heart of this book (concerning truth versus ideology and liberation versus domination) would be fundamentally to assert that science was a vehicle for the former in each case, even while it was

.ssential to struggle against appropriation by the forces of ideology and domination. Ironically, his work was in large measure appropriated by those forces. A tailored version of Bernal's 'orthodox Marxism' laid the foundation for a massive expansion of science in the interests of capitalism and power. It was a less orthodox form of Marxism, as will be discussed in Chapter 6, itself heavily influenced by 'bourgeois sociology' in the West, that became the frame through which many of Bernal's most radical insights and challenges were to be carried forward into contemporary Marxist sociology of science.

## The Sociology of Science

Robert Merton was the first person to develop a 'sociology of science'. This was in no small measure a systematic attempt to rebuke the claims of Marxists. In particular Merton was keen to challenge the claims of Boris Hessen (who had in part converted Bernal to Marxism) that scientific knowledge could be explained, at least in part, in relation to the economic conditions underpinning its production. Merton's investigation into the development of science in seventeenth century England was an attempt to develop some of Weber's suggestions about the 'elective affinity' between puritanism and the rise of 'occidental rationalism' (1970[1938]). Weber sought to demonstrate the relationship between certain non-rational religious teachings and the rise of instrumental rational capitalism and bureaucracy (1930[1905]). Merton sought to demonstrate the link between such a puritan view of the world as godless and corrupt and the rise of a scientific willingness to account for the world in mechanistic rather than in supernatural terms. Following Weber in looking at the socio-psychological drivers of modern thinking, Merton resisted, as did Weber, the temptation to question the 'truth' of modern western science. While non-rational motives may have played a part in the formation of the scientific outlook, such non-rational elements did not discredit the content of scientific knowledge. How could this be? Merton (1942, reproduced in Barnes 1972a) came to develop an account of the 'institutional' norms and values that regulated the practices of scientists. In this his account becomes more Durkheimian, but retains many affinities with Weber's accounts of the 'ideal typical' bureaucrat, capitalist, lawyer or scientist.

Merton outlines four dominant values which are said to regulate science. These are as follows:

### Universalism

This refers to the regulative assertion that all scientific knowledge should be universally true. This is not to say that because gravity makes one apple fall from a tree that all apples must fall, or that if they don't the theory of gravity is refuted. It is only to say that what the theory of gravity must seek to do is explain the 'general principles' which account for particular phenomena. All sorts of intervening factors may limit the effect of a universal law, but not its existence. Science asserts that the truth it seeks is not culturally specific, and that the underlying laws it seeks to uncover are 'true' regardless of whether people agree with them or whether they even know of them. This would be the basis of the suggestion often made by defenders of science's 'objectivity' that: 'If you show me a relativist at 20 000 feet without a parachute, I'll show you a hypocrite.' Universalism is a benchmark. Claims made in science are expected to live up to this exacting standard.

## 'Communism'

Communism (which Merton placed in quotes) refers to the regulative assertion that science functions, and can only function, through the preparedness of its members to share with each other the findings of their research. Such a gift economy is a non-capitalist system of exchange. Scientists who keeps their findings a secret will not gain the recognition of their peers, and are likely to loose out to others who publish similar findings before them and so claim the status of 'discoverer' or 'inventor'. Unlike in commercial activity, where patents give innovators exclusive rights of access and use of new ideas and tools, science encourages the sharing of ideas and the greatest tribute goes to those whom others follow and draw from. Publication, prizes, research funding, career positions etc. act to motivate the scientist to give all they know away. The citing of a scientist's work by other scientists is the measure of that scientist's status within the scientific community, not financial income. If to be cited is the reward others give to those whose ideas they have drawn upon (without financial payment), to use the ideas of others within the scientific community without citing their work constitutes intellectual theft. To take from others and to keep your own discoveries a secret would undermine the principles of scientific 'communism' and thereby undermine the creativity of the scientific community.

## *Disinterestedness*

This refers to the requirement of scientists to take a distance from the statements they seek to test except in so far as truth or falsity is demonstrated by evidence. A scientist should not assume a vested interest in a particular point of view. Their social position is based upon their methods of evaluation, not on the outcomes, for better or worse. Scientists should be prepared to abandon theories that do not conform to evidence, even when these theories are ones they have invested time and energy in, and which their name has become associated with.

*Organized Scepticism*

This refers to the institutional process of questioning that is supposed to ensure that personal opinion and residual vested interests are weeded out of scientific-ally generated knowledge. Peer-reviewing for academic publication and for research, as well as for appointments and prizes, is said to ensure that one person's view is always subject to the highest possible level of scrutiny. A scientist who is accused of taking something for granted would be seen as a bad scientist.

Merton believed that knowledge was always influenced by the social context in which it was generated. However, in his sociology of science he suggests that the institutional values around which scientific practice is structured ensured the production of 'truth', rather than partial or distorted knowledge. For Merton, the emergence of external conditions and internal norms and values conducive to the production of objective knowledge represent one of the greatest social achievements in human history. Writing in the 1930s and 1940s, Merton was keen to defend the social norms and values that he believed structured the social interactions of the scientific community from the distorting influences of political ideologies, both communist and fascist. Merton did not believe that such distorting social forces, external to the community of science, were as strong in Western liberal capitalist societies, and it was in such societies, he believed, that the four principles outlined above could best be practised and defended successfully. To sustain the argument for the relative detachment of science from economic and political influence, Merton's account of scientific history focuses almost exclusively upon academic science in a small number of universities. Practical application, and the involvement of prominent scientists such as Boyle, Newton, Wren and Hooke in the economic and political systems of their day are underplayed, while the wider development of science in relation to industry, trade, government and warfare is likewise neglected (see Weingart 1978).

Merton's sociology of science remained dominant until the late 1960s. W. O. Hagstrom's (1965; extracts 1972a, 1972b) *The Scientific Community* developed a Mertonian account of the functional role of norms in 'big' science after the Second World War. This approach asks how such institutional practices as 'gift exchange' function to maintain rational and efficient practice when it might (in capitalist society) be assumed that direct financial reward would be a better incentive. Hagstrom also addresses the dynamics of scientific growth into ever wider sub-fields, using analogy with the 'animal kingdom' (the search for resources and limiting competition). The question of whether science is true is not asked.

At the same moment Soviet sociologists of science asked the same questions. Ignacy Malecki and Eugeniusz Olszewski (1972) identified trends in science towards complexity, and vertical and horizontal integration in application, as well as increasing disciplinary differentiation, but never questioned the nature of scientific knowledge. For them the value of sociology is to act as a 'science of scientific activity' (1972:165) to further the management of science policy. The work of Derek J. de Solla Price (a British historian and follower of Bernal) set out the transformation of science since the seventeenth century. Exponential growth by all available measures, the fusion of science and technology, and the qualitative shift from individual and small-team-based research towards huge state- and business-funded collaborative research programmes all represented a shift from 'little science' to 'big science' (Price 1963, 1972). The Manhattan atomic bomb project in the West and the Sputnik space programme in the Soviet Union were testament to the power of socially organized science. The role of the Western functionalist sociologist and the Soviet scientist of science planning was to map and facilitate this 'progress', not to question its 'truth' or 'utility'.

## Thomas Kuhn's New Historical Approach to Science

Thomas Kuhn's *The Structure of Scientific Revolutions* (1962) transformed the study of science (socially, historically and philosophically), but not quickly, nor in any one single direction. Kuhn's work was a relatively open canvas upon which a diverse array of emerging perspectives and social movements projected their interpretations and legitimated their challenges to established philosophy, history and sociology of science. Kuhn's perceived challenge to the traditional philosophy of science lay in his assertion that science trains its novices to see the world through the prism of particular theories. These theories then cannot be simply tested by means of observation. What you see is dependent upon the theory you already hold. Any link between theory and evidence is as much the result of the theory-laden nature of the observation as it is the result of independent triangulation between what the theory predicts and what actually exists. Therefore, to understand science, we must look at the socialization and regulation processes operating within science as an area of social interaction. Kuhn's description of science as 'paradigm-dependent' opened up even the most abstract theoretical or rigorously experimental fields of science to sociology, though Kuhn was not a sociologist.

Kuhn's historical account of the transformation of twentieth-century physics, the shift from the acceptance of a Newtonian model of reality to an Einsteinian model, demonstrated that evidence alone was not enough to prove one model true and the other false. The Newtonian model generated predictions that in most instances conformed to observable reality. Certain limits and anomalies had been observed in the Newtonian account, but the strength of the model in predicting most observations was taken to be grounds for confidence. It was generally assumed that further research within the existing framework would eventually allow such limits and anomalies to be overcome. Kuhn likened this process to working within a puzzle (1962:35–51). If certain pieces do not go in one place it is assumed that in time their correct location will be identified as other pieces are fitted into place within the already existing big picture.

Kuhn argued that in many areas the Newtonian model remained productive, generating micro-questions within its overall account of reality, micro-questions that led researchers to interesting and innovative 'discoveries'. Those working at the more macro levels of astrophysics and theoretical physics encountered anomalies that challenged their faith in the overall model, but it was still possible to remain hopeful that these would one day be resolved. All models have anomalies. It was not evidence alone that compelled the physics community to abandon the Newtonian model. Kuhn argued that it was only the development of an alternative model (in this case Einstein's relativity theory) that generated the new puzzle within which new generations of scientists could be trained to look for the micro-questions that emerged from its new big picture (1962:111–35). Initially, Einstein's approach offered solutions to particular anomalies. However, the model he put forward generated significant anomalies of its own in relation to what was already understood to be the case. Given the weight of existing 'evidence' (evidence generated within the existing Newtonian model), Einstein's relativity theory appeared hopelessly riddled with flaws. For Einstein's model to become accepted, it was necessary for a great deal of existing evidence to be reinterpreted.

What Kuhn was proposing was that models do not emerge one fact at a time. Models allow evidence to be sought, evidence that requires the model to give it the meaning it is assumed to have. Generations of scientists had been socialized to look in certain ways and in certain places for certain things. Their thinking and their practical activities were structured within what Kuhn called a 'paradigm', a big picture, a puzzle. For radical new developments to occur it was necessary for a new pradigm to be developed, and for it to gain support from within the existing scientific community. Considering the expectations of that community, such a new account would be counter-intuitive given the number of clashes the new model contained relative to all they had come to take for granted. Transition takes place as much as a result of older generations retiring and/or dying off and being replaced as it does by these older cohorts being won over to the new thinking.

Kuhn's work challenged the view that evidence could ever be immune from the theoretical framework through which or in which it was developed. The naïve view that a theory could be proved correct simply by demonstrating evidence in support of that theory was demolished. Even the supposedly more sophisticated view, that while a theory could never be proved unquestionably true on the basis of confirming examples, at least it would be possible to disprove a theory by means of empirical examples that contradict the theory (Popper 1972–Chalmers 1982), could no longer hold. If evidence itself is always paradigm-dependent, and all paradigms contain at least some anomalies, then single instances of apparent contradiction between evidence and theory are never enough on their own to debunk a theory. Glitches can be explained either as misinterpretation of the data in need of further theoretical elaboration or as faulty data-collection in need of more sophisticated empirical techniques or technologies.

Kuhn himself was simply seeking to show how science progresses through a combination of slow developments within particular puzzles and rapid, revolutionary bursts when one paradigm comes to replace another. His concern lay more in strengthening the capacity of the United States' scientific community to operate on a large scale, to collaborate and to meet the challenges of what was becoming 'big science' in the cold war arms and space race (Fuller 2000). Gone were the days when scientists worked alone or in small teams. So it was necessary for scientists to abandon the idea that facts emerged one at a time from the fragmented actions of isolated laboratories. Kuhn was not a relativist. He believed scientific knowledge grows and improves. He was hostile to those who took his work to imply that any paradigm was as good as the next (see Kuhn 1970 for his 1969 postscript to the 1962 original).

What Kuhn had highlighted was the community nature of scientific practice and the community nature of scientific knowledge production and belief. He offered no critique of science, nor any account of why periods of stability should suddenly give way to periods of change. He merely noted that this was what happened. New theories emerge all the time. Most are dismissed. Why a new paradigm gains or does not gain support is never explained. In this sense, Kuhn's is a history or ideas, not a sociology of science. Kuhn's 1962 text was initially disregarded by sociologists for this reason. They could find no 'explanatory' social account within it. It was rather regarded as a curious chronicle of changing ideas and, at best, a social psychology of community belief. It is testament to the vagueness of Kuhn's account, however, that by the late 1960s his work was being taken up by a new generation. For them, his work acted as the intellectual justification to focus upon just those aspects of human interaction and belief previously disregarded by mainstream sociology of science. While Kuhn did not call for a sociological account of why people believe what they do, a new generation of sociologists believed he did or should have, and used his name to justify their own project of developing a sociology of scientific knowledge.

## The New, Radical and Divergent Sociologies of Science

Michael Mulkay's (1969) 'Some Aspects of Cultural Growth in the Natural Sciences' and (1972) *The Social Process of Innovation* use the space opened up by Kuhn to challenge Merton's sociology of science, even while challenging Kuhn's paradigm theory. Mulkay suggests that Kuhn's account of transformation in physics cannot and should not be uncritically generalized. Mulkay opened the way for 'internalist' perspectives in the contemporary sociology of science (interests and ethnographic discursive perspectives). His work in part paralleled, and in part preceded, the work of the Edinburgh School, to be discussed in Chapter 4. At the same time a new radical science movement also developed. Hilary and Steven Rose's (1970[1969]) *Science and Society*, and their (1976 – [original 1972]) *The Radicalisation of Science* exemplify and document the rise of critical or radical science and its study. This movement was linked to anti-war, socialist and feminist movements and laid the foundations for 'externalist' perspectives in the contemporary sociology of science (Marxist and feminist approaches). Some in the radical science movement also drew upon the language of Kuhn's paradigm theory to challenge the authority and objectivity of science.

## Attention to Internal Interests

In effect Mulkay allied a Mannheimian sociology of knowledge to Merton's sociology of science. What if Merton's scientific norms and values were the 'ideology' of a particular group, in this case scientists? Mulkay suggested that the picture Merton paints is exactly the one that scientists would most like us to believe. It is the scientific community's ideal image of itself. While scientists might recite the above principles to each other and to the world, and believe in them, this does not mean that these principles actually govern scientists' behaviour. Values may be what you say guides your action, but selective application and interpretation mean that such values become veils, all the more useful, given their constant use, as covers to obscure other motives and pressures.

Immanuel Velikovsky's (1950) *Worlds in Collision* was published in popular form before being reviewed by the scientific establishment. Velikovsky challenged the established methods and theories (paradigms) in astronomy, geology and biology. He was vilified even before his research had been examined. Many reviewers admitted not to have even read his scientific papers. His work was not repeated to test his results. His personal integrity was questioned. Some who supported his right to publish lost their jobs, and publishers who handled his work were threatened with boycotts. Even while some came to support Velikovsky's right to publish, the Mertonian view that science applies standards of universalism, disinterestedness and organized scepticism is unable to account for such behaviour, which is not unique. Far from encouraging openness, the socialization process in science encourages closure (Mulkay 1969).

What for Merton represented a virtue may in the light of Kuhn represent a restrictive force. The years of training which scientists undergo involves con-tinual assessment based upon conformity to group expectations and practices. Only after one has proved oneself fully submissive to these expectations and routines is one allowed to engage in 'creative' work, but even this creativity is regulated to remain within the dominant puzzle. Deviance is heavily punished. '[S]tudying science becomes stenography plus memorisation' (Jevons 1969:140, cited in Mulkay 1972:19). Scientists proclaim Merton's values, but share information selectively, evaluate each other's work in terms of career advantage and collaborative and/or competitive potential, defend their vested interests in particular theoretical models with vigour, and effect strong pressures to conformity, in terms of topics to be researched, methods to be applied and acceptable conclusions to be drawn (Mulkay 1972).

Kuhn's (1962) account of scientific developments in physics should not be taken automatically to be a universal account of science. Physics is often considered as the paradigm of good science. Because Kuhn's study is about physics, his questioning of its 'self image' has rippled out into a general questioning of science as a whole. What Kuhn then suggests to be the 'reality' of physics, its highly developed paradigm dependence and its strong enforcement practices by which the current paradigm is enshrined, has been taken almost as a universal statement about science. Kuhn (1962:preface) distinguishes paradigm sciences and non-paradigm sciences. This has usually been taken to refer to the distinction between the physical and the social sciences, the former hard, ordered and strong, the latter soft, disorderly and feeble.

Far from achieving order and paradigm centrality, with occasional revolutionary shifts, in the cases Mulkay discusses there are rebellions rather than revolutions. Rather than abolishing old centres, rebels within scientific fields branch out to create new fields. This is often in response to the lack of space in which to develop one's career as a young academic unless one generates something new. However, to do so is hard when faced with the established power of older members of your field. The easy option is to create a new sub-discipline, produce new conferences, journals and professional associations to promote its work, suggest new applications and so bypass the need to confront the old guard.

This is what happened with the emergence of psychology (Mulkay 1972, drawing upon Ben-David and Collins 1966). Anatomy was a growth area in German academic medicine early in the nineteenth century. Rapid growth led to a wave of new academic chairs. Professorships were filled by young academics who would not retire for decades. The generation beneath them got very little chance of promotion within anatomy and so 'promoted' physiology as a 'new' sub-field for which lots of new professorships could then be created. However this had the same effect on the next generation. Wundt's 'invention' of psychology created a new space in which to prosper. If physics changed by revolution, other fields emerged out of rebellion and detachment. Mulkay (1969) suggests that scientific innovation happens less at the heart of a paradigmatic puzzle than through dispersal of old models to new 'areas of ignorance' or at the point where two paradigms confront each other or cross-fertilize.

Different scientific fields have different social relations and histories. These need to be studied. Mulkay demonstrated the need for sociological study to be carried out across a range of scientific fields rather than for one generalizing model to be applied across the board. The contemporary 'internalist' sociology of scientific knowledge seeks to further these two aims (identifying the social roots of belief and the divergent histories of different scientific fields). Mulkay (1972) also suggested the need to link studies of the social relations of scientific knowledge production to wider social conflicts and practices. Mulkay's brief 1972 text did not develop this third dimension. While some within the 'internalist' tradition have sought to do this, those holding to a more 'externalist' research focus argue that greater attention needs to be paid to wider social relations of power and domination than is achieved by focusing attention primarily at the internal dynamics of the scientific community.

## *Attention to External Interests*

Bernal's (1964[1939]) *The Social Function of Science* maintained the classical and orthodox Marxist faith in the progressive and liberating nature of science, and in its capacity to produce objective truth. Western and Soviet development of 'big science' was integrated within, and in the service of military, political and economic power. Towards the end of the 1960s Bernal's faith was becoming increasingly difficult to sustain for a growing number of young scientists and others critical of capitalist and bureaucratic systems. In 1964 Harold Wilson's Labour Party came to power in Britain, amidst promises of social transformation in the 'white heat' of technological and scientific innovation. Bernal had been consulted, at one step removed, in the composition of Labour's 1964 manifesto (Goldsmith 1980). However, Bernal's reflections in *The Social Function of Science*, republished in 1964, sought to emphasize that more science was never going to be enough on its own, as long as science acted in the service of an economic and political minority over the majority.

Hilary Rose and Steven Rose (1976e:8[1972]) suggest that being blamed for the nuclear age and reacting against the politicization of science in the Soviet Union led scientists in both the West and the Soviet bloc to adopt a stance of 'neutrality'. This amounted to the assertion that scientists only engaged in the production of objective knowledge, while it was 'society' that decided how such knowledge might or should be applied. Whether knowledge was used for good or ill, so the argument of scientific neutrality ran, was not the ethical responsibility of the scientist, or the scientific community. While physicists might have developed the theory and split the atom, it was for 'society' to choose whether this knowledge be applied to the making and using of nuclear bombs, for the production of electricity in nuclear power stations, or not used for either purpose. If biologists and chemists were able to identify genes, it was for society to decide whether any consequent discoveries should be used to pursue eugenic programmes or not. In exchange for expanded budgets and social status, science had, in large measure, withdrawn from questioning the established order.

The doctrine of scientific neutrality is premised upon the separation, first, of science and society, such that one can engage in purely objective work, while the other is solely responsible for ethical decision-making. Science is seen as detached from ethical considerations, while society defers to science for truth. Second, the doctrine of scientific neutrality is premised upon the separation of science and technology, such that science provides knowledge, while technology refers to the production of objects with social, economic and/or military utility. Chapter 3 challenges the separation between science, technology and society. Here, it is only necessary to point out that, not for the first or last time, the doctrine of scientific neutrality was deployed to serve a particular set of political purposes. However, the late 1960s saw this doctrine increasingly questioned.

The Vietnam war marked a watershed in the intensification of the 'industrial-military-scientific complex' (Rose and Rose 1976e:15[1972]). Protesting against the war led students and others to uncover the deep and extensive links between the military and university scientific research, most intensive in the United States, but also across all advanced industrial societies (including the supposedly demilitarized West Germany and Japan). Delegations sent to assess civilian casualties in North Vietnam charted the use of horrendous and new explosives as well as the use of illegal chemical weapons on a mass scale and deliberately targeted against civilians. The latest university and industrial scientific research in aviation, navigation, communication and computing was all being channelled into the routine and ever more efficient conduct of crimes against humanity. 1968 saw the founding of the British Society for Social Responsibility in Science (Rose and Rose 1976e[1972]). This was an eclectic association of groups and individuals without a specific political programme and having links to a diverse array of mainstream scientific bodies and associations as well as a range of new left and new social movement groups and causes. By late 1969 this movement had around 1000 members (not all of whom were natural scientists). Also, at this point, divisions emerged between those calling for greater attention to the systemic relationship between science and capitalism, and those who saw science as ideally neutral, but being subject to misuse. Similar debates emerged elsewhere in Europe and the United States within the emerging new social movements that fed into and developed after the events of 1968. (For a discussion of developments in Scandinavia and the Netherlands, see Eyerman and Jamison 1991; for Germany see Habermas 1971[1970]; for France see Touraine 1971[1968]; and for the United States see Gouldner 1976). New left and new social movement radicals, whether focused upon the rise of new working-class radicalism, student politics, the civil rights movements, women's liberation, ecology, anti-imperialism or peace, began to ask questions about the role of science in the maintenance of domination in both material and ideological terms.

While writers like Hilary Rose and Steven Rose were, in the late 1960s and early 1970s, socialists, they were not Marxists, and others, like Jerome Ravetz (1973), were libertarian and anarchist. It was only later, as these new questions and debates filtered into a new and radicalized sociology of science, that much of this attention to the external relations of science came to centre around new Marxist and feminist theoretical frameworks.

# 2

# The Perspective of This Book: Reflexive Epistemological Diversity

## The Sociology of Science and Scientific Knowledge Today

Mulkay's social theory of scientific specialization challenges both traditional accounts of functional specialization and Kuhn's theory of scientific revolutions. The radical science movement too, though attending to very different issues, challenged the traditional account of scientific power and objectivity. The sociology of science, arising from both strands, though with these most often in isolation from each other, has, since the 1970s, produced a wide range of studies, from theoretical accounts to studies of particular academic fields in the present or in history and detailed ethnographies of everyday scientific life. It has been through these studies that many of the tensions discussed in the introductory chapter were highlighted and developed as productive sites of further study. Chapters 4–7 outline current work in these new fields. The social-interests perspective, or the strong programme in the sociology of science, developed directly in keeping with Mulkay's work. The ethnographic and discursive approaches emerged directly out of, and in criticism against, the social-interests school. Contemporary Marxist and feminist perspectives emerged from the radical science movement, and from allied social movements of the late 1960s and early 1970s. Marxist research developed through the rediscovery and reinterpretation of older debates in the light of new social conditions. Feminist perspectives in part developed from a critique of the gender-blind nature of other perspectives, but also from developments in the wider feminist movement and in the ongoing transformation of women's lives in technocratic capitalist societies.

Before these perspectives are outlined, it is necessary to give greater attention to the theoretical framework being proposed in this text, and to address key conceptual issues concerning the terms 'science', 'technology' and 'society'. Thus this chapter elaborates the perspective of reflexive epistemological diversity, while Chapter 3 defends the claim that science subsumes technology within contemporary risk society.

This chapter outlines the core elements and tensions within the four dominant contemporary perspectives in the sociology of science. At the heart of these tensions within and between perspectives is the question of causal attribution. How far is it possible to identify 'causes'? How far is it possible for sociologists to question scientists' explanations of their own findings without bringing into question the validity of their own causal explanations? Does sociological questioning undermine sociological explanation? Is this a problem or a positive invitation to a more modest way of knowing? These are 'epistemological' questions. Epistemology is the field of philosophy concerned with asking how it is possible to gain true knowledge. Each perspective within the sociology of science adopts a different epistemological position, as do different disciplines within the physical sciences. The easy solution to epistemological difference is to defend the supposed principles of one's discipline or field, and to dismiss challengers on the grounds that they do not conform to what 'clearly' works in the eyes of your community of practitioners. This approach is common within the physical sciences, within the social sciences, and between the physical and social sciences.

Yet the assumption that, because one epistemological approach 'works' (within its own terms of reference) it must therefore be the only way of knowing, is as inadequate as the view that any one approach can be immune to blind spots, anomalies and areas to which it cannot be successfully applied. A willingness to accept insights from other epistemological traditions is not to confirm the total falseness of any one epistemological approach. This chapter shows how entrenchment within forms of reductionist and relativist epistemology can and should be moved beyond.

# The Move Towards a Study of Scientific Knowledge Itself

Contemporary sociology of science is often referred to as the sociology of scientific knowledge. This is to distinguish what is currently prevalent from what has gone before. For all the differences that exist within current sociologies of science, one thing remains a significant, unifying focus of attention. The founders of sociology were more concerned to attach to their activities the status and power of science. Thus, for all the critical insights their work was later to generate, at the time of their writing Marx, Weber and Durkheim had little to say when it came to questioning the truth of scientific knowledge. This respect for the validity of scientific knowledge was also characteristic of the writings of Karl Mannheim and Robert Merton. While Merton established the sociology of science and Mannheim the sociology of knowledge, Merton did not seek to question the authority of scientific knowledge and Mannheim did not seek to apply his relational theory of knowledge to what he referred to as the 'exact sciences'. The Marxist J. D. Bernal had explored many aspects of science's intimate integration within the politics, economics and ideology of the society of which it is a part. His work was, however, appropriated by those who wished only to highlight the positive influence of science upon society, its superior and neutral 'truth'-generating function, and not any ideological aspect it might contain. In the aftermath of the Lysenko affair Bernal himself stepped back from questioning the objectivity of mainstream Western science.

The work of Thomas Kuhn opened the door for a fusion of Merton's examination of science and Mannheim's approach to knowledge. While Kuhn's specific account of physics was historical, his attention to the communal process of learning to see, of the socialization process that trains each generation to ask certain questions and to work with the world through particular 'puzzles', or paradigms, was the point of departure that separates what went before from today's 'sociology of scientific knowledge'. Even though Michael Mulkay's (1969, 1972) early statements of what a sociology of scientific knowledge might be were in part a questioning of the application of Kuhn's model to the explanation of other areas of science, Kuhn's attention to the social process of scientific seeing marks a watershed. The sociology of science today is a sociology of scientific knowledge. Whether in seeking to explain or to describe, the object of study is what science claims to be the 'truth'. The question of domination versus liberation has also come to the fore, although mainly in the work of feminists and Marxists rather than in that of those more concerned with 'internal' questions of scientific practice and belief. This focus upon the external relations of science, both in relation to the truth of scientific knowledge and in its relation to the question of domination versus liberation, was forged (or reforged) in the new left and new social movements of the late 1960s and beyond. The bringing together of insights from both 'internalist' and 'externalist' approaches has remained relatively elusive. This text, while tracing the separations, also highlights significant scope for collaboration.

# Dominant Perspectives within the Contemporary Sociology of Science

Contemporary approaches to the sociological study of science display considerable diversity. Those working from a social-interests perspective focus attention upon conflicts within science as a means of highlighting what Harry Collins calls 'interpretative flexibility' and the 'closure mechanisms' therefore required to enable disputes to be contained. Vested interests are drawn upon as explanatory resources in such accounts. Interests are both those of career and status within the scientific community and those operating within the wider social, economic and political world. As Barnes (1974) suggests, the interpretation of interests and beliefs will always display an openness between the interpretations of the researcher and the actors being researched. Ethnographic and discursive approaches focus attention less upon conflict than upon the routine performance, interaction and language of science. Ethnographic and discursive researchers adopt a more sceptical tone towards attempts to provide 'explanations' for what happens, whether these explanations are from physical scientists or social researchers. Rather, EDA focuses attention upon description of action, talk and especially the performance and rhetoric that gives the impression of order, routine and agreement in the midst of complexity and not a little chaos (every-day life in the laboratory). Marxists and critical theorists attend to the role of science and technology within capitalist society. Science is shown to have both ideological and material 'effects' in its applications, while at the same time social influences, in cultural, political and economic terms, are shown to influence the conduct, direction and interpretations prevalent within science and technology at any particular moment in history. Feminists address a range of questions concerning the position of women within the institutions of science, the representation of women in scientific research, the impact of science upon women's lives, and the question of whether science should be entered and improved, challenged and transformed, or rejected altogether by women.

Within each approach there are tensions. Within the interests approach there is scope to dispute the extent to which empirical evidence about the physical world can seep through the filters of social interests. As will be seen in Chapter 4, Collins and Pinch's (1993) account of Pasteur and Pouchet draws upon evidence that came to light after both biologists had long been dead. This new evidence allows Collins and Pinch to 'explain' why things may have appeared the way they did to those not party to this new knowledge. It also shows that other (non-physical) factors must have intervened to produce an outcome seemingly at odds with what would have appeared to be the case at the time. This relies upon the view that, now, we can look back and see what really happened, while at the time, on the cutting edge of knowledge in that period, evidence could not be successfully calibrated. Elsewhere, Collins (1985) suggests new research insights are 'black-boxed', contained in taken-for-granted rules of thumb and mass-produced artefacts, as much as in conscious hindsight. Just because people are no longer arguing, does not mean that the truth has been formulated explicitly and for all time. Thus, the extent to which yesterday's disputes can be resolved on the basis of today's more settled judgements may be viewed either as unproblematic or still open to question. Whether the scope of social-interests research is only at the cutting edge of new knowledge, where novelty breeds uncertainty, or whether such an account can apply to science in general remains open for dispute and negotiation, which, of course, from a social-interests perspective, is as it should be.

Ethnographers and discourse analysts display a tension between a focus upon social interaction by anthropological observation and a focus upon abstracted talk (via interviews) and/or text (in the analysis of written work such as conference papers and journal articles). Ethnographic attention to interaction and the even more narrowly focused ethnomethodological attention to the everyday production of the appearance of order tends towards an account of human actors working to create their own strategies, rhetorics and routines. Attention to text, in the study of written discourse, tends towards an attention to the structure of language. While the former tends towards a humanistic account of creativity, the latter leads to the generation of accounts that appear to show how language, categories and grammars shape human thinking and action. This maps onto a tension between forms of Anglo-American qualitative social research methods and forms of French literary theory. As will be seen in Chapter 5, the attempt to create an actor network theory, an attempt made by a mixture of ethnographic and discursive researchers, was torn apart by competing conceptions of what an actor was (either a human agent or a field of discursive, material and network constructions).

The Marxist tradition contains a tension between critical theorists and critical realists. Critical theorists have placed emphasis upon the ideological role played by science in the generation of systems of domination and in their ongoing legitimation. Critical theorists have also drawn attention to the distorting effect of dominant economic and political systems upon the direction and content of scientific research. Critical realists are more positive about science, seeing it as part of the productive forces that offer hope of a future free from want. Critical realists are critical of the way science has been harnessed by dominant groups to serve their interests and are keen to see science liberated for the good of humanity. Marxists from different sides of this divide dispute the extent to which science is internally biased or externally abused. Realists fear the scepticism of relativists, as this doubt in reason and modernity has echoes of conservative and religious rhetoric. Critical theorists also fear relativism, but seek to explain why such beliefs are popular both within and beyond science. They suggest dogmatic belief in science as explanation for all things can be just as dangerous and irrational as the dogmatic rejection of all scientific advances in knowledge.

Feminist approaches to science are divided between those who seek to promote greater female participation within science and those who are sceptical about the value of such participation as long as science remains biased in the knowledge it produces about women. Feminist empiricism seeks to highlight the underrepresentation of women within the scientific community, both in total and in senior positions. They suggest that the history of sexism expressed in the way science views women and nature would best be corrected through increased numbers of women being in science itself. Feminist standpoint theory argues that a greater slice of a dubious cake is not the best solution. Writers like Sandra Harding and Hilary Rose argue that women's outsider position in society and science allows women a perspective upon society that is not afforded to those whose positions of security and power make the world as it stands appear both natural and right. In particular, the nature of contemporary science is seen by standpoint feminists to reflect the desire to dominate and control nature and women. Whether because they are excluded from society's positions of domination (as is suggested by Rose and Harding), or because women are 'naturally' more attached to other human beings and to nature (as is suggested by Vandana Shiva), or both, women are less prone to see this desire to control life as synonymous with knowing it. Feminist standpoint theory promotes knowing, based upon learning through attachment, listening and empathy, rather than through detachment, looking and control. Feminist post-modernists reject any belief in one true superior form of knowing and suggest women should be sceptical about all claims to knowledge, or any singular female position from which to 'know'.

## Internal and External Approaches

One key difference often highlighted in contemporary sociology of scientific knowledge is that between internalist perspectives and externalist perspectives (Webster 1991). Marxists and feminists start from a theoretical account of the wider social world and begin to work in towards an account of how these factors influence and are aided by science. Interests theory and ethnographic/discursive research places greater attention upon the internal social processes within science, whether within the laboratory or within the broader realms of the scientific community, such as in conferences, publications or the general interactions that go on within disciplines, universities and research teams. While social-interests approaches tend to start from the internal dynamics of disputes within science, it is common practice to link these disputes, and the closure mechanisms by which they are contained, to the wider society and conflicting interests at work there. Interests theorists are criticized by ethnographers and discourse analysts (Woolgar 1981) for drawing too heavily upon external explanations that are beyond the immediate scope of the researcher to observe. At the same time they are attacked by Marxists and feminists (Rose 1994) for focusing too much attention upon the internal relations of science and too little upon the implications of science for the wider world and the impact of the wider world upon science. While this dispute would appear to fracture the sociology of science, such a characterization is misleading. Extreme claims on either side of this dispute over the right and wrong ways of understanding science are based upon a false dichotomy. This false binary opposition is between those who claim that social causes can be proven to explain scientific knowledge fully and unproblematically and those who argue that it is possible to suspend such causal explanations altogether.

## The Question of Attribution Beyond Appearance: Causes

As will be highlighted in Chapter 5, the ethnographic and discursive researchers' claims to have suspended the attempt to provide causal explanation, focusing instead only upon providing descriptive accounts of events within scientific everyday life, is overstated. Latour and Woolgar's (1979, 1986) *Laboratory Life* contains numerous attributions of explanation. The offshoot of ethnographic and discursive approaches, 'actor network theory', was itself torn apart by competing attributions of causal explanation (between those who saw actors as human individual agents, and those who saw actors as sites of cross-cutting networks of social and physical causes). What distinguishes EDA from interest accounts, Marxists and most feminists is (rhetoric aside) a different focus of attention, and therefore a different set of causal attributions. Once this is recognized, it is possible to see Woolgar's (1981) critique of causal explanations in the sociology of science as a rhetorical devise. Woolgar seeks to undermine one focus of attention in order to give greater authority to another, at that point underdeveloped, focus and method of study, that of day-to-day interaction and language in science. Woolgar highlights the difficulties of making causal attributions to 'wider' social forces, said to be operating beyond the immediate situation observed by the researcher, yet his and Latour's *Laboratory Life* makes many such claims. Even the claimed ability to identify rhetorical and linguistic devices that 'naturalize' and 'externalize' the constructions produced by scientific researchers, requires an attribution of effects that cannot be immediately verified, either within the immediate experience of an observer, or by means of more structural models of social influence. Potter (1996) is right to highlight the danger of Collins's (1985) non-rhetorical rhetoric (to be discussed in Chapter 5). The naïve belief that what people say, about how they were persuaded, is true, and not just another attempt to persuade, must be questioned. However, this danger is ever present. What is important is to be aware of this, and to seek strategies to evaluate what researchers are being told. Potter's claim that the best strategy to avoid the naïve view (the view that while some language is rhetorical, other language is 'true') is to assume that all language is rhetorical and that all explanations are contrived is doubly questionable. First, it is not in fact what discourse analysts themselves do. Discourse analysis regularly attributes explanatory force to rhetorical language. Second, to adopt such a view is so dogmatically anti-reductionist as to become the mirror image of the dogmatic reductionism it seeks to oppose. The collapse of reality into language and the collapse of language into reality is a reversal that yet leaves the same symmetrical correspondence. To assume that everything is simple rhetoric is to say that the only analysis required is discourse analysis. This is an exclusivity that is no more justified by evidence or argument than the counter-claim that the only factor required to explain reality is empirical data and the universal 'scientific' methods required to collect and order such data.

## Differences of Focus or Fundamentals: Reductionism, Epistemological Diversity or Epistemological Chicken?

Harry Collins and Stephen Yearley (1992) suggest that the flight from causal explanation in the sociology of scientific knowledge can best be likened to the game of chicken:

> The game of 'chicken' involves dashing across the road in front of speeding cars. The object of the game is to be the last person to cross. Only this person can avoid the charge of being cowardly. An earlier crosser is a 'chicken' (noun), that is, a person who is 'chicken' (adjective). (1992:17)

The sociologist of science who can claim that they have detached themselves most fully from the authority of the physical sciences, that is the authority of causal explanation and universal knowledge claims, may be seen as having carved out the biggest 'epistemological' space for themselves, that is the space where social researchers are equipped to 'know best'. Any concession to the view that causes and universal explanations can be found with the tools of physical science or any attempt to mimic such methods in the social realm can be seen as being 'chicken'. Collins and Yearley focus attention on the work of Latour and Woolgar. They conclude that such accounts offer great value as provocation, forcing those seeking to provide causal accounts to consider the possibility that their accounts are flawed and inevitably limited. However, anti-causal accounts, in so far as they engage in the game of 'epistemological chicken', are driven to a form of insularity that parallels the most naïve forms of reductionism. In the end, Woolgar and Latour see all claims other than their own as naïve. No other approach is seen as valid. This is similar to the view adopted by reductionists, who believe that only their 'deeper' explanation is correct and that everything else is naïve. Reductionists believe that, properly understood, everything will, one day, be reduced to their level of explanation (from society to biology, from biology to chemistry, from chemistry to physics and perhaps then eventually from physics to mathematics). Eventually, for reductionism, all other levels of explanation can be done away with. All things will be explained in terms of the lowest level of things, that is the basic building-blocks. For the kind of relativism adopted by some ethnographic and discursive writers, the reverse is true and everything that can be investigated is in language and interaction. Thus the only work worth doing is ethnographic and discursive. Reductionism and relativism end up as mirror images of each other. Collins and Yearley conclude that the game of 'epistemological chicken' renders the social sciences immune from the knowledge claims of the physical sciences, but also has the reverse consequence of making the social sciences irrelevant to the physical sciences. The game of 'epistemological chicken' is a rhetorical strategy that gives the impression that ethnographic and discursive approaches do not rely on causal models and explanations when in fact they do. The rhetorical immunity afforded by playing 'chicken' is illusory. To escape reductionism and dogmatic forms of relativism, we need to abandon epistemological chicken and adopt reflexive epistemological diversity.

A frog sits by a pond. A snake is approaching the frog. The frog jumps into the pond. Steven Rose's (1997:10) five accounts of 'What caused the frog to jump?' (physiological, ethological, developmental, evolutionary and molecular-biological) are all 'true', within the limits of their disciplinary frame of reference or focus of attention. According to Rose, while each discipline poses the question of cause differently, the truth of one does not invalidate the truth of the others, except in so far as each invalidates the claims of the others to be the whole truth. That each can be sustained does not mean each can be reduced to one basic 'explanation'. Rose proposes 'translation', not 'reduction'. Order is systemic. Organization conditions and constitutes component elements just as the component elements represent conditions required for higher levels of complexity to exist. Rose (1997:76) cites a talk given by Karl Popper entitled 'Eight Reasons Why Biology Cannot Be Reduced to Physics'. In the talk Popper argued that the organization of physical elements into complex chemical forms produces structures that themselves act to organize the physical elements they are made of. The same is true when chemical units are organized into biological structures. Any attempt to fully explain a level of order requires attention to that level and all the levels below it. A full account cannot be given simply by focusing upon one level and attempting to reduce all other levels to it, or suggesting that a higher level is completely self-explanatory without reference to other levels. Rose concludes that while the world may be an integrated whole (what he calls an ontological unity) the best way to understand this complex whole is to approach it at a number of levels, so as to identify the range of factors that contribute to 'explaining' any one outcome. Rose calls this 'epistemological diversity'. Epistemological diversity is not the view that any approach is valid. It is simply the view that causation occurs at many levels and that specific events are caused by complex sets of factors.

What Rose is suggesting comes from a critical-realist perspective. Critical theorists, most feminists, social-interests theorists and ethnographic/discursive analysts place a greater emphasis upon the role of alternative epistemologies in limiting the claims made by the physical sciences to totality and universality (the ability to explain everything everywhere). While highlighting the limits and distortions, they are also, whether explicitly or not, proposing alternative epistemologies. While critical realism emphasizes the complementary nature of different epistemologies, against forms of reductionism and relativism, other sociology of science perspectives emphasize the critical function of different epistemologies.

This returns us to the question of focus or fundamentals. Is what divides the sociology of science and the natural sciences, one from the other and within each, simply that different schools and disciplines choose to focus attention upon different factors in the causal web (such as the different fields attending to explaining why a frog jumped into a pond)? Or are different perspectives fundamentally at odds, each account therefore challenging the validity of the others? As Chapters 4–7 show, there has been a great effort to present differences within the sociology of science as fundamental differences of mutual exclusivity. However, this has been overstated for intellectual and career interests. As much difference originates in the choice of focus (on physical, chemical or biological, class, gender, career/organization language and/or interactional factors).

It is not the case that beneath the heat of boundary-setting and career-building in the sociology of science there is a clear set of mutually supporting sub-fields. Nor is it the case that the different agendas pursued by Marxists, feminists, interests theorists and ethnographic/discursive researchers would, if understood correctly, fit neatly together as different but compatible pieces in a big picture. However, the binary distinction between epistemological chicken and epistemological reductionism (whether this be exclusive causal reduction to particles, molecules, genes, classes, gender, social interests or language/interaction) can be moved beyond. A position of reflexive epistemological diversity offers far more than is offered by any one single approach set off against all the others. This is for two main reasons: more and less explanatory validity.

Reflexive epistemological diversity (RED) does not mean simply accepting that different disciplinary perspectives contribute unproblematically to one unified and singular explanation. RED recognizes that the significance of different contributions to any overall account force us to reflect upon the limitations of each singular explanatory approach. Differences encourage reflexivity if they are actively engaged with. 'Reflexive epistemological diversity' is distinct from a simple 'epistemological diversity' based upon stacking up the results of insular research traditions confined within specific and self-referential disciplinary fields. To limit the explanatory power of any one dimension of explanation is not to dismiss it out of hand. When playing 'epistemological chicken', sociologists of science may appear to, and sometimes do, dismiss the epistemologies of the physical sciences, and those of sociologies of science other than their own. RED requires that we are open to the possibility that empirical findings are influenced by social factors, whether these be of class, gender, career or linguistic origin, while at the same time recognizing that such results also relate to the physical world, if never directly or absolutely. The desire to assert the significance of the social in the work of scientists should not lead to an insecurity complex, one that seeks to deny the input of physical reality. Equally, sociologists of science need to suspend what Mason *et al.* (2002a, 2002b) call 'a priorism', the presumption that the elements their method is best designed to highlight are always the most significant in explaining any particular set of events. This applies to all epistemologies, from the micro to the marco, in the physical and in the social sciences.

## Non-paradigm Science or New Reflexive Paradigm?

The possibility of dialogue based upon reflexive epistemological diversity, between the natural and social sciences, as well as between different branches within both, raises the question of whether sociology of science should be a unified field or the attempt to bridge diverse fields. For Kuhn (1962), what characterized physics was its paradigmatic focus, the unity around which those socialized into the field were trained to see the world in terms of particular questions, puzzles, problems and procedures. The sociology of science does not possess this unified quality, and appears more like the rebellions and detachments described by Michael Mulkay mentioned in Chapter 1. What Mulkay described was a series of splitting-off manoeuvres designed to close off fields of study from their competitors, so allowing greater career advancement for the members of the new field. This use of epistemological separation might best be called boundary work rather than evidence for the intrinsic incompatibility of perspectives. Such boundary work limits the scope for reflexive engagement between different epistemological fields. Even while boundary work is endemic within the contemporary sociology of scientific knowledge, the value of SSK lies in resisting these pressures and in opening up scope for reflexive epistemological diversity.

Gerard Delanty (1999, 2001, 2002) sets out to define the new intellectual terrain opening up in the movement beyond scientific reductionism and social relativism. Social scientists once sought to distance themselves from the 'positivism' of reductionist natural science. However, the constructed nature of the latest techno-science (in particular genetics and computing), and the involvement of such techno-science in the reconstruction of 'nature' and 'society', has led to a breakdown in the distinctions both between 'nature' and 'society' and between natural and social science. Language and interaction have become increasingly powerful metaphors within the natural sciences, even as mechanical and reductive metaphors have declined in both the social and natural sciences. Delanty supports a version of constructivism that recognizes the significant, if never clear and partially fluid, limits imposed by the 'reality' posited in realist accounts of science. This constructivism can best address the radical potential for established boundaries, truths and realities to be undone and rewritten in what he calls 'the "post-scientific" age of techno-science' (2002:285). The best way to describe such a position is as 'reflexive epistemological diversity'.

## Instrumentalism, Romanticism and Beyond

Helga Nowotny (1979:1–25) observes the tendency for scientists, and the defenders of the 'institution' of science, to label counter-movements as irrational and anti-science. Anti-nuclear, peace and environmental activisms combine a complex mix of movements and stances in relation to science. Romantic anti-science, pseudo-science and 'institutional' science interact. Anti-science and uncritical establishment mirror each other in their inability to accept any criteria of rationality other than their own. Anti-science romanticism can express a perfectly rational rejection of the imposition of instrumental rationality upon 'lifeworld' interactions, even while it contains an irrational rejection of science in realms where objectification may be legitimate. Scientists need to avoid a blanket instrumental rationality when confronting romantic reactions to science.

Gernot Böhme (1979:105–25) seeks to transcend opposition between two extremes. One is a pro-science view that does not question scientific knowledge, only the ownership and control over it. Böhme identifies this with J. D. Bernal's question 'Whom does science serve?'. This form of Marxist pro-science is opposed to an anti-science romanticism that Böhme associates with Martin Heidegger (1978). This view is that instrumental domination is built into the very fabric of modern techno-scientific ontology. In the first outlook, truth offers human progress, while in the second, scientific truth is to grasp reality rather than to understand it in the non-controlling sense. Böhme advances a Habermasian version of critical theory. Böhme is critical of those critical theorists more sceptical of science than Habermas. Böhme rightly identifies in the work of Adorno, Horkheimer and Marcuse the view that modern science embodies a will to instrumental control. However, he ignores the explicit rejection of romantic anti-science in their work (see Chapter 6), when equating it with the mysticism of Martin Heidegger. Böhme suggests that the British interests perspective offers some scope for a more measured account of the complexities and contradictions of science (beyond the stark either-or of science/anti-science). However, such an internalist approach must itself be supplemented by an orientation to wider social conditions.

Böhme highlights the belief popular in scientific circles in the late 1970s that science was close to providing a final account of basic physical reality, such that efforts could soon be placed fully into the task of applying such knowledge to human needs. He responds with a sceptical view, but one that suggests the scope for improving, not rejecting, science. We cannot simply acquire all the answers and then apply them to problems previously neglected. The nature of answers in science will change when the questions being asked by science are themselves changed:

> The rules according to which one makes something the theme of a scientific study depend in part on the manner in which such a something has become one's

(*cont'd*)

problem. This, the interest one has in an object, may have consequences for its formal properties. In this sense, the sociologists of knowledge, from Scheler to Habermas, have asserted that for modern natural science nature only becomes an object of interest to the extent that it becomes interesting to manipulate it technically. (Böhme 1979:114)

The question is not how to apply neutral science, or to abandon it. Rather, it is to create a society where the priorities are not for war, profit and domination, and where the treatment of people like objects is not the dominant logic of economic and political life. Only then would such values and pressures cease to shape scientific knowledge.

## The Value of Diversity

Chapters 4–7 outline the four dominant contemporary traditions. In Chapters 8–10 the value of reflexive epistemological diversity will be demonstrated in relation to three fields of science. This value will be shown in two senses. First, it will be shown how different sociological perspectives can highlight different aspects of a field and so add to an overall account of the issues in question. Second, it will be shown that different perspectives facilitate reflexive challenges to the authority claims of each other, so overcoming misconceptions, enabling intellectual development and challenging domination.

## Reflexivity, Scepticism and Relativism: Risk, Trust and the Science Wars

At a time when there is a sense of greater scepticism towards science and the knowledge it generates, it is important to be able to investigate the claims made by both the critics of science and those who would seek to defend it. Adopting the position of reflexive epistemological diversity, rather than either the dogmatism of epistemological reductionism or epistemological chicken, the sociology of science offers the best means of balancing the need to question all taken-for-granted assumptions and the need to respect a range of explanations. This is not to accept all knowledge claims or cling to one form of knowing without question.

## Experts, Democracy and the Big Picture

Barbara Katz Rothman (1998:30–41) makes a parallel between the exclusion of non-genetic experts in medical and/or scientific decision-making and the decision whether or not to install electric lighting in a lakeside holiday village she and her family regularly visit. Participation in deciding whether to go ahead did not require a degree in electrical engineering, even if the opinion of an engineer was sought in the process. Decisions should be based upon the possible consequences and the wishes of the users. Apart from advising on possible unforeseen consequences, 'experts' have no more right or ability to judge than anyone else does.

In a similar vein, but in relation to the debate over screening for genetic markers that may predict susceptibility to certain forms of cancer (see Hallowell 1999), Rothman questions the value of ever more micro-focused research into genetic differences and dispositions. Such research generates ever more obscure expertise and claims to decision-making authority, while diverting attention from more socially inclusive policies and democratic decision-making processes. She writes (1998:170):

> I have no idea what individual, cellular, internal factors account for variations in susceptibility to cholera. And I don't care. I opt for a safe water supply. And so, I believe, it can be with cancer... To switch our attention from power lines to cell lines in the search for causes of cancer, to keep looking down instead of up, is dangerous. To individualize the disease obscures the role of the social world in causing cancer... Cancer is the product of mutations. But it is also the product of society. We need more than one map if we are to imagine solutions.

This is an invitation to reflexive epistemological diversity. Science is driven by political and economic dynamics in Rothman's account. It is not that such science is wholly false. It is simply the case that a half-truth can be the most powerful deception.

# 3

# Risk and Technoscience: The Fusion of Society, Science and Technology Today

## The Colonization of Technology by Its Own Sub-field, Science

Recent innovations within genetics and computing have focused attention upon the relationship between science, technology and democratic decision-making. Defensive and offensive portrayals of science run through media discourse (both in news and in fiction). Science is pictured either as irresponsible Frankenstein or Big Brother, as a pawn in the pocket of states and multinationals, as a heroic exposer of deception, or as a vehicle for the passage to a new and better future (Turney 1998a and 1998b). Science's assumed 'otherness' tends to expose it to such extreme representations (whether it is seen as amoral or impartial – or both). While the revolution in computing is often depicted as the product of techno-geeks in garages or back sheds, the revolution in genetics is more often depicted as the work of super-eggheads in clinical laboratories. Such stereotypical images of 'outsiders' (playful amateurs and 'blue-skies' scientists) belie a radical transformation of science and technology over the course of the twentieth century. The boundaries between science, technology, politics and economics have always been porous. To separate them at all has always been problematic. Yet three world wars (two hot, one cold), the rise and fall of national economic and political management, and the new global world order has seen the rise of a new synthesis between science, technology, politics and economics. Far from emerging from the margins of social life (in back sheds and ivory towers), the new revolutionary innovations in computing and genetics reflect and reinforce this ongoing technocratic integration. The collapsing of the boundaries between science and technology and the erosion of distinctions between science, politics, economics and ethics requires us to ask serious questions about the state of the society we now live in.

35

As has already been discussed in Chapter 1 (pp. 18–19), the doctrine of 'scientific neutrality' played an important role in presenting science in the cold war era. Science was to be seen as neither responsible for the practical application of its knowledge (the separation of science and technology) nor directly driven in its focus or in its findings by the interests of those funding research (the separation of science and society). Here, the relationship between science, technology and society is given a more systematic treatment. The very title of this book, *Science in Society* (rather than for example 'Science and Society'), implies that these two terms are not separate. The choice of 'Science' alone, rather than 'Science and Technology in Society', underlines the view that science and technology are united. These two propositions are defended below. First, while modern science has always been a sub-field of instrumentally oriented technical control over nature, what makes the present unique is the extent to which science has come increasingly to incorporate the whole technical field from which it emerged as a subcategory. Second, it will be argued that while science has never been detached from its social context, what makes contemporary 'risk' society distinct is the extent to which this integration of science in society is now increasingly explicit and impossible to ignore.

This book does not seek to present a singular definition of science. It is not the author's intention to legislate over the inclusion or exclusion, from the category 'science', of social science, medieval alchemy, renaissance artists, Chinese medicine, Indian mathematics, Babylonian astrology, ancient Greek classifications of nature and logic, or the 'sciences' developed in the Islamic world. All these questions are of great interest and significance but lie beyond the scope of this text. The focus here is upon the dominant institutional fields of science today, the natural and physical sciences that emerged in Western societies in the period since the so-called scientific revolutions of the renaissance and the seventeenth century. It cannot be disputed that other traditions fed into this dominant 'modern Western science'. No single characteristic unites all elements of today's dominant science, nor sets it apart utterly from all other traditions of knowledge and discovery. Nevertheless, it is the very institutional dominance of that which is commonly called science today that commands attention, and which forms the focus of the following discussion.

Gernot Böhme *et al.* (1978) suggest that from its inception in the Italian renaissance, modern Western science was always instrumental in orientation, making it a part, even if an innovative part, of the technological undertakings of its age. These authors give an account of the shift in medieval cathedral-building, from a craft-guild-based system that built from experience towards an approach that sought to theorize the potential and limitations of new structures in advance of their ever being constructed. Leonardo da Vinci (1452–1519) is cited as a pioneer of this approach in a number of technical fields. What distinguished such a theoretically driven approach to knowledge from the 'science' of ancient

Greece lay in the new approach's overarching emphasis upon knowledge as a means of controlling nature, not simply as a method for knowing it passively. Modern scientific knowing has always been driven by an instrumental conception of 'knowing' as 'grasping'. It is a cognitive sub-field of technical control. Modern Western science was from its inception a branch of technology. Böhme *et al.* go on to chart the changing nature of this emerging science. The period 1660–1750 saw the practical integration of science with service to trade, state and production, while also establishing a separation of science and technology at the levels of representation and institutional setting. The industrial revolution again witnessed this dual process of technical integration with ideological and institutional demarcation. The period from the end of the nineteenth century through two hot world wars and one cold saw a more intensive integration of science within state and economic technical priorities combined, once again, with a revised institutional ideology of separation from both practical direction and application.

As Hilary Rose and Steven Rose (1976c:19) suggest, 'The point is that, despite the paradigm within which bourgeois historians, philosophers and sociologists of science have operated, modern science and technology are indivisible'. While it was, at least in the past, a badge of honour for scientists to claim that their work was of no practical utility, pursuing truth for its own sake, science has, in the main, focused upon issues of value to the societies of which it has been a part. Gunter Küppers (1978) highlights the practical integration of science and technology with particular reference to combustion technology, thermodynamics and fluid mechanics. While 'science' claims 'general relevance criteria' different from those of 'technology' ('truth' rather than 'efficiency'), these differences can only ever be partial. As is discussed more fully in Chapter 4, 'truth' relies upon criteria of technical 'calibration', just as 'calibration' requires criteria of theoretically predicted outcomes to validate its claim to ensure an 'accurate' measure. As development generates both greater specialization and sophistication, the experiment becomes one site of integration between science and technology (truths and tools), just as does the practical application, machine or product. Böhme *et al.* asserted that the late twentieth century would be the age of 'theoretical technology', or as they also put it (1978:219) 'the scientification of technology'.

Following the colonization of technology by its own sub-field, science, increased attention is being paid to the fusion of the sociology of science and the sociology of technology. Trevor Pinch and Wiebe Bijker (1989) suggest that the sociology of scientific knowledge and the social construction of technology fields are increasingly fused together. While philosophers have failed to move beyond the flawed separation of 'scientific discovery' and 'technical application', and while governments and scientists debate the relationship between practical problem-solving and 'blue-skies' research, a sociology of science and technology is emerging. Pinch and Bijker adopt the three-step model proposed by Harry

Collins (see Chapter 4 for details) for the sociological examination of disputes over the status of scientific 'facts':

1.  Identify 'interpretive flexibility'.

2.  Identify how flexibility is closed down (how disputed interpretations are 'stabilized').

3.  Show how such closure can be related to wider social relations of power and influence.

They combine this approach to closing down 'facts' with attention to technical 'artefacts' and the social constructivist approaches to such objects developed within the sociology of technology. In their account of the rise of the 'safety bicycle' Pinch and Bijker argue that the social process of producing and stabilizing facts and artefacts is fundamentally the same, and each feeds off the other at every step. Pinch and Bijker draw most heavily upon the social-interests perspective within the sociology of scientific knowledge, when demonstrating the value of bringing together the sociology of science and technology. However, they also cite the work of the Marxist David Noble (1984) and the ethnographic/ discursive researcher Michel Callon (1989) as exemplars of the new fusion. Feminist approaches are not addressed in their discussion. I will suggest that feminist research into the social construction of facts and artefacts forms a central part of the new sociology.

As was pointed out in Chapter 1 (pp. 8 and 19), war in the twentieth century was a powerful factor in the intensified integration of science and technology within society. Science increasingly subsumes the general category of technology from which it originally arose. The category of science should be understood today to include the fields of advanced technology discussed in Chapters 8, 9 and 10. It is for this reason that I have called this book *Science in Society*.

One clarification should be made at this point. Steve Fuller (1997) usefully warns of the attempts by scientists to project their current incorporation of technology backwards into history. Fuller reminds us that scientists did not invent the steam engine or the aeroplane. To assert that modern Western science is wedded to criteria of instrumental and technical control is not to say that all successes in the history of instrumental and technical control have been examples of 'science' as currently defined.

## Science Is 'In' Society

The second theme, the position of science within society, rather than something external to society, can be dealt with fairly quickly, given much of what has previously been said, both in this chapter and in Chapter 1. In addition to what has been said already, about science as a sub-field of social life, I only wish to cite the following observation:

> [A]ll those many books entitled 'Science and Society' (also including one by authors who should have known better) are, as Levy Leblond and Jourert observe, sociologically incorrect, in that they juxtapose as, distinct if interacting, scientific and social systems. (Rose and Rose 1976c:19)

Just as modern Western science has always been a sub-field of instrumental technical thinking, but one that has come increasingly to colonize the field in which it arose, so science is a sub-field of social life that has come increasingly to colonize all aspects of the social (and non-social) lifeworld. Gernot Böhme and Nico Stehr (1986:8) argue that 'Contemporary society may be described as a knowledge [post-industrial/information] society based on the penetration of all its spheres of life by scientific knowledge.' These authors identify seven dimensions of the growing reorganization of social relations upon scientific knowledge (itself socially constructed). First, everyday practices are redefined in terms of scientific research and developments. Diet, relationships, fertility, childrearing and exercise are all current examples of this 'scientization' of social action. Second, professionalization and credentialism increase the role of science as a source of credibility in defining competence in every aspect of work and expertise. Third, science becomes an increasingly 'immediate' productive force (in rapidity, intensity and in its location in physical and cultural terms in relation to the economy). Fourth, science gives rise to whole new economic sectors with increasing rapidity. Fifth, science becomes the primary means of legitimating social policies and economic strategies, while, sixth, technocratic government uses 'science' almost as a secular religion, in a supposedly 'end-of-ideology' era of 'neutral' and 'rational' 'modernization'. However, at the same moment, the rising number of university-educated professionals creates the foundations for a new class, a new politics of social movements, and new sciences/counter-sciences. For Böhme and Stehr, science shifts its ideological position from the social superstructure to the productive base, but they reject both technological-determinist and end-of-ideology conclusions. As society becomes 'scientized', it is essential to recall that science is itself socially constructed. What occurs is a shift in the nature of social relations, not a shift from social determination to that of some external logic. New conflicts emerge within the knowledge society, and 'the increased distance from nature [and its increasingly radical transformation and manipulation] may mean that nature can affirm itself catastrophically in knowledge societies' (1986:20). This is an intimation of the 'risk' society to be discussed in the next section.

World wars focused the attention of government upon the social position of science within society. The Vietnam War awoke a new generation of critical voices concerning the integration of science within militaristic and hierarchical societies. However, the position of science within today's so-called 'risk' society is being highlighted as never before and in the consciousness of ever greater numbers of people.

## Science in Contemporary 'Risk' Society?

Helga Nowotny (1977) made the observation that the question of risk assessment in relation to the nuclear industry increasingly exposed the scientific establishment to the accusation that scientific knowledge is unavoidably political, not only in its application but also in its construction. When asked to evaluate the risk involved in relation to the nuclear industry, scientists are being asked to make calculations based upon a combination of probabilistic risks that cannot be predicted in any absolute way. No single and universal methodology can be impartially prescribed. The selection of calculation methodologies becomes open to the accusation of political motivation. Science becomes caught between the expectation that it can answer questions of risk likelihood and condemnation for political bias in any claims it actually makes. Science cannot move beyond a certain level of uncertainty on these questions, but is expected to do precisely that to maintain its social prestige. Yet, if it takes an authoritative line on such matters, it is open to the accusation of having been selective in its criteria and/or in its calculations. Science's reliance on a presentation of 'cognitive immunity' (1977:249) comes under threat when confronted by such highly emotive risk issues. Science's historical involvement with the nuclear industry, combined with its need to secure its own position with authoritative knowledge claims where none can be given, threatens to demystify science, and overturn the belief that science can stand above society.

Almost all contemporary issues and debates have been linked to 'risk' in the years since Nowotny's article was published. The concept of 'risk' has become one of the central organizing principles in social theory today. Issues such as AIDS, foot-and-mouth disease, BSE, salmonella, genetically modified food, cloning, nuclear waste, loss of biodiversity, the destruction of the ozone layer, medical and recreational drugs, and a whole host of other products and practices have all come to be discussed within the broad theme of risk. What unites this array of issues is the perception that these problems are, in part at least, the products of human actions. Also, whether in regard to the causes of these problems, our ability to identify their existence and extent, or in relation to 'our' ability to solve/prevent them, all these issues are linked to the power of science and technology in modern society. Science appears divided as a source of both security and insecurity, knowledge and doubt, solutions and more problems.

The sociological–anthropological 'debate' about risk consciousness is characterized by two separate debates that have almost entirely failed to engage with each other. These two debates are centred around the respective works of Mary

Douglas and Ulrich Beck. The near total lack of dialogue between the two 'camps' is the result of theoretical and political starting points that are mutually incompatible. The former adopts a communitarian stance, the latter a libertarian one. Work produced from within one 'camp' appears self-evidently misguided from the perspective of the other, so leaving very little to be said. The occasional fragments of comment that pass between the camps are dismissive and do more to shore up existing commitments than to raise questions. Recent works by Lupton (1999a, 1999b), Allan (2002) and Irwin (2001) have sought to draw upon the work of both Beck and Douglas. While such works address interesting issues and identify particular paradoxes, the gulf between the two theoretical approaches remains great and significant in what it highlights about knowledge, trust and science in contemporary society.

So, what does the current debate on risk come down to? Two themes unite and divide the work of Beck and Douglas:

1. Beck and Douglas are united in observing the rise of 'risk consciousness', the perception that 'we' are increasingly at risk from the consequences of human intervention in nature. Is our heightened sense of insecurity in 'risk society' the result of a greater consciousness of self-generated ecological risk, or is our belief in heightened risk the result of greater social insecurity? Mary Douglas is more prone to the latter view; Ulrich Beck argues it is both combined.

2. How can an ecologically motivated politics hope to reappropriate the same rational resources of modernity (science, technology and bureaucracy) which are so central to the ecological crisis in the first place (a criticism of Beck made by Zygmunt Bauman in his (1993) book *Postmodern Ethics*)? Beck suggests society, and science as a part of society, must both be more 'reflexive' in their acceptance of expert knowledge. For Douglas, it is the very questioning of all forms of authority, including science, that leaves human beings feeling insecure and vulnerable in the first place. Douglas asserts the need for re-establishing trust in scientific authority. Beck suggests re-establishing trust in science by encouraging science to act in a less authoritarian fashion.

## *Risk as a Stick to Beat Authority With*

Mary Douglas attempts to apply principles of Durkheim's (1989[original 1897]) general sociology to the understanding of pollution and taboo. Initially (1966) this was in relation to the traditional object of anthropological study: small-scale, 'premodern' societies. In her later work the same analysis is applied to modern society. Risk consciousness manifests collective identity and solidarity needs. Collective representations of 'risk' are representations of what puts the collective at 'risk'. The central claim behind Douglas's account of modern risk perception is that the contemporary breakdown in social solidarity, and of the conscience collective, has produced an individualism whose consequence is 'pathological' insecurity. Not only is social solidarity not strong enough to counteract these pathological fears, but these fears are themselves vehicles for the continued assault on 'authority' in the name of 'emancipation'. 'Risk' becomes a byword for the dangers to which individuals are exposed by 'the system'. Risk is always associated with modes of responsibility and of blame. Modern emancipatory individualism escapes responsibility by blaming those 'in charge' (Douglas 1996:161–2).

Douglas provides a synthesis of Durkheim's account of regulation and integration as keys to the formation of social solidarity (Douglas 1978). 'Grid' refers to systems of social regulation. 'Group' refers to systems of social integration within subgroups (see Table 3.1). Social relations manifest different levels of regulation and integration, shaping individuals' lives and experiences.

Douglas presents us with four 'institutional personalities', the product of particular social circumstances:

- *Fatalists* combine high grid powerlessness and low group identification.

- *Hierarchalists* are integrated and regulated; they believe in the system and feel utterly dependent upon it.

- The free-marketeering *individualist* is prone to unregulated ambition and self-destruction.

- *Egalitarian* sect members combine a weak sense of social order (giving an anomic sense of normless chaos in the universe) with a strong altruistic identification with their group (the latter compensating for the former through extreme collective identification; setting 'us' against the 'corrupted' status quo).

### Table 3.1

**Grid and group**

|  |  | Group | |
|---|---|---|---|
|  |  | High | Low |
| Grid | High | (b) Hierarchalist | (a) Fatalist |
|  | Low | (d) Sectarian | (c) Individualist |

Adapted from Douglas (1978).

Douglas and Wildavsky (1982) apply Douglas's grid–group model to the analysis of 'environmental risk consciousness'. They present four modes of 'cultural bias', what their collaborators Schwartz and Thompson (1990) call 'myths of nature'. For the fatalist, nature is capricious. They feel powerless, so nature feels unpredictable. For the hierarchalist, nature is robust within limits. We are safe as long as we don't rock the boat too much. For the individualist, nature is robust. They do not see nature as risky, and believe things will turn out all right in the end. The egalitarian sees nature as both at risk and risky. Their suspicion of authority leads to a fear that all is not well and that 'the system' is storing up trouble ahead.

Douglas and Wildavsky are biased towards hierarchy as the best bet for a solution to modern insecurity, as projected onto nature. They conclude that only a restoration of faith in authority and social solidarity can enable society to absorb, through the productive but gradual reform of institutions, the patho-logical 'risk consciousness' (the evasion of responsibility) which they see as reflecting the normlessness and egoism wrought by modern individualism. Douglas concludes (1994:266) that

> unless we learn to control our cultivated gut response against the idea of hierarchy we will have no choice among models of the good society to counter our long established predatory, expansionary trend. By sheer default, among cultural forms hierarchy is the rejected Other... Yet hierarchy is the social form that can impose economies, and make constraints acceptable.

Empirical research carried out into the validity of these cultural types (see Dake 1992) suggests a strong fit between the theory and individual perceptions of risk (so-called 'myths of nature'). Durkheim's work has been questioned for the way empirical data is structured within and then used to verify his theoretical model of suicidogenic tendencies (for example, by Jack Douglas 1967). So Mary Douglas can be held to have created a hermetically sealed, abstract model that frames data collection, and so creates tautological self-confirmation. Of course, the sociology of science highlights the extent to which this is a generic issue in the relationship between theory and evidence.

Are Mary Douglas's cultural biases, her four institutional personalities, only the extreme outermost manifestations of the grid/group axes she sets up, or are they inclusive categories into which the whole field of environmental risk consciousness can be located? For Durkheim threats to the centre may invigorate the culture as long as the centre is itself strong. Mary Douglas, following Durkheim, suggests that a normative consensus within society enables threats to be dealt with. At certain points in her writing this centre is equated with the hierarchalist position. In others consensus is seen as some moderate combination of all four positions. The functional reduction of perception to collective identity needs in her argument leads her to present the four thought styles as fairly inclusive of human thinking when she adopts a debunking tone. This is when she wants to suggest that current risk perception results from the pathology of a modern emancipatory sentiment pitted against beleaguered hierarchy. Yet, this reductionism is toned down and the four extreme positions are pushed to the margins when she adopts a more reconstructive tone (that is when she seeks to rekindle the possibility of shared values and a willingness to accept the decisions of those in authority). The latter must be based upon a willingness on the part of the majority to accept compromises worked out between the extremes by those in power. However, such a possibility would be denied if the fragmentation of the conscience collective suggested in her account of modern anomie and egoism is to be believed. When she is being critical of others, relativism is deployed to reduce risk perception to expression of group identity. When hierarchy is being defended this relativism is reigned in. Douglas pulls the rug out from under her own feet.

## *Risk as Consequence of Self-Confrontation Within Authority*

Douglas's account understands the current social crisis to be one of individualism against hierarchy, with the hierarchy as victim but at the same time posited as redeemer. Authority could check rampant individualism if only respect for authority had not been so heavily undermined by rampant individualism. In Beck's account (Beck 1992, 1997; Beck *et al*. 1994), reversing the arrow of blame, technocratic domination is the problem. While Beck reverses the evaluative polarity between hierarchy and emancipation, his account of risk consciousness is very much in line with Douglas. In the process of modernity's self-development, individualization through differentiation, and the intensified division of labour, undermines traditional faith in institutions:

> Ultimately, what emerges from the fading social norms is naked, frightened, aggressive ego in search of love and help ... In this 'individualization process' people fall out of the nest of binding and guiding traditions, 'set free' in Marx's term ... This very logic makes it difficult or impossible to recognize the social character of the individualization process ... Modernity is a revolutionary-system wolf hidden in sheep's clothing of science, business, and technology. (Beck 1995a:40–1)

As regards the selection of risks to panic over, Beck is again in many ways in agreement with Douglas:

> To put it systematically, cultural indignation chooses between matters of the highest 'objective' urgency, and this choice is not guided by the issues themselves, but by cultural symbols and experiences that govern the way people think and act, having their origin in their history and in societal living conditions. (Beck 1995b:47)

Contemporary risk consciousness is intimately bound up with the breakdown of established social conventions. Just as feudalism's legitimating principles – the divine ordering of heaven, society and nature – was undermined by the plague, so

> [t]he entry into risk society occurs at the moment when the hazards which are now decided and consequently produced by society undermine and/or cancel established risk calculations. (Beck 1996:31)

The industrial society emerged in the wake of feudalism's material and ideological collapse. The feudal ordering principle had been the hierarchical governance of heaven, man and nature. Industrial society created its own principle of hierarchical ordering to compensate for the newly introduced insecurities (or risks) associated with the transition from 'traditional' ways of life to modern society's urban industrial mobility and rapid change. This hierarchical institution was the modern nation-state, built upon bureaucratic administration as well as scientific and technical prediction and control. The 'social contract' between state and society is based upon an exchange of individual freedom for a degree of personal security. State legitimacy, and the right of hierarchical authority to 'rule', is premised on the promise to safeguard the well-being of the individual rights-bearing citizen:

> To that extent, the calculus of risk and the idea of assurance represent more than just one institution among the others of industrial society. They are the institutional arrangement, the invention, with which industrial modernity anticipates and compensates the insecurities of its own creation. In this way the 'assurance state' (*etat providence*) arises as a pendant to 'risk society'. (Beck 1995b:109)

Risk society emerges as faith in the *etat providence* begins to wain. 'In the ruins of detraditionalized life forms and lifeworlds, the crisis of identity is spreading like an epidemic' (Beck 1995a:59).

To maintain their legitimacy, the economic 'technocracy' must intervene more radically in nature (*intensifying production*), while the political 'technocracy' must seek to increase their knowledge of the world by which the citizen can be safeguarded from natural and self-generated dangers (*intensifying prediction*). *Intensifying production* comes increasingly to undermine itself through unintended consequences, as intensification in the production of economic goods leads to intensification in the production of 'ecological bads'. *Intensifying prediction* comes to undermine itself as increasingly sophisticated knowledge of nature reveals the 'self-generated risks' of production, hitherto unsuspected risks, and weaknesses in what was assumed to be unproblematic prior knowledge. This combination generates what Beck calls a self-confronting reflex action within the 'sub-politics of technocracy'. The very self-contained nature of technocratic authority, the ability to govern largely without the involvement of the non-technocracy, while largely retaining their passive consent, through the legitimacy of scientific, technical and bureaucratic rationality, becomes problematic when those on the inside start disagreeing. The technological-determinist ideology of legitimate authority becomes a liability as that very technocratic ideology starts to undo itself from within its own logic.

Meanwhile, to achieve intensification of production and prediction, 'technocracy' accelerates the division of labour, social mobility and individuation. This accelerated fragmentation of life Beck refers to as the 'sub-politics of experience'. The sub-politics of technocracy is the self-confronting reflex action within arenas of decision-making. The sub-politics of experience is the radical self-reflexivity this leads to in everyday life. The taken-for-granted securities of identity, family, sexuality, career, locality etc. begin to fracture and appear more and more transient and contingent. Such an insecure and individuated population become more likely to panic in the face of media-rendered accounts of the contradictions raging within the sub-politics of the technocracy.

The higher-educated are both more socially mobile and more keenly aware of the contradictions in their own lives and in the society of which they are a part. They also make up the group located at the margins of the technocracy itself. They carry the sub-politics of experience inside the sub-politics of technocracy. Beck suggests that this 'explains why the environmental movement recruits especially from milieux and groups where disenchantment and the loss of unquestioned assumptions have reached an advanced stage' (1995b:56).

There are similarities here with Douglas, but in Beck's view such an anomic situation is more characteristic of middle-class radicals on the margins of the elite than of marginal groups on the fringes of society. Douglas would no doubt agree that '[w]here consensus about progress begins to crumble, "rationality of risks" becomes both necessary and impossible. It becomes necessary in order to manufacture acceptance, and impossible because rationality shatters in the spectrum of cultural perceptions' (Beck 1995b:91) that would have enabled such acceptance:

> The 'revolution' of hazard is carried out by the situation [technocracy] and its agents via its denial, in a kind of involuntary moonlighting – more thoroughly and impressively than anything the short arm of social movements could ever achieve. (Beck 1995b:104)

Experts falling out in the media do more damage than protesters. The reflex confrontations of experts do more damage to the system than the action of radicals on the margins. Lawyers, doctors, engineers, scientists, politicians, civil, servants, insurance brokers and accountants fall out over the failure of each group's criteria of success, safety and efficiency to match those of the others. One expert's judgement is shouted down by another. The authority of experts in general is dragged down. Beck appears to be suggesting that a palace coup in the corridors of technocratic power is going to be the main liberating factor in the shift to a 'new modernity'. However, Beck does not want to abandon politics altogether and suggests scope for new democratic spaces: 'Where science robs itself of its own scientific character, however, it opens the door to public disputes, fears, and viewpoints and to shared decisions. Democracy sneaks in' (1995a:105). However, quite how this is the case is not made very clear in Beck's work (for a more detailed critique see David and Wilkinson 2002).

Douglas and Beck see much the same picture of contemporary society. Each evaluates that picture differently. Crucial to the difference between Douglas and Beck is the answer each seeks to give to the question of whether science and technocratic elites can claim authority in deciding questions of truth and/or questions about the 'best interests' of humanity. In line with their theoretical commitments, but based upon limited evidence, Douglas asserts that we should believe they can, while Beck is more sceptical. Yet, regarding truth versus ideology and freedom versus domination, Beck sees an ironic reversal. Science, in the service of domination and ideology, comes increasingly to expose the truth and liberate the individualized populous. Mary Douglas seeks to collapse the distinction between freedom and domination, while truth and illusion are dealt with in an even more elliptical fashion. In her work, the authority of truth seems more important as a regulative and integrative ideal than does the question of whether science actually tells things like they really are. Both Beck's optimism that the instruments of domination and persuasion are in the throes of enlightening and liberating us, even against themselves, and Douglas's eliding of categories for political purposes are unconvincing. This volume seeks to provide a more grounded approach to answering these questions.

### Risk, Science and 'Lay Expertise'

Brian Wynne's research into the 'fallout' from the 1986 Chernobyl nuclear accident focuses upon interactions between scientists and sheep-farmers in the Cumbrian high fells in the North West of England. Shortly after the nuclear accident scientists from the Ministry of Agriculture, Fisheries and Food (MAFF) imposed a ban on the sale of sheep from the high fells. As this threatened the farmers with economic ruin, reassurance was given that the ban would last for only three weeks, since the scientists had 'utter confidence unqualified by any hint of uncertainty' (Wynne 1996a:63) that radiocaesium would be chemically locked into the soil within 20 days, so eliminating further risk to the food chain. These claims were false. Scientists had applied principles drawn from clay soils to Cumbria, where acid, peaty soils leave radiocaesium chemically mobile. Local expertise, which could have highlighted this difference, was not sought. The farmers sought to balance their own knowledge with that being asserted by the scientists, while the scientists relied on their own methods and models. While the restrictions were later modified to allow the sale of sheep for non-human consumption, and the area of the restrictions decreased over time, this action highlighted the danger of assuming universal knowledge, the problem of scientific arrogance and ignorance, and the value of 'local' 'lay' expertise.

Wynne notes that, contrary to Beck's account of reflexive modernity, the uncertificated, rural and conservative farmers showed greater reflexivity than the 'modern',

(*cont'd*)

urban and supposedly self-critical scientific community. Scientists displayed an unreflexive faith in their universal truth claims. As one farmer's representative put it: 'When a scientist says he doesn't know, perhaps there's hope for the future!' (Wynne 1996b:32). Wynne counterpoints the scientists' culture of certainty and control, with the farmer's cultural frame of reference and way of life. The latter admits to and practically engages with contingency and uncertainty on a daily basis.

Farmers came to notice that the crescent of land where restrictions remained in force for years was an arc around the Sellafield (originally Windscale) nuclear power station and reprocessing facility. This had been the site, in 1957, of the world's largest civilian nuclear accident prior to Chernobyl. Government scientists once again proclaimed definitive knowledge. The different half-lives of the radioactive isotopes caesium-137 and -134 meant that, over time, the ratio of intensities between the two isotopes' respective gamma-ray frequencies would change. This, it was said, provided a dating method by which 1986 emissions could be distinguished from earlier ones. Armed with such a methodology, scientists set out to show 'the so called Chernobyl fingerprint, making an analogy with a form of evidence which is never questioned in law' (Wynne 1996b:30). Showing Chernobyl's 'fingerprint', government and nuclear industry scientists sought to reassure the public that the problem was 'Russian' in origin. Years passed before it was admitted that the Chernobyl 'fingerprint' accounted for only 50 per cent of the observed radiocaesium.

Wynne points out how farmers' actions and attitudes were always ambivalent, reflecting both suspicion and reliance upon scientific expertise. The economic centrality of Windscale/Sellafield to West Cumbria and the power exercised by MAFF scientists over their lives meant farmers were reluctant to speak out. However, this did not demonstrate unproblematic trust. Wynne traces distrust of scientific expertise as a longstanding thread that precedes Beck's announcement of the 'risk society'. Alternative forms of 'lay expertise' have always existed. The will to certainty and control still persists within the 'culture' of science, even in today's supposed age of reflexivity. All forms of 'expert' knowledge are bound up within ways of cultural life, social interests and economic relationships.

# Science in Society

Two fundamental questions arise about science from contemporary risk society theory. These are:

1. Is science a threat to humanity, or the promise of greater security and well-being?

2. Does increased reflexivity over the objectivity of scientific knowledge claims undermine science or improve it?

These questions are permutations of the two key questions running through this book. Sociological research into media representation of science and the public understanding of science (Allan 2002; Anderson 1997; Petersen 2002; Wilkinson 2001; Wynne 1996a, 1996b) highlight the paradox faced by scientists. Media representations of scientific claims often present 'facts', 'proof' and 'causal links' in black-and-white terms. Such representations draw upon and uphold the image of the scientist as an authority figure, to be trusted and believed. However, such absolute claims are often met with equally black-and-white counter propositions. Set against authoritative expectations, such conflict appears to undermine the credibility of science in general. Presenting less absolute claims, based upon probabilities rather than absolutes, also presents difficulties when journalists, corporations, governments and the public want 'answers', and expect science to provide secure knowledge about what to do. In recent years, many scientists have reacted negatively to the claims made by sociologists of science, claims that appear to limit the power of science to generate authoritative knowledge. The so-called 'science wars' will be discussed further in Chapter 6. In the contemporary 'risk society' government and corporate research sponsors, the media and the public all call for science to answer their anxieties. However, none are willing to trust the scientists when they cannot agree about what those answers might be. It is important, in such conditions, to reflect on what science really is, and what it can realistically deliver. It is necessary for science to reflect upon its strengths and its limits, and for the wider society to do so too. I seek to demonstrate that the failure of absolutist science, the view that one way of knowing can answer all questions fully, should lead to the acceptance of epistemological diversity. Reflexive epistemological diversity or RED (the approach advanced in this book) represents the rejection of reductionism (to any one level of explanation), and recognition of the critical and limiting value of reflexive confrontation between different approaches to knowing the world (within and between the natural and social sciences as well as beyond). Such a framework offers the most constructive way forward for debate and action.

### Cognitive Norms and Knowledge Interests

Drawing upon Habermas's theoretical framework of cognitive norms and knowledge interests, but also making direct links to the work of Mulkay and the then emerging social-interests school in the sociology of science, Gernot Böhme (1977:69–102) presents an account of early debates in 'experimental psychology'.

Debates over the best method to select a sample to participate in experiments are focused upon. Was it best to draw a random sample or one based on strict controls to ensure a group with similar baseline characteristics? Böhme highlights that while the German researcher Titchener was interested in the general characteristics of the human mind, his United States rival in disputes over sampling methods, Baldwin, was

(*cont'd*)

interested in the differences between individual human minds. The Marxist scientist Stephen Jay Gould (1996) points out that the economic and intellectual foundations of psychology in the United States lay in selling itself to private employers and the army. What psychology sold was the promise that it could provide a supposedly objective (though in reality spurious) method for measuring differences between individuals in terms of a fixed and singular level of intelligence. Such a fusion of scientific and social criteria is what Böhme, after Habermas, calls the interlinkage of cognitive norms and knowledge interests.

Robert Franck (1979:39–56) extends the Habermasian approach with a more general observation on the ideological value of the separation between knowledge and opinion. The ideological value of such a separation lies in the ability of dominant groups to deploy the category of 'objective knowledge' in describing their own positions, while denigrating the views of those without access to high-status knowledge resources as 'subjective opinion'. As Habermas argues (1972), the distinguishing characteristic of human interaction lies in its non-reducibility to objectification (and its resistance to attempts to reduce it to such a level of control). The attempt to disqualify the non-objectified knowledge from rational decision-making is the attempt to abandon democracy in favour of domination by technocratic economic and political power.

# Part Two
## Theoretical Approaches

# 4

# Science and Institutional Interests: The Strong Programme and Beyond

## Introduction

The basic premise of the interests perspective is that any piece of empirical data can give rise to more than one interpretation of its meaning. Any 'finding' can be rejected as an experimental error or as the consequence of faulty logic. Thus persuasion and belief within scientific communities rely upon more than brute fact. How the scientific community establishes the credibility of some accounts and marginalizes others should and can be studied empirically within the routines of scientific practice and, by more theoretical accounting, within the wider social world. The strong programme in the sociology of science, and the many offshoots it has spawned over the last 30 years, has established a tradition of research that offers key insights into the 'social construction of scientific knowledge'. Whilst this tradition has received major criticism for its 'relativism', these attacks conflate two meanings of that term: one that denies the possibility of absolute certainty about external reality and one that denies the existence of an absolute reality to be known. The interest perspective adopts the former, while often being accused of promoting the latter.

The interest perspective in the sociology of science paralleled and develops the work of Michael Mulkay (see Chapter 1). It emerged in the 1970s under the banner of the 'strong programme' (strong in the sense of adopting a strong relativism, at least at an epistemological level, as will be explained below). The programme was strongly associated with the Edinburgh University Science Studies Unit and so its adherents are sometimes called the 'Edinburgh school'. The interest perspective is associated with the names of David Bloor, Barry Barnes and Harry Collins among others. Here I outline the core of the perspective, drawing on the work of Barry Barnes, David Bloor, Harry Collins and Trevor Pinch. Barnes's work (1972a, 1974,

1977) laid down much of the foundations. Bloor's *Knowledge and Social Imagery* (1976) represents an early canonical text – outlining basic tenets in programmatic form. Harry Collins's *Changing Order* (1985) carries out a similar task for what Collins calls the 'empirical programme of relativism' (a sibling or parallel to the 'strong programme'). Collins and Pinch's *The Golem* (1993, 1998a, 1998b) series is perhaps the most accessible introduction to the programme and its 'granular' approach (the use of numerous case-studies of scientific disputes).

After outlining the foundations of the programme, examining an illustrative case-study, and exploring the key notion of the 'experimenter's regress', this chapter sets out the basic principles of the interests account. The interests approach is then distinguished from ontological relativism. Three further case studies will then be used to highlight the significance of tacit knowledge, the local nature of knowledge within science and the fusion of 'technical' and 'social' criteria when something is said to 'work'. Both the elaboration of the experimenter's regress and the three case-studies are boxed to set aside materials designed to reinforce the main argument from the flow of the argument itself. In the next section the core assumptions and findings of the perspective are restated and three key criticisms are aired: first, that the perspective fails to research science in a truly scientific manner; second, that the interests approach is insufficiently reflexive about its own claims to have proven the determining power of social causation, and to have suspended claims to 'truth' (both key 'principles' of the approach); third, the primary focus upon the internal social dynamics of science as a community raises serious questions about autonomy and causation as competing explanatory resources. These three specific criticisms are then related to the two dominant questions being asked in this book; i.e. the relationship between science and (1) 'truth' and, (2) 'freedom'.

## Foundations

Inspired by Kuhn (and Polanyi 1957), and influenced by Mulkay's (1969) ground-breaking work, Barry Barnes's work initially 'does not attempt to develop a new framework' (1972b:269). Rather, Barnes only attempted to apply established sociological theories of belief to the realm of science. If truth does not force us to believe it, the question of why scientists believe what they do is open to sociological investigation. The causes of conformity with and deviation from socially established belief require explanation. The traditional anthropologist found it hard to suspend their own 'epistemological' belief in the superiority of their own knowledge over that of those they studied (Peel 1969). The sociologist of science faces the reverse 'epistemological' preconception that what scientists believe is believed because it is true. Barber (1961) sought to explain scientific 'errors' in terms of cultural bias, inertia and loyalties, but Barnes asserts that while cultural influence may lead to error, it can also lead to insight. Loyalty to neo-Platonism meant Copernicus could hold on to the notion that the earth went around the sun, even in the absence of 'reasonable' evidence. Early Darwinians held to evolution despite Lord Kelvin's assertions, 'impeccable in terms of the physics of the day' (Barnes 1972b:276), that the time-scale involved was impossible. Facing such seemingly overwhelming evidence '"truth" triumphed by ignoring it for thirty years' (276). The desire to believe sustained belief. For Barber 'truth' is like gold, 'permanent and immutable'. Scientific explanations become discoveries, rather than constructed theories. Barnes concludes that there is no universal benchmark by which truth can be simply 'recognized' whenever it appears. The only way to account for belief at any point in time is to examine the beliefs of scientists and other actors from within their own frame of reference. This is a sociological question. It suspends judgement on what is or is not 'true', only to ask what people *believe* to be true and why they believe it.

Barnes went on to develop the critique of accounts of scientific knowledge based upon pure empiricism and induction (1974), and as non-contemplative seeing (1977). Once faith in pure empirical or universal rational principles is suspended, Barnes concludes (1974:43), '[t]he sociology of science is no more than a typical special field within the sociology of culture generally'. All areas of culture are special. Science is no more special with regard to the need for its beliefs to be studied as a product of its culture. If truth does not compel belief, then we are as much in need of a causal account of why people believe true beliefs as we are when explaining false beliefs. Barnes therefore insists that scientific knowledge, like any other, should be studied, sociologically, in a symmetrical fashion. It is not enough to say someone believed something because it was true, any more than it is enough to say someone believed something on account of it being untrue. There is no universal scientific method for the sociologist to research. Therefore Barnes suggests 'a piecemeal approach based upon sociological and historical materials' (1974:48). Opposed to both purely internal accounts of scientific practices and beliefs, and crude reductionist accounts of scientific beliefs as straightforward products of economic or political necessities, Barnes advocates a case-by-case approach where particular situations are examined in detail. Barnes cites the work of Mulkay (1969), Forman (1971), Young (1969, 1971, 1972) and Cowan (1968, 1972) as prototypes for such an approach. Barnes (1974:121–2) identifies four key sites for sociological research in the social relations of scientific knowledge: (1) scientific culture; (2) processes of disciplinary and field specialization; (3) the emergence of science from early, pre- and proto-science, when the science–society distinction was being defined; and (4) the boundary work that goes on to define what is and is not legitimate to transfer across the supposed science–society boundary (funds, research priorities, staff, metaphors).

Once social influence is recognized as universal in all knowledge formation and not necessarily a source of bias and distortion, the use of the term 'ideology' becomes in part universally applicable, but also potentially misleading if it appears always to infer error. Barnes does not reject the need to identify error where it occurs, but does not suggest that this is the role the sociologist is best qualified to perform. He concludes (1974:154) that a sociology of science should be materialist, methodologically sceptical (impartial), symmetrical and reflexive (applying its own principles to itself).

Barnes sets this framework against the work of Mannheim and Marxists like Lukács (1971) and Habermas (1972). Mannheim's critique of Marx was that the latter had failed to follow through on his historical and materialist account of ruling-class ideas with a materialist account of his own beliefs (see Chapter 1: p. 6). Barnes asserts that Mannheim himself failed to follow through his own sociological explanation of belief when it came to the knowledge claims of the relatively detached intelligentsia (scientists and would-be social engineers like Mannheim himself). Attention to the specific historical and material causes leading to particular scientific disputes and discoveries enabled Barnes to claim that his approach was more historically materialist than those of Lukács and Habermas. Similar criticisms of earlier Marxists like Bernal were being made by Marxists such as Hilary Rose and Steven Rose at the same time (see Chapter 1: pp. 9 and 18). Why would anyone be required to believe a fully symmetrical, sceptical and reflexive materialist account, one that openly acknowledged itself to be 'the product of its time' (Barnes, 1974:155)? Barnes suggests it would be in keeping with such times for at least some people to do so. In this sense (1974:156) 'its justification lies within itself'.

# An Illustrative Case

Harry Collins and Trevor Pinch (1993, 1998a) give an account of a dispute that occurred in France in the 1860s. Could new life emerge spontaneously in a suitable medium of nutrients, or did the growth of organisms (moulds and bacteria) only ever result from spores deposited by the air? Louis Pasteur supported the latter view. Felix Pouchet defended the former. Both agreed that air was essential to the emergence of organisms. It was generally agreed that flasks of nutrients, boiled to render them devoid of living organisms, and then sealed, saw the development of no living cultures. Was the introduction of air essential because it allowed the introduction of spores and seeds of already living organisms or was air necessary to allow 'spontaneous generation'? The introduction of 'sterile' air (air devoid of bacteria, spores, etc.) was seen as the test for this vexing question. The question then would be; would living cultures grow in flasks of nutrient filled with 'sterilized' air? In simplified terms there are two expectations and two possible outcomes. If you predict one thing and that prediction is confirmed, you will feel vindicated. Collins and Pinch point out that Pasteur's experiments were fraught with difficulties and he abandoned a large number of his results as he was convinced his air must have become contaminated with germs or suchlike, despite all his efforts to avoid this. His published findings relied mainly upon the minority of results that confirmed his prediction. When responding to Pouchet's letters, letters in which Pouchet highlighted results that confirmed his own predictions, Pasteur was equally quick to dismiss his rival's results as the consequence of faulty methods (methods which, Pasteur asserted, must have allowed germs to enter Pouchet's flasks accidentally). Pouchet defended his methods and asserted that his 'positive' results (those which confirmed his prediction) were evidence for the spontaneous generation of life. However, flasks which did not show signs of living cultures growing, flasks that Pasteur would claim confirmed his view, were said, by Pouchet, to have been 'spoiled', either by the boiling process, or through exposure to the various chemicals used to clean and seal the flasks (in particular mercury); see Table 4.1.

What resulted was a standoff. Each side in the dispute was capable of reading the evidence, whichever way it came out, in such a way that the theory they held to would still remain intact. Evidence was not enough to force conversion. How was this dispute resolved if not on the basis of the evidence? The French Académie des Sciences appointed two commissions to investigate. Collins and Pinch (1998a:87) suggest that all those appointed to both commissions were hostile to Pouchet's ideas, many announcing as much even before seeing any of the evidence. Pouchet withdrew from both competitions. Twice humiliated, Pouchet's case was lost. Pasteur still reigns in the pantheon of scientific geniuses.

---

*Table 4.1*

**Interpretive flexibility and the problem of the experimenter's regress: the disputed evidence and the disputed interpretations in the case of spontaneous generation of life and the dispute between Louis Pasteur and Felix Pouchet**

| | | Believe in spontaneous generation | |
|---|---|---|---|
| | | Yes (Pouchet) | No (Pasteur) |
| Result in any one case-study: life grows after introduction of 'pure' air | Yes | 1. Proves Thesis | 2. Air accidentally contaminated |
| | No | 3. Air spoilt by treatment | 4. Proves thesis |

Adapted from Collins and Pinch (1998a:83).

Collins and Pinch suggest three reasons why the commissions sided with Pasteur when the evidence could not force a decision one way or the other:

1.  The 'pasteurization process' gave Pasteur the greater scientific and economic status.

2.  Pouchet's claims challenged the notion that life required a divine intervention and so upset a still dominantly Roman Catholic French society.

3.  Pouchet's ideas were too close to those of the British scientist Charles Darwin for the highly nationalistic French scientific and social elite.

Given the failure of the evidence to be sufficient to resolve the dispute it falls to the sociologist to highlight the 'social interests' at work in the situation. Collins and Pinch note that at the time it was generally believed that the boiling point of water was the level sufficient to kill all life. This is now no longer held to be the case. Even given sterile air life would grow in nutrients only boiled to 100 degrees celsius, because many spores contained in the nutrients would have survived the heating. The evidence at the time would have appeared to favour Pouchet's thesis even if the cause of such 'evidence' was not what either Pouchet or Pasteur would have imagined. Still, as the case-study suggests, 'science' did not follow the 'evidence'. It is evidence, and its interpretation, that tends to follow the social consensus established within the scientific community.

## The Experimenter's Regress: The Achilles' Heel of Science

Harry Collins outlines what he calls 'the experimenter's regress'. He analyses a dispute over the possibility of detecting gravitational radiation (1985; Collins and Pinch 1993, 1998a). Collins argues it is never possible to repeat someone else's experiment in such a way that, if the conclusions do not match, the first researcher will be forced to admit that they were wrong. Claims made by one physicist (Joseph Weber) were disputed by a second (given the fictional name of Quest). Collins seeks to show how each party to the dispute defended their own evidence while denying the validity of evidence presented against their case. Failure to generate the same results was explained away in terms of faulty procedure on the part of the opposition. What Collins calls the experimenter's regress is the logical possibility of always calling for another test to test whether a previous test was a sufficiently accurate replication of the test that went before it. The consequent problems that this regress generates, in disputes over what scientific evidence should lead us to believe, forms a central part of Collins's approach. Collins identifies what he calls the problem of calibration. How can you know your instruments are accurate when at the cutting edge of science? If the thing being measured and/or the instruments being developed to measure it are always open to being questioned you cannot prove that the reading is an accurate measure of 'reality'.

## Elaborating the Experimenter's Regress: The Case of Weber and Quest

Collins refers to the experimenter's regress as a philosophical problem with a socio-logical solution. The sociological solution is not a philosophical solution. Rather it is a means that allows the research community to carry on as though the philosophical problem had been resolved, when , in principle, it remains. The philosophical problem is that of induction (Chalmers 1982; 1990). Scope for disputing the meaning of evidence always remains. The solution is the enforcement of closure around one interpretation of disputed evidence, using various forms of non-evidence based social status and influence (Collins 1985: 145–8). The problem of induction lies in the inability to say that just because something has happened regularly in the past it will continue to do so. The turkey that predicts that it will be in for a good feed tomorrow on account of its experience up until that day is a classic case in point. If tomorrow is a feast day then the turkey is in for rather a nasty surprise. Every new situation will be just that little bit different. We can never be quite sure whether the difference next time is going to really make a significant difference.

Collins suggests that there was no significant dispute over the existence of gravitational radiation, or that the movement of large masses in space generate gravitational waves. What was open to question was whether such background radiation could ever be distinguished from the mass of electrical, magnetic, thermal, acoustic and seismic forces acting upon any instrumentation designed to pinpoint the gravitational wave fluctuations resulting, it was generally believed, from such things as exploding supernovae, black holes and binary stars (Collins 1985: 79). Weber's critics believed such a level of accuracy could not be achieved. This can be seen as a problem of calibration. How can you check the accuracy of a measure when the only way you have for identifying the thing being measured is the instrument with which you are measuring it? Where subsequent research produced results that clashed with Weber's original findings Weber was able to suggest that this latter work must have been insufficiently accurate in its efforts to repeat his methodology.

Collins goes on to catalogue the claims of a range of physicists over who they believed in the Weber versus Quest dispute, and their reasons. All respondents asserted that their belief was based upon what they saw to be the better science. In the absence of absolute criteria, given the experimenter's regress, Collins (1985:88) identified a series of proxy measures by which quality was assumed. These were:

1. Faith based on prior working partnerships with a party to the dispute.

2. The personality or intelligence of the researchers.

3. The reputation of running a huge lab.

4. Industry or academia bias.

5. A previous history of failures.

6. 'Inside information'.

7. The style of presentation of the results.

8. The psychological approach to the experiment (attributions about the state of mind of the researchers).

9. The size and prestige of the university in question.

(*cont'd*)

10.   Integration within various overlapping scientific networks.
11.   Nationality.

As things turned out, Quest was able to mobilize the greater resources to his cause and Weber was sidelined. Mobilization of the scientific community by an array of non-evidence-based means is what Collins calls the sociological solution to the problem of induction. Where physical evidence is open to interpretation (which it always is) then closure is achieved on social grounds.

## 2, 4, 6, 8, . . .

Just as Wittgenstein (cited in Collins 1985:14) suggested that no rule can carry within itself the rules for its own application, so any description of an experimental arrangement will contain within itself room for interpretation. As Collins (1985:56) points out, following the sequence 2, 4, 6, 8, . . . correctly may require the expression 10 or the expression 'Who do we appreciate?', depending on the context. Wittgenstein's point was that cultural rules do not explain themselves and their correct enactment is always sensitive to the situation in which it occurs. That situation is always open to interpretation.

### *Repeatability . . . Popper vs. Popper*

'Press scientists and in the last resort they will defend the validity of their claims by reference to the repeatability of their observations or the replicability of their experiments. This is usually a matter of their *potential* replicability' (Collins 1985:18). The infinite availability of points of dispute creates a crisis for any account of verification or falsification based on the notion that evidence will settle a dispute. Karl Popper suggested that the existence of a falsifying instance is enough to discredit a theory (1972), but he also admitted that no two experimental conditions could ever be absolutely identical. Thus the condition of repeatability necessary to *falsify* a theory can never be indisputably achieved. 'All repetitions which we experience are approximate repetitions . . .' (Popper cited in Collins 1985:26). Thus there is always scope for refusal to accept a refutation of one's work based upon what others claim to be contrary evidence drawn from the supposed replication of the original research.

The interests approach seeks to develop a general account of scientific practice through the elaboration of particular disputes. It is to this general theory or account to which we now turn.

# Basic Principles

Two attempts to outline the basic principles of a sociological approach to scientific knowledge, as understood by the strong programme/interests perspective are presented here. These are David Bloor's (1976) 'four tenets' and Harry Collins's 'three stages in the empirical programme of relativism' (1985).

## *Bloor's Strong Programme: Four Tenets*

Bloor outlines four basic tenets of the strong programme. All these tenets had been presented in the earlier work of Barry Barnes (1972b, 1974), but were given a more programmatic 'manifesto' treatment in Bloor's work. They are as follows:

### *Causality – All the Way*

Bloor argues that science can be understood in a scientific fashion only if it is accepted that scientific knowledge is caused. Just as physical events have causes, so too do brain states and social relations. It is suggested that there is no realm outside causation. Perceptions and conceptions, theories and the willingness to accept certain things as true are all best understood in causal terms. Various factors cause us to believe a proposition is true, just as an array of factors cause leaves to fall from trees. These causes may be complex, but complexity must not be confused with non-causality. It is the job of sociologists to look at the social processes that form a part of the causal chain.

### *Impartiality – Sociology Can't Judge*

Sociologists are not in the business of saying that one scientific theory is more true than any other. The sociologist is not qualified to do this. It is the sociologist's job to show that social relations play a significant role in how scientists make such judgements. Sociologists are not saying they can do physical scientists' jobs better than the physical scientists themselves. The sociologist's job is to study why people believe the things they do. Physical scientists are people and so sociologists are in a good position to explain why such people accept some things and reject others. This challenges the physical scientists' belief that they believe things only because they are true, even while other people believe things because of ideologies and prejudices, self-interestedness and delusion. Physical scientists might complain that any attempt to show their beliefs are caused, at least in part, by social factors, represents an attempt to discredit their beliefs. Bloor rejects this view. The sociologist should not judge, only explain.


### Symmetry – True and False Beliefs are Equally Caused

Just because a belief has a social cause does not make it false. It is only if one believes that true beliefs are accepted simply because they are true, that one would believe that any social causality must act to pollute the truth. Bloor asserts that if naked empirical observation were a superior source of truth to socially constructed ways of seeing, then animals would be better scientists than humans. They have less social mediation in their experience of the world. Science prides itself on being an unnatural form of perception beyond appearances (see Wolpert 1992). Thus all scientists know that naked observations play no role in science. All worthwhile seeing is structured by theory and theory-validated apparatus. Once it has been accepted that the truth is not self-evident to the naked eye, truth can no longer be a simple criterion (standing prior to expectation and belief), allowing us to decide what to believe. You cannot see a cause simply because it is there. How would you know it was true? Thus Bloor argues that social processes of organizing perception into meaningful things must always occur for us to make sense of the world, even if sense perception may give us a fairly accurate set of basic inputs. A scientific belief that is 'true' requires just as much social causation to make people believe it as would a false one. Whether the world is flat or round does not determine which option is believed. It is necessary for scientists and laypersons alike to trust the research, interpretations and experiences of others in forming beliefs of their own. The truth does not compel assent. The sociology of science is not about exposing the social corruption of science, the intrusion of distortions into otherwise clear perception. It is about a symmetrical study of the social causes of all scientific beliefs without regard for whether they are true or false (a distinction that can be made only within the social frameworks of acceptable belief at any one time in any case).

To reiterate, while it may seem that a focus upon the social causation at work in science must, of necessity, be a form of debunking, Bloor denies this. To say that the way a thing is seen reflects something other than the nature of the thing itself may suggest a faulty way of seeing, one that has been interfered with, distorted, or otherwise corrupted. Surely a socially caused way of seeing is a distorted one, rather in the manner of Mannheim's ideologies and utopias (discussed in Chapter 1). Yet Bloor argues this is not the case. As was explained above, the interests account starts from the basic observation that sense can only be made of naked sensation by means of concepts, and concepts cannot be extracted self-evidently from nature. It would only be possible to write off socially organized knowledge as inferior knowledge if a superior knowledge could somehow be made available. It cannot. Socially structured ways of seeing are not perfect, but they are the only ones that exist.

Bloor asserts a form of epistemological relativism, the claim that there can be no absolute foundation for knowing the world and that all such claims are generated and sustained or rejected in and through social relationships. The standard argument against relativism is the accusation that if relativism were true then the claim that relativism was true would therefore have to be relative and therefore not *true*. This argument appears to show that relativism is an intellectual position that undermines itself, because to uphold it as *true* would contradict relativism. Bloor dismisses this argument. He points out that such an argument assumes that a belief cannot be both relative and true at the same time. It may be the case that we could never be sure that a particular belief was true, but to say that we cannot be sure that something is true is not the same as suggesting we can be sure that it is not true. It simply means that there is no absolute vantage from which to establish its truth. Something does not have to be believed for it to be true. This is for exactly the same reason that something does not have to be false just because someone wants to believe it. Epistemological relativism asserts that physical reality and belief are two distinct realms. These realms interact but can never be rendered identical. Thus there is always scope for interpretation and dispute.

### *Reflexivity – Applies to Sociology as Well*

Finally, Bloor suggests that what applies to the physical sciences must also be applied to sociology. If social relations underpin what is accepted or not accepted as true in the realm of the physical sciences then this must be equally the case in the social sciences. The same principles must be applied by the sociologist to their own claims to truth as are applied by the sociologist to the beliefs of others. In so far as Bloor asserts that the demonstration of social causes in the realm of scientific beliefs is not a form of debunking, he is also able to assert that turning the spotlight back on sociology is itself not a form of debunking the debunkers. Nevertheless the same logic highlighted in Collins's discussion of the experimenter's regress means that any claim made by a sociologist is open to question. Any evidence presented or argument put forward can always be given an alternative interpretation.

## *Collins's Three Stages in the Empirical Programme of Relativism*

Harry Collins (1985) re-elaborates the principles of the strong programme in relation to the empirical examination of scientific disputes. He presents a three-stage process model, as follows:

*Demonstrate 'Interpretative Flexibility'*

Here the sociologist identifies the absence of empirical closure. In other words, in scientific disputes the evidence is not enough to compel agreement, because the competing parties give differing accounts of the data. In their account of Pasteur's disproof of the spontaneous-generation-of-life thesis (1998a, discussed above), Collins and Pinch show that Pasteur's supporters and his opponents interpreted the same data either as proof of their case or as a manifestation of faulty technique. In other words when the data does not support your theory it is always possible to question the data collection process or the inferences drawn in the analysis of data. Data can always be read in more than one way. It is never sufficient to settle a dispute. Interpretative flexibility causes the experimenter's regress discussed above.

*Describe Closure Mechanisms*

If there is always interpretative flexibility, how are disputes settled? Here Collins suggests that the sociologist must look for institutional and social-network-based closure mechanisms. Within the scientific community opinion is mobilized by various means around the various parties to the dispute. Alliances set about each other. If one side achieves the upper hand their claims will be taught as truth to subsequent generations, at least until they are themselves deposed. In certain cases both parties to a dispute are deposed by a third force. In particular cases closure of a kind is achieved by the separation of the disputing parties into discrete subdisciplines.

*Relate Closure Mechanisms to Wider Social and Political Structures*

Collins's third step is to relate the closure mechanisms within the scientific community to wider political and economic disputes and resources. This then relates the internalist concerns of the strong programme to those of more externalist approaches to the study of science in society. Collins is keen however to avoid any premature leap from particular disputes and their resolutions to wider forces in society. He asserts the need to give attention to the institutional dynamics of particular scientific communities, fields and eras before attempting to make links between such specific formations and the wider economic, social, political and cultural situation in which they are located.

# Is the Truth Out There? The Difference Between Ontological and Epistemological Relativism

The assertion that belief should be studied and explained in terms of social causation (by interests) is to parallel the materialism of the physical sciences, not to reject it. The strong programme/interests perspective seeks to study science scientifically. It is important to understand that the strong programme is materialist in a particular sense and they do not suggest the non-existence of a physical world or of a social world. To deny the existence of a reality outside our thinking would be ontological relativism (a belief that reality itself is relative to how you see it). Such a perspective would suggest that what is believed in large part moulds the real. This is not as absurd as it might at first seem. Certainly, in social life it is very often the case that what is believed by people has a major impact on the reality of social life. Through human action much of nature is moulded and transformed. Thus there is no absolute separation between thought and world. However, ontological relativism goes a stage further than simply asserting that ideas affect the real and are not merely mirrors of reality. Ontological relativism asserts that there is no real beyond belief. What the interest school asserts is an epistemological relativism. This is the belief that there can be no absolute way of knowing the world with certainty. Thus no claim to knowledge can be sure of the conditions of its own knowing. The world may well be out there, but that is the point. It is not in here (in our theories and ideas), and neither can it ever be. Out there is the real. Truth (a quality related to how ideas relate to things) cannot be simply out there. The strong programme asserts only the relativism of the latter (epistemological) kind. This is an important distinction to keep in mind. Critics from within the scientific community have often mistakenly criticized the strong programme for being ontologically relativist, while those who could more accurately be called ontological relativists (see Chapter 5) accuse the strong programme of retaining too much of the naïve realism and materialism of the natural sciences. For the strong programme truth is a quality we attribute to meaningful claims. Truth is a quality of language. Reality is out there. Our only means of seeking to grasp the real is through language, and language is always social.

### Further Case-Studies

The study of particular disputes within science offers a rich seam of case-study material for the sociologist of science, whether these case-studies are first-hand empirical projects or based upon secondary sources. In the first study, the notion of tacit knowledge is explored. Here, it is suggested that scientific knowledge is as much craft knowledge (an embodied material practice that can never be fully translated into abstract language) as it is a set of formal theories, formulas and algorithms. In the second case-study, disciplinary boundaries are explored. Who counts as an expert and what counts as acceptable knowledge will depend upon the intellectual discipline you belong to. Border disputes between disciplines highlight that what appears to be universally accepted knowledge to those within a discipline are more akin to local knowledge and tribal lore. The third study highlights how political interests shape technical criteria.

*(cont'd)*

## Participant Research: Making a Laser

In participatory research into the creation of early lasers in the 1970s (1985), Harry Collins explores a number of themes about knowledge generation.

## Tacit Knowledge

By this (and following the work of Michael Polanyi, 1957), Collins (1985:56) refers to knowledge held but not available to abstract articulation. Just as one might ride a bicycle without being able to put how to ride a bicycle into words, so a lot of what gets transmitted through shared and hands on experience within a laboratory is not put into words. Collins gives the example of a particular piece of wire, the length of which was said to be important. It had to be short, but how short? It was not simply a question of saying, 'Keep making the wire shorter until the laser works.' To assume that things were as simple as that would assume that the researchers knew that the length of the wire was the only possible problem. Perhaps there were hundreds of such ambiguous specifications. To run through every permutation would take forever. Only after the fact was it possible to discern what the relevant anomalies were, and even then many acquired bits of know-how were tacit, that is unspoken or taken for granted. Collins found that only those teams that had had members with hands-on experience in other teams that had already successfully built a laser were able to build one themselves from scratch. Once components became manufactured rather than hand-crafted by laboratory technicians, some of the essential technical specificity became embodied in the components rather than in the heads and hands of human actors.

## 'Wise' After the Event ... Wisdom gets 'Black-Boxed'

Once a consensus has been arrived at and also as manufacturing techniques have been set in motion to produce components that require less understanding of their inner workings to use, so technologies can become more user-friendly to those not present at their inception. However, this is only to invert the tacit-knowledge argument, rather than to refute it, as by this stage users do not have to understand the things they use. Thus science is once again not defined by articulate knowing, only this time the how-to is inside the object. Yet again it is not open to full articulation. This is what Collins calls 'black-boxing' (1985:64–5). The argument that science must be true because the technologies work confuses 'truth' with 'function'. Being able to ride a bicycle and being able to explain how to ride a bicycle in abstract terms are two different things. Science works through an array of tacit knowledge and manufactured objects, not simply because its abstract formulations are true, which they may or may not be. Still there is the question of what it means to say that something works.

(*cont'd*)

## What Counts as Working Properly?

Surely the best way to measure the success of a measurement device is to set it against the thing it is set to measure. But how are we to do this? Surely if we already know how to measure successfully the measuring device we are seeking to develop is not necessary. It is all very well setting your watch by the speaking clock, but how are we to set that clock? This then creates another form of regress. At the cutting edge of science things are more problematic. There is a degree of consensus about the measurement of time, and this consensus in itself allows relative conformity, which is good enough for most purposes (purposes themselves being set by the means available to enable them). However, at the cutting edge of science, there is no consensus. The question of calibration becomes very difficult (as was noted in the case of Weber versus Quest). How are you to calibrate your measures if the thing you are seeking to measure with the new measuring device has itself not been mapped? The device needs to be set against the thing it is set up to measure but the thing it is being set up to measure is only knowable if the device works. How then are we to know whether or not it works? This is what Collins calls the problem of calibration (Collins 1985:100).

## Informational or Algorithmical Versus Cultural Practice Model

Collins distinguishes knowledge that is hands-on and written or algorithmical information. The latter can only carry so much and must always be supplemented with elements of the former. Abstract symbolic forms cannot capture or communicate *tacit knowledge* and without these tacit forms of practical knowing there can be no translation into successful application. Collins suggests scientific knowledge is not the pure abstract information it is often portrayed as being. Science is as much a craft as it is the practice of abstract formulation and representation.

## Secondary Data Analysis: The Paranormal

In a study, based on secondary sources, of the application of polygraph testing to plants (Collins 1985), experiments suggested that plants reacted to (felt empathy with?) shrimps that were being dropped into hot water. Collins highlights the way biologists sought to discredit the researcher (Clive Backster, himself the inventor of the polygraph), asserting that he was not a biologist. Similarly Collins looked at the boundary disputes between parapsychology and other more mainstream sciences over 'scientific'. Each group has its own definitions, criteria of evidence and vested cognitive interests. Evidence that would count for one does not count for the other. Each sees the other as narrow-minded and dogmatic for failing to take its claims on board. What appears to be universal knowledge within the community of one discipline appears more like local belief and custom when we note that there are many such communities, and, thus, many universal truth claimants.

(*cont'd*)

## Interview-Based Research: Stellar-Intertial Guidance

Donald MacKenzie (1988) researched the development of nuclear missile guidance technologies from the 1950s to the 1980s in both the USA and the USSR. Stellar-intertial guidance (positioning by reference to stable star identification) became the method of choice for both superpowers to enable missile self-realignment when long distances between launch site and target, mobile launch location and 'hard-target' accuracy became political-military priorities. MacKenzie documents how political-military criteria ('Is it needed?') structured technical selection, development and testing criteria ('Does it work?'). 'Negotiating *acceptance* of the technology was simultaneously negotiating what it *was*' (1988:229). The United States and the Soviet Union, with significant awareness of each other's developments, pursued divergent 'technical' strategies to address the same political–military 'problem'. This 'problem' was how to build star-mapping guidance into missiles so as to allow mobile submarine-based weapons to 'hit' tightly defined targets from distances far enough away to limit the threat from enemy defences. This divergence highlights the non-existence of a purely 'technical' definition of what was 'optimal'. With greater access to United States sources MacKenzie documents the economic, political and bureaucratic-military interests at work in the negotiation of an 'optimal technique', a solution to the question of 'accuracy'. System testing was never simply an 'empirical' exercise. 'First, both stellar-intertial guidance itself, and the testing of stellar-intertial guidance, are, to use a philosopher's term, "theory-laden" in similar ways' (1988:225). Engineers at Kearfott had developed the statistical models (referred to as Mexican arithmetic by some military personnel not able to follow it) by which their version of stellar-intertial guidance was programmed, and by which it was to be evaluated. Those selling the goods were the only ones capable of saying whether it worked. They claimed it did! Second, assessment cannot be fully 'algorithmic'. Human judgement was always central to interpreting test outcomes. Third, evidence from other US missile testing programmes highlighted the frequency with which testing-error models were significantly revised in the light of the failure of systems to succeed by the established criteria. In short, moving the goalposts was common practice. By the late 1970s stellar-intertial guidance was 'stabilized' as the self-evidently optimal technical solution to a political-military problem. It seemed obvious that political strategies set the task and scientists and/or technicians went about providing the best functional solution. MacKenzie demonstrates how such a separation of political problems and technical solutions was itself a negotiated fiction designed to balance the interests of competing factions within the government, military and private sectors, behind a veneer of discrete but cooperating realms. Maintaining the impression of neutrality is the best political strategy to win contracts and manage public relations, just as the impression of technical optimality is the best strategy to win a cold war.

# If Social Influences Are Not Intrinsically Distortions, When Is Critique Appropriate?

The strong programme/interests perspective sets out to explain scientific knowledge in a scientific way. By this is meant that scientific belief is to be accounted for in causal terms, and in a symmetrical and impartial fashion. This is to mirror the materialism and neutrality which natural scientists claim as the hallmarks of their knowledge-generating trade. The experimenter's regress, interpretative flexibility, closure, tacit and local knowledge all move explanation away from idealized accounts of pure method, evidence, knowledge and logic towards the material and practical, while at the same time rejecting the suggestion that such a move away from idealized accounting represents a form of debunking. While subversive in many ways, the strong programme also seeks to be a sub-version (or version) of the very thing it seeks to research. As we will see in the next chapter, this attempt to be a science of scientific communities has drawn much criticism from those who would go further in the subversion of faith in science. Here it is sufficient to point out three key criticisms.

## *A Pale Imitation of the Real Thing?*

The first criticism that can be raised is that, for all its claims, the strong programme does not do science in the manner commonly associated with natural science. The strong programme presents theory as emerging from the accumulation of case-studies in classically inductive fashion. It does not test its theories in the more deductive mode associated most classically with the experimental method. The strong programme's theories have not been tested. Rather they have been formulated as an interpretation of prior data-collection. This is a general accusation often made by physical scientists against the social sciences. The generalizability and validity of findings based upon accumulating case-studies can be questioned in the absence of rigorous random sampling and controlled conditions. That such conditions might be impossible to provide in a study of scientific practice and belief, just as they are often impossible when researching other aspects of social life, represents a limiting factor on any attempt to offer a sociology of science that seeks to be a science of scientists. The strong programme may be as scientific as it can be, but it can never replicate the physical sciences. But then, as we have seen, the physical sciences can never absolutely replicate their own prior work or their own ideal methodological principles. The problem of induction cuts both ways.

## Failing its Own Methodological Principles?

A second criticism (discussed further in Chapter 5) is that the interests perspective fails to live up to its own methodological principles, in particular its contention that it is necessary for the sociologist to be reflexive – to apply their social explanations to their own social explanations. The physical scientists are convinced that it is physical evidence that leads them to draw the conclusions they do. The sociologist highlights that such evidence is open to interpretation, and so cannot determine for itself how it should be understood. Why not go on to point out that social influences may be equally open to interpretation? Are not social factors as open to interpretation as physical ones? If interpretative flexibility is given free reign, would a person not be as open in the interpretation of their interests as they are of empirical evidence? At one level Bloor asserts this very thing in his outline of the strong programme's basic premises. Yet such mindfulness is perhaps too quickly forgotten in accounting for specific disputes, as social interests are given the role of hidden causal force while their interpretation by actors is underplayed relative to the emphasis given to actors' interpretations of physical evidence. Taking this issue of reflexivity one step further, should we not seek to reflect upon the social interests of sociologists in promoting social explanations? Is it the evidence from case-study research that convinces the sociologist of the validity of a social explanation, or is it their cognitive, professional and material interests? From an interests perspective we have to opt for the latter explanation, though as Bloor would point out, this would not represent a debunking. Another methodological principle breached is that of impartiality. In the study of Pasteur and Pouchet, Collins and Pinch use subsequent evidence as a benchmark of 'truth' by which to highlight the social influences upon previous beliefs. Thus the interests approach may not be so far removed from either the conventional scientific assumptions of truth-seeking or the Marxist and feminist concern to distinguish false and true knowledge.

## Facing Two Ways At Once?

A third line of criticism is that the interests perspective places itself in a contra-dictory position in relation to the autonomy of science as a practice and its social explanation. The empirical programme of relativism seeks to relate the social processes within the scientific community (by which closure is affected in cases of dispute) to social interests in the wider society. In so doing however emphasis is placed first of all on the social interests operating within the scientific community. There is a strong desire to avoid premature reduction of power relations internal to science to external power relations in the wider society. Immediate reduction of dispute resolution within science to, for example, capitalism or patriarchy is avoided. Such a defence of the relative autonomy of science presumes that science, as a set of institutions, has some capacity to restrain direct external determination of its operations. Can such autonomy be maintained? Marxists and feminists question this ability (to varying degrees as will be examined in Chapters 6 and 7). If a degree of autonomy can be maintained, why are the institutions of science not capable of the far greater autonomy from social determination suggested by Merton and Mannheim (as discussed in Chapter 1)? If external social interests can be tempered to some degree by science's internal cognitive, disciplinary and career interests, this would justify the interest perspective's primary focus upon them. However, were this true, might not such internal interests offer a social basis for the claims made by scientists themselves, and earlier sociologists and philosophers of science, that science can offer impartial knowledge, detached, in however limited a fashion, from crude social determination? In brief, the interests perspective does, tacitly and sometimes explicitly, acknowledge the superiority of science as a set of social institutions in sustaining a level of intellectual autonomy in knowledge production free from reduction to such social forces as capitalism and patriarchy. In this regard it is not as far from Merton and Mannheim as perhaps its own proponents believe. It does so in order to defend itself from Marxist and feminist critics, who see such an approach as defending a view of science that denies, ignores or underplays science's relationship with social domination and exclusion. Focus upon the internal disputes arising within a community of predominantly white, middle-class men is unlikely to focus upon the absence of other groups, or the relationship between the knowledge produced and such a partial cross-section of humanity (Rose 1994).

Nevertheless, the interests perspective maintains a far more sceptical regard for the power of science's autonomy from social determination than did earlier generations of sociological researchers interested in science's internal relations. The interest perspective has opened up research into the role of career, cognitive and disciplinary interests far beyond what would have once seemed possible. The perspective has challenged scientists, social researchers and society in general to reconsider idealistic accounts of belief and knowledge generation, even while its focus and priorities generate limits and biases. As will be seen in subsequent chapters, and as has been alluded to earlier, such challenges are always open to interpretation. In opening the doorway to a form of *relativism* (however this is qualified with provisos against being a blanket debunking of all claims to authority), the interest perspective cannot help but to have denied for itself the assurance of an unquestionable foundation. Insofar as the *empirical programme of relativism* invites reinterpretation of the claims it makes, from whatever stance such reinterpretations might come, it has forced discussion onto its own terms.

# Conclusions: Science in Society?

The 'internalist' focus of the social-interests approach places the perspective at one step removed from a primary focus upon science's relationship with domination/liberation. The claim to be suspending judgement over the 'truth' claims of science also seems to distance the interest school from the question of truth/ideology. Yet, on both fronts, the situation is more complicated than it at first appears. While emphasis upon internal relationships may create blind spots, such as with regard to gender and class dynamics within science, this need not be the case. As the Pasteur–Pouchet case illustrates, wider power relations can and are addressed from an interest approach, even while other studies, such as those looking at gravitational radiation in physics and laser building in engineering, manage to pass over the almost complete absence of women in those fields. Regarding truth versus ideology, the claim to being agnostic is itself rarely sustained. The general principle, that social influence over belief need not result in false knowledge, can be upheld. Yet studies that conclude that all beliefs examined had social foundations often go on to suggest that one set of socially determined beliefs was more in accord with reality.

Attention to the power of career and cognitive interests within scientific knowledge formation enables attention to be given to relations between social domination and 'ideology' (even where ideology is not crudely countered to a self-evident and unproblematic truth). That those who have built careers focusing upon the internal dynamics of scientific career-building should be in dispute, over where the emphasis should be placed, with those who have built careers addressing external relations, should not come as a surprise. The interests approach provides valuable insights, even while attention to those areas of neglect highlighted by its critics increase such insights.

# 5

# Science and Language/ Interaction: Ethnography and Discourse

## Introduction

The ethnographic and discursive approaches (EDA) to the study of science seek to focus attention on the importance of language and interaction in the construction of science and its representation. Both these perspectives (and often they are fused together – see Zeitlyn *et al.* 1997, 1998, 1999; and David and Zeitlyn 1996) grew out of a critical reaction to the 'depth' explanations put forward by 'interest' theorists, feminists and Marxists alike. What ethnographers and discursive analysts claim they direct attention towards is the immediate and the apparent. They are suspicious of all attempts to attribute to hidden processes the capacity to explain surface phenomena. As will be pointed out, ethnographic and discursive approaches adopt a stance that questions the very distinction between surface and depth. This chapter begins with an account of the criticisms levelled against the interest-based approach by discourse analysts and ethnographers. These criticisms laid the foundations for the new approaches. The ethnographic, discursive and ethno-methodological approaches themselves are then described. The following sections address the limits of ethnography, the attempt to overcome these by fusing ethnography and discourse analysis within an actor network theory (ANT), and the failure of this attempt. The final section addresses the value and the limits of accounts claiming to suspend causal attributions, and discusses the ethnographic and discursive approaches in relation to the general themes of 'truth' and 'freedom'.

## Critical Foundations

Jonathan Potter, in his book *Representing Reality* (1996), argues that the interest perspective (of which Harry Collins's works are taken to be indicative) engages in a subtle form of sleight of hand. On the one hand interest theorists question the ability of physical scientists to see the world except through the lenses of their 'interests', while at the same time social-interests-oriented sociologists of science exempt themselves from this necessity. Potter examines Harry Collins's (1981, 1985) account of the conflict within the physics community over gravitational radiation (discussed in Chapter 4). Collins suggests that it was really the influence of Quest that decided the final fate of the dispute. Quest's ability to win over the scientific community, based upon a variety of institutional, personal and academic resources, is seen as decisive. Potter argues that this is impossible to prove. How is it possible to go back in time and rerun events minus Quest in order to see how things would have turned out without him? It cannot be done. As such Collins relies upon what appears to be a logical account, but this is nevertheless vulnerable to 'interpretative flexibility' and perhaps even more so than the 'evidence' disputed by Quest and Weber.

### *Epistemological Relativism About the Physical World, but Realism About the Social World*

Potter claims that what Collins and the interest perspective in fact do is create a two-tiered world in which there is a realm of epistemological relativism and a realm of epistemological realism. Relativism is applied to what the physical scientists can know, while realism underpins the accounts of the social world to be given by social science. This is an atypical reversal of the usual opposition between realism in the physical sciences and relativism in the social sciences. Potter does not suggest this inversion is the intention of the interests authors. It is merely the consequence, Potter claims, of trying to use 'interests' as causal mechanisms in the determination of knowledge:

> Although the relativist position allows Collins [and the interests account in general] to be disinterested in the truth or otherwise of scientists' utterances about the natural world, his need to provide a definitive version of what is going on in the social world forces him to make exactly such judgements concerning scientists' utterances about the social world. (Potter 1996:32)

What Potter wants to say is that once you let the cat out of the bag you cannot simply put it back just when it suits you. Once relativism is used to corrode the certainties of the physical sciences then it will surely bring into doubt claims to objectivity from every quarter, not least the claims made by those using it. This is the classic relativists' double gambit. This is usually employed to discredit relativism (reaffirming faith in truth by doubting the doubters). However, Potter is using the double gambit to widen the scope of doubt (the doubt that leads us to question the doubters still forces us to doubt claims to authoritative knowledge as well). Discourse theorists claim that they question all claims to explanation and/or causation. This is a claim to being more symmetrical than earlier approaches that sought to be so (i.e. the social interests approach). Discourse theory evaluates all claims only in terms of the linguistic devices used in making such claims. It seeks thereby to show the rhetorical and literary character of even the most supposedly empirically based statements (for a defence of the interests approach see Barnes *et al.* 1996):

> Rhetoric is central to his [Collins's] account because it provides closure to controversies... Yet... he [Collins] does not explore its senses or develop an elaborate theoretical account of the notion. When he provides examples of rhetoric they are often in the form of rhetoric attributions... We therefore have to take it on trust that these speakers can give an accurate account, not only of the influence of Quest's work on a large number of other scientists, but also exactly what feature of the papers was responsible for the influence. The irony in Collins' analysis, then, is that he is elevating rhetoric to a position as the crucial lubricant for controversy closure – yet he is treating the accounts which supposedly show this as non-rhetorical. (Potter 1996:33)

Collins's claims are based upon interviews in which physicists claimed that they had been swayed by Quest. However, just because that is what those scientists said influenced their decision, and irrespective or whether those saying so actually believed it, it cannot be proven that this is actually what made them change their minds. The consensus that emerged after the event, and recalling that Collins's interviews were also carried out after the event, may have developed for any number of reasons. Yet Collins is satisfied to take scientists' accounts of their social beliefs at face value, even while questioning the accounts given by the same scientists when it comes to the causes of their beliefs concerning the physical world.

Potter's critique of non-rhetorical rhetoric is paralleled in Steve Woolgar's (1981) critique of the attribution of naturalism in social-interest-based accounts of scientific disputes (in particular Barnes 1977; Barnes and Shapin 1979; MacKenzie 1978; Barnes and MacKenzie 1979). Woolgar points out that the term 'naturalism' carries at least two meanings. One is an attachment to the materialism and neutrality supposedly characteristic of the physical sciences. The second is an attachment to non-intrusive methods and the avoidance of imposing prior theoretical models or laboratory-based controlled conditions. Interest theorists, according to Woolgar, hold on to the status to be gained from attachment to physical science models, while at the same time questioning science's validity. To Woolgar, it seems contradictory to question the very method you then claim underpins your own authority claims. Woolgar suggests it would be more honest to abandon the former naturalism for the latter, to reject causal accounting and embrace ethnographic description (see below). Potter's critique of attributions of causation to supposed hidden social interests is also paralleled in Woolgar's work (1981, 1988). Ethnographic and discursive perspectives developed, often together, from a shared claim to be rejecting causal attribution.

# Talk and Text

## *Rules – Merton's Rules and Fuller's Martians*

Steve Woolgar's 1981 broadside against the social-interests perspective derives from the ethnomethodological tradition in sociology (to be discussed later in this chapter). Woolgar is as scathing of those who think they can explain human action in terms of causal interests as he is critical of those who would claim to explain human action in terms of following rules (the foundation of the early Mertonian sociology of science). Woolgar bases his critique on the work of Harold Garfinkel. Garfinkel's basic guiding principle (1967) was to point out that a person has to interpret a rule in order to act upon what they take the rule to be asserting. Any act that is said to be an act of following a rule is also an act of interpreting that rule. Humans are not electronic computers and social rules are not mathematical formulae that can be expressed unambiguously. Steve Fuller (1997) nicely shows how Merton's four value orientations (see Chapter 1) cannot act as determining forces in the conduct of scientific research and can only be discursive resources to be deployed in scientific practice. Fuller tells a story about Martian anthropologists coming to earth. Would they be able to identify the normative compulsion that Merton believed his values imposed, or is it rather the case that each rule would be found to be open to different interpretations by different groups or at different times? Fuller suggests the latter. Fuller points out that Merton's principle of universalism can be seen as a form of dictatorial imperialism, while 'communism' might be seen as a coercive impulse to give up your assets to the group. Disinterestedness and scepticism might be seen as moral abstention. In all cases evidence can be presented to show that practising scientists have in some situations chosen, when describing their actions in terms of Merton's principles, to interpret the rules in one way and in other situations another way. What Merton assumes to be good might as easily be taken as bad. Scientists are also capable of suspending a supposed principle for what they describe as a higher good. How these rules are interpreted and used by scientists must be studied, not assumed. If their meaning cannot be prescribed it is important to study their use.

## *Bloor – Causality, Impartiality, Symmetry and Reflexivity*

From Steve Woolgar's perspective (1981, 1988), the same can be said of Bloor's four tenets for the empirical programme of relativism (see Chapter 4). Bloor's

(1976) call for the sociology of science to operate by principles of causality, impartiality, symmetry and reflexivity cannot dictate how such principles are to be interpreted and applied. Potter and Woolgar can assert that any attempt to dictate how such rules could be interpreted and applied in practice would be partial. However, in so doing they also limit their own criticism. If Bloor's standards cannot be specified, how can he fail to live up to them? At this theoretical level, a stalemate emerges. What is more productive is to identify what the ethnographic and discursive perspective might offer in terms of practical methods and findings.

## Ethnography: *Laboratory Life*

At the heart of Bruno Latour and Steve Woolgar's *Laboratory Life* is the concept of 'literary inscription', the production of documents, the contents of which are seen and said by scientists to have resulted from, and to seek to represent, physical activities at the lab bench. The process of literary inscription is seen by Latour and Woolgar to involve the process of 'working up', the production of 'facts', neutral external objects, out of the messy activities of researchers in complex and highly artificial experimental contexts. *Laboratory Life* builds upon Latour's fieldwork carried out between October 1975 and August 1977 at the Salk Institute in California. The primary research focus of the institute was neuroendocrinology, the study of the relationship between the nervous system and the hormone-producing and -releasing endocrine system. While some attention is devoted to the history of the sub-field and of the laboratory, the primary research was an ethnographic study of everyday life in the lab. Based upon interviews, conversations and archival materials, however, the book contains detailed accounts of historical developments in the field as well as the more ethnographic details of events within the remit of the anthropological gaze. Latour and Woolgar (1986:54–63) note the taken-for-granted assumption within the institute of a shared history. This sense of a shared history was not regularly questioned or explicitly stated. There was always scope for interpretation. This flexible history stood as a mythic character in the day-to-day routines of those in the lab.

The case of TRF(H) (1986:105–50) exemplifies the focus upon 'literary inscription'. Ironically for a text often hailed as the most important text in establishing the ethnographic tradition in the social study of science, the TRF(H) case-study is based solely on secondary sources and second-hand accounts. Even while key players in the case were working in the Salk Institute at the time of the fieldwork, the events that marked the construction of this particular 'fact' occurred between 1962 and 1969. The case of TRF(H) is described as the construction of a fact. TRF(H) stands for thyrotropin-releasing factor (Hormone). As such the name describes the effects of this factor/hormone, rather than its specific composition/nature. The exact chemical structure of what was having this effect was what researchers sought to discover. A network of competing and cooperating researchers sought to solve this puzzle, a puzzle posed in terms of isolating and identifying the structure of this causal agent. Using the methods and models available to them, researchers set out to identify what was assumed to be a singular and objectively present yet currently unidentified object.

Two research teams claimed credit for the 'discovery' in 1962. However, each characterized what it was they believed to be the one true object of their attentions in a different way. One team claimed to have 'discovered' a 'hormone'. The other team claimed they had discovered a 'factor'. In terms of composition, at a highly detailed level, the two formulations had slightly different properties, and descriptions of composition and structure were also distinct. At the point of supposed discovery in 1962, two distinct theoretical constructs were being presented. By 1969, the redescription of both using the language of analytic chemistry allowed the prior differences to be rendered invisible. This was rather like the differences between apples and oranges being rendered invisible by use of the general term 'fruit'. A single and abbreviated description, that only highlighted common features, allowed different constructions to be rendered identical for all practical purposes and thus the different constructions could be regarded as accounts of the same object. TRF(H) had become a 'fact'. Latour and Woolgar (1986:148) conclude by saying that 'once one and only one purified structure had been chosen out of all the equally probable structures, a decisive metamorphosis occurred in the nature of the constructed object'. Once selection (choosing one) was successfully represented as purification (finding the essence of the only one), this 'one' could then be mass-produced and circulated to anyone with money to spend, regardless of understanding of TRF(H)'s composition or its alternative constructions. Once detached from its origins and construction processes, TRF(H) became a 'fact'.

Literary inscription refers to the process by which representations, complex theoretical constructions, devised to summarize the content of highly complex and confusing data, collected in highly artificial contexts, are turned into the passive reflections of external objects, out there in the world and supposedly transparently obvious, to be empirically observed. While looking and ways of looking precede seeing, in literary redescription of the discovery process this is reversed and 'seeing is believing'. Latour and Woolgar's account of this work focuses particular attention on these processes at a number of levels. Tidying and reversing the priority between constructing and 'discovering' are played out in practical experimentation, theoretical and conversational interaction in the laboratory, office and staff canteen, as well as in academic conferences, in funding meetings or applications and in publications. These fact-making devices are also deployed in the 'cycles of credit' that Latour and Woolgar characterize as the processes of career and scientific development.

In conclusion, Latour and Woolgar (1986:236–44) identify six dominant themes in their analysis of scientific everyday life, as follows:

1. The transformation of artefacts (constructions) into facts (discoveries).

2. The agonistic nature of such constructions (born of debate and differences of interpretation rather than, as they become characterized, as objects presenting themselves to a passive observer).

3. The recruitment of material objects in the passing off of constructed artefacts as neutral facts (highly controlled actions and interpretations are presented as the technical outputs of laboratory apparatus – such that the active involvement of human actors at all stages of design, conduct and interpretation are rendered invisible). This is particularly significant in the tidying-up process by which laboratory notes, documenting who did what and when, are transformed into formulaic outlines of formal procedures for the purposes of presentation in conference papers and journal articles.

4. The deployment of established forms of credibility in deciding how ambiguity is to be resolved, and the construction of credibility in the establishment of interpretive dominance.

5. The circumstantial nature of fact construction.

6. The constant requirement to write off the majority of findings as 'noise', the need to legitimize the selective nature of what counts as a finding and what counts as experimental error.

According to Latour and Woolgar a sense of order is created out of disorder by means of the six practices. They refer to this process as 'stabilizing' (1986:244).

Each of the six points is heavily referenced in relation to the contemporary French and English language social theorists popular at the time when the text was written. This tension between ethnographic claims, to be presenting local events in a particular place at a particular time, and the constant use of theories and examples from beyond the researcher's own data collection to explain the meaning of those data, parallels the ethnographic and discursive analytic criticism of interest theory. While interests theory draws upon causal inferences that cannot be directly demonstrated or proved by the data, so the ethnographic and discursive approach draw upon theoretical models and secondary sources to construct its account of the events it claims to be focused upon. Physical scientists use a variety of devices to achieve stability in their account of reality. Those from the interest perspective use the notion of causal interest to stabilize their account of reality. So ethnographers and discourse analysts draw upon a variety of resources external to their available data (whether ethnographic or textual) to achieve the same end. This point will be returned to later in this chapter.

---

### What's In a Sub-Title?

In an interesting appendix to the second (1986) edition of their text, Latour and Woolgar explain that in the first edition the subtitle of *Laboratory Life* had been *The Social Construction of Scientific Facts*. By the time of the second edition, seven years later, the authors felt it best to delete the 'social', changing the subtitle to *The Construction of Scientific Facts*. When the first edition was published, the authors claim, they had wanted to challenge the traditional sociology of science as exemplified by Merton (see Chapter 1). For Merton, 'the social' was seen as being significant in creating or limiting the conditions necessary for the institution of science to develop. However, once established, a part of the institutional apparatus of science was to enable science to insulate its content (the conduct and analysis of objective research) from 'the social' (that is political and cultural bias and economic manipulation). Latour and Woolgar sought to show that the very heart of scientific everyday life and all that flowed from it was 'social'. However, by the time of the second edition, the authors' felt the very distinction between science and society was a false dichotomy that was being sustained in the claim that the 'social' 'constructed' 'scientific facts'. Latour and Woolgar claim (1986:250) that as all human actions and interpretations are constructions, and because science is a human social activity, to say that science is a social construction is saying nothing more than saying science is a construction. To imply there was a difference would be to imply that some kinds of human constructions were not social. The distinction often made is that between the social and the technical. Latour and Woolgar reject this distinction. Woolgar (1988:89) suggests that because science is team-based rather than individual, technical criteria are constructed and maintained by group processes. Because scientists orient to the judgement of other scientists, not to an external reality unmediated by prior socialization within the scientific community, the technical is as much a subset of the social as is science. As such, Latour and Woolgar claim that the use of the term social in relation to human constructions is superfluous. Critics of ethnographic and discursive approaches (Rose 1994) argue that this move warrants a focus on the internal nature of science as a sociological arena, at the expense of attention to the relationship between science and other human social activities (see Chapters 6 and 7). Establishing that science is social does not justify exclusive focus upon science's internal social relations, even if this would be convenient for the small-scale, interaction-and language-focused researcher.

---

While not the first ethnography to be carried out within the routines of scientific practice, *Laboratory Life* has become the most referenced account of science from an ethnographic vantage. The book established a new agenda for an ethnographic approach to the study of science (even while this was not entirely in line with the content of the text).

*From Interviews to Ethnography*

Importantly, the method of data collection shifts from interviews to ethnography. This, it is said, enables a greater understanding of the practice of science in its everyday routines.

*Construction over Discovery*

Crucially, the researcher is interested in how the scientist builds up a picture of what it is they are doing and what it is they are seeing or collecting. The active role of the scientists in 'constructing' the object of perception becomes a key site of research. It is important to say 'scientists' rather than 'scientist', as it is through the study of interaction on a day-to-day basis that ethnographers hope to gain insight into how the world is made sensible by scientists together.

*From Controversy to Routine*

It is suggested that a major failing of the interest approach is that, despite its claims not to want to be evaluative in judging the validity of scientific claims, its foci of empirical attention are disputes within science. As such the method of identification of 'interpretative flexibility' requires us to focus attention on abnormalities within science. Relying on the scientists to fall out every now and again in order to give the sociologists opportunities to pick over the bones leads to an account that presents science as more conflict-ridden that is perhaps the case. The ethnographer seeks to study everyday interaction within science without the need to go in only when the scientists have started to fight amongst themselves. The study of 'business as usual' may, it is suggested, enable a focus on the methods of representational and practical management that are the routine rather than the perverse or extreme.

*Discursive accounts of Out-There-Ness*

One of the routine practices of everyday science is the discursive practice of rendering what one has interpreted from observations in complex and highly contrived systems of observation and measurement into things out there beyond the instruments and the minds of the scientists.

*Effecting Disinterestedness – Submerging Agency and Perspective*

It is not the same thing to say that someone observes a rule as it is to say that that person obeys the rule. Scientists display a finely tuned capacity to represent and describe themselves in terms of the Mertonian values of science discussed in Chapter 1. Because they present and describe themselves in these terms does not mean they are obeying, or that they are not. What the ethnographer/

discursive analyst focuses upon is the act, the description given, and the way the two are linked together in the accounts given by the scientists.

# Inside Out: Externalizing Devices

## *Discourse*

Nigel Gilbert and Michael Mulkay's (1984) *Opening Pandora's Box* is based upon interviews with 34 biochemists along with analysis of published papers. Gilbert and Mulkay claim that they are not interested in what science is, but what scientists say it is! The authors were particularly impressed by the capacity of scientists to account for their own actions in such a way as to emphasize both their creativity and their conformity to supposed rules. In particular Gilbert and Mulkay identify what they call an 'empiricist repertoire' by which researchers present their findings. Here scientists demonstrate a capacity to talk about the world as if things were fairly easy to identify, even if this requires apparatus. The concepts and the measures are downplayed and objects are given a capacity to almost speak for themselves (or at least that is the impression that is being managed). Empiricist language is built upon a number of devices.

## *The Empiricist Repertoire*

Three broad themes are identified (Gilbert and Mulkay 1984:55–8). First, the grammatical form in which papers are published is such that the researcher appears more as a bystander than as a participant. Rather than writing that 'when person A added factor X, person A noted effect Y', what is written will be more like 'the addition of factor X led to the outcome Y'. Second, data is treated as primary as if the results were not the outcome of the research but rather its cause. Verbs normally applied to humans are applied to objects. 'The chemicals showed' replaces 'the chemist observed'. Finally, laboratory action is described as being driven by rules, identified and applied without ambiguity, dispute or need for interpretation. By these three means, empirical data appears to drive the research process, rather than being its constructed product.

Gilbert and Mulkay identify a secondary repertoire (1984:39–62). The empiricist repertoire is used to account for what the speaker believes is correct research. However, when the speaker is keen to distance themself from the findings of another scientist a different set of devices are employed. This is what Gilbert and Mulkay refer to as the 'contingent repertoire'. Here scientists account for errors by pointing to all the contingencies that mean that what appear to be valid results could be contaminated. These descriptions (1984: chapters 3 and 4) display the capacity of practising scientists to deploy all the arguments put forward by sociologists of science against the unquestionable nature of 'evidence'. However, this is only done in relation to other scientists whose results they disagree with. Gilbert and Mulkay (1984:90–111) go on to show how the potential conflict between an empiricist discourse that presents data as unproblematic and the contingent discourse that highlights the scope for interpretation is defused. Scientists tend to suggest that 'the truth will out' in the end. This TWOD (the Truth Will Out Device) is an act of faith and a trump card.

Jonathan Potter's (1996) account of discourse-analytic approaches, some of which are ethnographic, though others are interview-based or base their analysis on textual data (such as publications, transcripts from conferences, or media coverage), identifies a range of representational practices that parallel those described by Latour and Woolgar, as well as Gilbert and Mulkay. Potter describes these processes as 'constructing out-there-ness' (1996: Chapter 6).

## Ethnomethodological Imports – Variations on Indexicality and Reflexivity

Strands within the ethnographic and discursive approach draw upon the tools of ethnomethodology to bring into question the notion that 'surface' talk and interaction somehow relate to processes, structures and truths that lie somewhere 'underneath' or 'above' the action. Steve Woolgar suggests (1988:21) that the sociologist of science should always remember that the boundary of the field being called science is itself constantly fought over (are sociologists, psychologists and philosophers in or out?). What counts as science should not be taken for granted. Woolgar suggests such a view would be 'essentialist'. Against the view that science has unconstructed and incontestable boundaries, Woolgar proposes a 'nominalist' approach, based upon the ethnomethodological view that social arrangements are just the arrangements that people make. To take for granted the constructed nature of science would be to reinforce the sense that science is an object, rather than a socially negotiated arena. Woolgar's debt to the work of Harold Garfinkel has already been mentioned. Here, the basics of an ethnomethodological approach to science are now outlined.

### Indexicality and Reflexivity

These two terms represent the fulcrum of ethnomethodology. Indexicality means pointing at things while reflexivity means referring to categories. The former describes pointing out examples while the latter refers to the 'groups' that all the little somethings are examples of. Specific things and events are made meaningful as examples, by referring to categories, and categories are made meaningful through the pointing out (indexing) of supposed examples. The basic premise of ethnomethodology is that social interaction draws constantly on this double act of examples and generalities to sustain the notion that 'order' exists out there beyond the surface of talk and interaction. The constant recreation of the myth of order is the nearest thing there will ever be to a social order beneath social interaction. It is not the social order out there that is being sustained in the talk, only the idea of it, and this is, in the end, only talk. The sustaining of a fiction of an external social order is paralleled with the practices in science. 'Facts', the institution of 'science' and its 'norms', 'methods' and 'practices', are constantly declared, as regulative points of reference, through the myriad of interactions in which these terms are drawn upon as unquestionable objects 'out there'.

---

### A Parallel with the 'Convict Code'

Woolgar (1981:383) uses the illustration of Wieder's 'convict code'. Wieder's (1974) study of interactions between staff and residents in a halfway house for ex-convicts recently released from prison highlighted the constant reference made by all concerned to a supposed convict code, a set of unwritten rules that were said to regulate interaction between the residents and the staff. Splitting and grassing (slang terms for betraying other ex-convicts to the authorities) were acts said to be in violation of 'the code'. However, as the code could only ever be defined in the act of its interpretation, it was always possible for one action to be defined one way or the other depending on the goals and strategies being deployed by parties to any interaction at any particular moment. What counted as 'grassing' was said to be clear-cut. However, this clarity was more an assumption than a reality. All interactions between staff and ex-convicts were potential sources of suspicion. Interpretation determined what counted as 'grassing' and what did not. What counts as science, and what counts as a violation of scientific principles, are always interpretations. Using examples to prove a theory and using that theory to define, characterize and select examples creates the circularity that sustains the illusion of external order.

---

### Triangulation

A criticism of such relativism is that science gets to the truth beyond talk and social interaction by means of 'triangulation', the confirmation of an external point of reference by means of more than one observation taken from different points in space and time and/or by different people. The parallel here is with map-reading, whereby one's location can be identified as long as one can take compass bearings from that point to two other points with known grid references. Triangulation in science assumes that the two or more confirmations of the same event or result were independent of each other (Woolgar 1988:72).

The danger is that an act of networking (echo effects) will be taken for genuine impartial confirmation. If all parties to a confirmation share some underlying assumptions about how evidence is to be gathered and interpreted, or at least share a common language through which their evidence is interpreted, what may appear to be independent confirmation, or be said to show it, may be collusion. Collusion may be too strong a word, as it implies intention, when all that is required to effect the impression of triangulation is the coordination of shared assumptions.

## Discovery

Are the objects of scientific enquiry ever discovered? This is to assume that what the scientist has in their theory is a real X, Y or Z. What they have is a theoretical construct that is said to map onto things out there in the world. As such, what the scientist has 'got' is better described as a construction. Scientists hope and claim that their constructions have a relationship to real things out there, but it still remains the case that what they have has been invented rather than discovered. Woolgar (1988:61) points out that conflicts over who discovered a particular scientific breakthrough, such as the structure of DNA, the principles of evolution or the make up of TRF(H), act within the scientific community to reinforce the belief that what is happening is a form of triangulation, a race to a real external point. This discovery metaphor also has a powerful consensus-building power, as whatever is currently the dominant theoretical model can be presented as something found, not made.

## Realism as a Post-hoc Justification of the Present Arrangements

The idea that what we think reality is today truly is reality is always confounded by tomorrow's 'discoveries' or 'reconstructions'. As such to project today's idea of what reality is out there onto reality, and to say it was what you discovered, is to get the tail to wag the dog. Woolgar asserts (1988:67) that 'realist ontology is a *post-hoc* justification of existing institutional arrangements'.

## Appeals to Authority

Just as theory is used to justify our interpretation of a particular example, and just as examples are used to justify the 'truth' of particular theories, so authority claims are used to dampen down doubts that others might express about ideas. Science draws upon a wide range of such authority-inciting devices. Prestigious awards, titles, institutional addresses, networks of colleagues, etc. act as resources that are discursively drawn upon to give weight to a point of view.

Woolgar refers to devices designed to minimize the significance of alternative interpretations, and to offset questions altogether, as methods for 'managing the horror' (1988:33–5). Inciting authority and presenting certain questions as being of minimal significance (mere technical hitches) allows the impression of consensus to be sustained. Interestingly, questions about why some groups wield authority and others do not are questions themselves offset and discounted within ethnomethodological accounts, and in the ethnographic and discursive approaches more generally. Such questions would require attributions of cause, reference to external social factors and perhaps even interests. Such attributions are in fact often made by ethnographers, ethnomethodologists and discourse analysts, even when the necessity, value and legitimacy of doing so are denied.

*Feedbacking*

Various discursive devices give the impression of an objective reality that is being observed. Through mutual reinforcement within a network the impression is given of independent verification. This form of feedback is reinforced when sociologists seek to research 'science', as this may reinforce assumptions of a thing called 'science' out there. What the sociologist needs to do is constantly generate an alternative feedback, constantly disrupting assumptions of a unified object of study both in science and in the sociological study of science (Woolgar 1988:36). This is to be achieved first and foremost through the ethnomethodological techniques of inversion outlined above.

# Problems with Ethnography

## Ritual and Disorder

To what extent is it possible to use ethnography to study science when what is being studied is the way scientists manage the presentation of 'science'? If the researcher is there to look at the scientists, surely those observed will act in an unusual fashion. Participation and proximity are not unproblematic (David 2002a).

## But It's Not All in the Lab!

Ethnographic attention to laboratory life carries the strong authority claim of 'being there', where the action is. However, most science goes on outside the laboratory. To make a fetish of the laboratory bench might be seen as an attempt on the part of the sociologist to get extra status. The social sciences have no laboratories. This difference may explain why reference to the exotic and revered realm of 'real' science will catch the attention of social scientists reading accounts written by the ethnographers. Spending time in the labs may give the ethnographer the sense of really 'being there' in the thick of things, when in fact there is a lot that goes on in offices, libraries, in the field and at conferences and editorial offices. Decisions made by governments, protest and lobby groups, and commercial actors will also fall outside such a restricted gaze. Latour and Woolgar's *Laboratory Life* draws very heavily upon non-ethnographic forms of data and theory-building in the construction of their case, while drawing upon ethnography to lend weight to the claim that their conclusions were based on 'being there'. The choice of title may best be read as a rhetorical device, used to focus the reader's attention upon one aspect of the research, rather than on other parts, and/or absences.

## *Wider Networks Are Hard to Track*

The problem with focusing on the laboratory is perhaps a natural outcome of an ethnographic approach. Ethnography is good at getting close to 'local' inter-actions and events. If the reality of science is in a range of wider networks then the ethnographer will have a great deal of trouble. Those who want to use ethnographic methods, but who want to avoid boiling science down to its empirical manifestations at the lab bench, are forced to make attributions about what is 'going on', attributions that run well beyond their empirical data. This brings such researchers into direct conflict with their own criticisms of others (namely social-interests theorists, Marxists and feminists) for doing the same. A focus upon discourses and language used in science allows a wider focus. However, attention to the rhetorical devices within scientific language can be justified only if it is assumed that this is a significant site of scientific activity, either as a prime indicator of influence or as the cause of it (or both) within the scientific community. Again, the move towards the attribution of causes is irresistible.

# ANT – Actor Network Theory?

Actor network theory sought to overcome the difficulties of ethnographic and discourse-analytic approaches when confronting large-scale social enterprises such as science. Writers using this theory have tried to use the notion of network to describe complex interactions that would normally be called social structures. They also sought to challenge the divide between agent and object with regard to the social and physical. As such, objects could be actors to. An actor was defined as any network of elements that affects consequences. The classic example is the hotel key attached to a large and heavy 'fob'. The design resists placement in a jacket pocket. This 'acts' to encourage the guest to return the key (because it is large and heavy). According to John Law (1999), ANT set out to investigate interactional achievements from the starting-point that networks are produced by actors, while actors are themselves formed within networks. However, regardless of whether actors were taken to be people (individuals or groups) interpreting their situation in relation to the various resources at their disposal, or whether actors were taken as interactional combinations of human and non-human elements capable of effecting action (such as the key in the jacket pocket), the notion of action still returns ANT to the need to attribute 'causal' power, the power to make something happen. ANT split between those who adopted a more discourse-analytic perspective on subjectivity and those with a more traditional ethnographic approach to the study of actors in everyday situations. The former placed more emphasis upon the constructive power of networks, the actor in this case being the site at which multiple factors intersect in generating effects. The latter emphasized the capacity of human actors to generate and sustain networks. Law (1999) and Latour (1999) conclude that ANT was never more than an attempt to disrupt assumptions about social order. When ANT became a theoretical model, they conclude, a theoretical account that people took to be an explanatory model of how things worked, it became the very thing it had emerged to disrupt, a model of social order. These are of course accounts of the demise of ANT given by those who had founded it. A less charitable account of the failure of ANT would be that any attempt to provide an account of social life will fail if any of the following is true:

1.  It denies the need for causal attribution.

2.  It is not explicit about the causal attributions that underpin it.

3.  It contains competing, but unspecified, causal attributions.

## Conclusions

Focus upon interaction, talk and representation in the work of ethnographic and discursive researchers represents a significant level of explanation in itself, and has enabled the sociology of science to be more reflexive, not just about science but about itself. However, the inability of ethnographic and discursive approaches to escape the necessity of invoking things outside talk and text (such things as causes or interests or structures) means that such perspectives can act only to make us aware of the limitations and dangers of such attributions. This encourages reflexivity, but cannot eliminate that which it encourages us to reflect upon, namely:

1.  The need to 'explain' why things happen (something that is required to some degree even in the attempt to only describe events) and

2.  The inevitability of believing more than you can know with certainty.

The failure to escape the need to make and defend causal attributions renders attention to discourses and everyday laboratory life only particular dimensions of any adequate accounting for science in society. As Rose (1994) observes, an inability to address questions of social and political power is routinely and rhetorically presented as intellectually defensible on spurious grounds. Refusal on the part of ethnographers, discourse analysts and ethnomethodologists to make reference to class, gender and race or ethnicity on the grounds that such categories require attributions of causal mechanisms beyond observable data cannot be defended on epistemological grounds, as such attributions are themselves unavoidable. Neither does attention to discursive construction and interactional negotiation, in itself, demonstrate that class, gender and race or ethnic categories are ontologically invalid. All that is demonstrated is that their existence is socially constructed (again implying causes). While attention to discourse and everyday interaction has generated fascinating and valuable data, the playing of 'chicken' (Collins and Yearley 1992) only serves to falsely present methodological focus as epistemological necessity (see Chapter 2). As will be shown in Chapters 8, 9 and 10, once shorn of its epistemological-chicken insularity, research addressing discourse and everyday interaction adds considerably to understanding the role of science in relation to 'truth' and 'freedom', even while such terms are alien to the ethnographic and discursive vocabulary.

# 6

# Science and Capitalism: Critical Theory and Critical Realism

## Introduction: Marx, Marxism and Science

Contemporary Marxist perspectives within the sociology of science engage in a dual process of rediscovery and innovation. The emergence of a radical science movement in the late 1960s and early 1970s was part of a wider movement which distanced itself from 'bourgeois' sociology of science and orthodox Marxist perspectives. The rediscovery of a 'humanist' Marxist tradition, in the work of Lukács and the Frankfurt school, came to form a bridge and an umbrella in which new perspectives developed. Other elements, such as French structuralist Marxism and Chinese Maoism, also played a part in this, but were themselves short-lived 'alternative' frameworks. This chapter begins by addressing the early flowering of Marxist research on the social origins of scientific knowledge, its decline, and the return to similar questions by a subsequent generation. The next section addresses how a new generation sought to address the ambiguous legacy of Marxist thought about science, in particular Engels' *Dialectics of Nature*, and the tension in Marx over the relationship between science and technology (as elements within the means of production) and social change. After this Lukács' conception of reification is set out, while the following section outlines the four key themes within the early Frankfurt school's account of science and technology in modern society: *Dialectic of Enlightenment*. The work of later members of the Frankfurt school, who were a part of the reinvention of Marxist scholarship in the late 1960s and early 1970s, is addressed next. The section after this outlines the critical-realist counterpoint to critical theory within Marxism. While critical of scientific knowledge, Marxists are also keen to defend rationality against relativism and irrationality. The so-called science wars are addressed at this point. The concluding section of this chapter recalls the key elements of the new Marxist approaches, while relating these to the central questions of truth and freedom running through this book.

Here, we will examine two Marxist interpretations of the work of Isaac Newton. At the start of the twentieth century Einstein's theory of relativity came to be accepted as a superior account of the physical universe, relative to Newton. Newton's model of the universe was very capable of predicting and explaining physical events (at least within certain limits). Einstein's account came to be accepted as better. Newton's account assumed a universe where elementary particles existed in a pre-existing infinite space. For Einstein space, time, matter and energy exist only in relation to each other. Newton's model was mechanistic. Why would the universe come to be interpreted in such a way in seventeenth-century England? It cannot be asserted that the universe came to be seen in this way because that is simply the way the universe actually is for two reasons. First, it is now commonly understood that elements of Newton's account are incorrect, and second, even were he correct, this would not explain why such an account emerged at the time and place that it did.

In 1931 the Soviet academician Boris Hessen (reprinted 1971) proposed, at a London symposium, that Newton's *Principia* was best explained as the product of the emergent bourgeois society of seventeenth-century England. To see the world in mechanistic terms, where each element could be detached from each other, simply reproduced in the physical world the mentality and practice of a society increasingly dominated by individualized trade and production. Newton's universe was made up of elements within a frame granted by God (the great watchmaker), while the society he lived in was made up increasingly of monetary exchange within a framework secured by an absolutist monarch. Hessen's Marxist emphasis lies in the changing relations of economic power at work in society. His attempt to explain ideas in terms of economic conditions works by association. He did not demonstrate the causal process at work in the historical association of ideas and circumstances. As was noted in Chapter 1, Hessen's account stimulated the emergence of an interest in the social relations of science in the West, both within a new generation of Marxists outside the Soviet Union like J. D. Bernal, and among anti-Marxists like Robert Merton. As was pointed out in Chapter 1, conditions in Stalin's Soviet Union constrained further developments in Marxist scholarship there. The school of critical theory that emerged in Frankfurt in the 1920s remained relatively marginal, in both mainstream sociology and in relation to Marxism until the protest movements of the late 1960s and early 1970s. This movement sought out radical perspectives not tainted by either of the dominant superpowers.

A new generation returned to reassess classic Marxist questions from a perspective informed by the Frankfurt school. A more sophisticated account of Newton's work was provided many years later by Gideon Freudenthal (1986). Freudenthal identifies in Newton's writing an underlying assumption about the nature of the universe that is not empirically demonstrated or theoretically justified. This is the elementary particle assumption (that is, the idea that the contents of the universe are reducible to base units and that everything in the universe can be explained in terms of the actions of such units). This unproven assumption is then explored. Why would such a notion seem self-evident to Newton and to those in his era and social circle? Freudenthal explains this self-evidence in terms both of the rise of a capitalist society but also with reference to the writings of Thomas Hobbes. Hobbes' account of social life as a mass of individuals in constant flux held in order only by an absolute monarch would have represented the dominant ideological frame of reference in Newton's day. This framework would have resonated with the experience of elites and the middle classes in the years after the English civil war.

It is important to recall that Freudenthal does not seek to debunk Newton. Freudenthal argues that while Newton's account is a product of his times, the work still represents a highly accurate means of predicting the physical world. That Newton's mechanistic account would have reinforced the authority of the new middle and rising upper classes of Newton's day, just as medieval accounts of nature and the universe had bolstered feudal elites (the divine chain of being: see p. 46), did not mean it was a pure fiction. Freudenthal suggests that the social influences and social effects of Newton's account lay in the language used and in some of the unproven assumptions incorporated into Newton's theory, not in the substance of the scientific research and analysis. Marxist accounts of science do not seek to debunk science, only to explain the social influences acting upon science and to expose elements of distortion and abuse within science and in its practical and ideological application.

If Robert Merton had aimed to develop a sociology of science that sought to reject the Marxist association between scientific knowledge itself and economic-political relations, the new generation of radical science activists sought to re-establish that very connection against Merton's, by then, orthodox sociological view. Hilary Rose and Steven Rose's (1970) *Science and Society* provides a wide-ranging account of the social roots and role of science within capitalist society especially, but also in Soviet Russia and Mao's China. The development of science is shown to be linked directly to economic and political power. The establishment of royal and learned scientific societies in England, France and elsewhere in late seventeenth and early eighteenth century western Europe is linked to the rise of capitalism and the transformation of the state (1970: chapter 1). Once established, the Royal Society in London oriented more to the London elites and their ambitions (astronomy, navigation and ballistics for empire building) than to the interests of the rising industrial classes. Birmingham's Lunar Society came to represent science oriented to the needs of the northern industrial revolution (Rose and Rose 1970: chapter 2). The directing of science towards the interests of economic and political domination is documented in relation to late Victorian industrial competition, the First (chemists) and the Second (physicists) World Wars, as well as in relation to the cold war.

Hilary Rose and Steven Rose (1970:265–6) show how the *Torrey Canyon* oil tanker disaster in the late 1960s brought into the open the operation of the British government's science advisory subcommittee, until then largely secret. In response to the oil spill the government asked for suggested solutions. The advisory subcommittee's chosen solution, to pour detergent onto the oil to break it up and sink it, was highly problematic. The detergent killed more sea life than the oil alone would have done. Interestingly, it was Britain's largest oil-producing and -refining company, British Petroleum, which manufactured the detergent, and for which the oil was destined. Were the oil experts in the scientific advisory subcommittee independent of the industry whose profitability underpinned their careers?

What Hilary Rose and Steven Rose seek to highlight is that the direction of scientific research and the uses to which science is put are driven by society. These authors believe in the value of science and are keen to see such value directed to the good of the majority, rather than the interests of the ruling class. The Roses highlight (chapters 1 and 13) how ideological dogma in Nazi Germany labelled theoretical atomic physics a Jewish science, not worthy of practical German attention. This led the Nazis to focus research money upon the development of rockets rather than nuclear bomb-making. The failure to realize the potential of atomic physics contributed to Nazi defeat. Similarly (again discussed in Chapters 1 and 13), it was ideological dogma that led a generation of Soviet biologists down a dead end, seeking to hold to the party line (asserted by Trofim Lysenko) that acquired characteristics could he genetically transmitted to future generations. In more recent years the Roses (2000) have sought to highlight that certain forms of genetic reductionism today reflect the interests of dominant classes in Western capitalist society.

## Confronting the Ambiguous Legacy of Marxism

The new radical science movement confronted the ambiguous legacy of Marxism's attachment to science, and in particular Engels' *Dialectics of Nature* (1940). This text propounded a fusion of Marxist dialectics and the natural sciences, and had become a canonical text in the dialectical materialist orthodoxy of Soviet Marxism (DiaMat). Marxist dialectical laws (the transformation of quality into quantity and vice versa, the interpenetration of opposites and the negation of the negation) were projected into nature, while Marxism was thus rendered a general science of physical and social reality. The emerging radical science movement tended to align itself with the criticism, made by the Hungarian Marxist Georg Lukács (1971[1919]) after the Russian Revolution, of such a wholesale merging of the social and physical sciences. It had been Lukács' 'humanist' Marxism, as distinct from more determinist forms of Marxism, which had laid the foundations for the Frankfurt School.

---

### The Lysenko Affair Revisited

The development of a new Marxist approach to science had to confront the legacy of Lysenkoism (see Chapter 1). Lysenko's attack on the reductionism of 'bourgeois genetics' as 'ruling class science', and his claims to have developed an anti-reductionist, dialectical, 'proletarian science' of the transfer of acquired characteristics, collapsed with the exposing of its flawed empirical foundations, and its repressive political backing. The affair consigned a generation of Marxist scientists to ridicule and subsequent retreat into a defence of science's political neutrality. Richard Lewontin and Richard Levins (1976:32–64) sought to evaluate the affair from a position unattached to either Soviet or Western propaganda. They identify four key elements in their analysis. First, while exaggerated for political advantage, it was legitimate in the 1930s and 1940s to criticize the unsubstantiated depiction of 'germplasm' common in the work of leading Western geneticists. The assertion of the existence of an unalterable 'germplasm', entirely detached from 'somatoplasm', and so unaffected by environmental conditions, was at the time unproven and highly speculative. The willingness of geneticists to lend their support to eugenics was also grounds for legitimate criticism of ideological contamination in their science. Second, the accepted refutation of Lamarckian theory, Weismann's removal of mouse-tails (and their subsequent reproduction of fully tailed offspring) misses its mark, as no selective advantage was built into Weismann's experiments. Lewontin and Levins go on to outline the existence of numerous research projects in the 1930s and 1940s suggesting that acquired characteristics, if selectively advantageous, could be inherited. After the exposure of Lysenko's misrepresentations, researchers in the United States (Schmalhausen) and the United Kingdom (Waddington) showed that Lysenko, and his supporters, could have gained the results they claimed, if not with the regularity or for the reasons they suggested. Latent genetic differences made manifest in different environmental conditions, rather than the acquiring of new characteristics thus, would have given results compatible with the Lysenkoist expectation (see Chapter 4 on 'interpretive flexibility'). As such, both sides had credible scientific foundations (given the knowledge available at the time), and both sides projected ideological bias into their work. Lewontin and Levins suggest, third, that an understanding of the material conditions of Soviet agriculture (both physical and economic-political) explain the inability to generate an assessment of 'normal' conditions against which to examine the claims made for the effectiveness of Lysenko's techniques. However, fourth, it is important to note that Western evaluations of Lysenko's work were themselves not immune to ideological bias. Even based on Western estimates of Soviet agricultural output between the 1920s and the 1970s, while never able to match US grain belt output per acre,

(*cont'd*)

Soviet agricultural production maintained its relative position even during the height of Lysenkoist practices. Western claims that Lysenko's 'ideological science' devastated Soviet agriculture have no basis in evidence, even while Lysenko's claims to Stakhanovite strides forward are equally to be dismissed. Lewontin and Levins conclude that the projection of myths of perfection onto nature (such as in Western eugenics and Soviet DiaMat) is a recurrent danger. They reject a priori assumptions of genetic determinism and infinite plasticity. They suggest a dialectical approach to variation and heredity avoids the dangers of eugenics, but that its users must beware of such an approach becoming a dogma itself.

Another ambiguous legacy in Marxism was Marx's view on the position of science and technology in relation to social change. For Marx the development of technology and science are bound up with the development of the material 'means' of production. Hilary Rose and Steven Rose (1976b:5–6) cite Marx, who writes:

[N]atural science has invaded and transformed human life all the more *practically* through the medium of industry; and has prepared human emancipation, although its immediate effect had to be the furthering of the dehumanisation of man. *Industry* is the *actual* historical relationship of nature, and therefore of natural science, to man.

However, the term 'material' is used in at least two ways. In one sense the material refers to the physical reality of life. However, in another sense, Marx writes about the material as the 'economic relations' that operate above the level of any individual's control. This is the sense in which Marx says that

Men [*sic*] make their own history, but they do not make it just as they please; they do not make it under circumstances chosen by themselves, but under given circumstances directly encountered and inherited from the past. (Marx 1978:9)

This double sense of the material (as physical and social constraint) is played out in Marx's discussion of technology. Technology occupies a position both in relations between humans and between humans and physical reality. People interact with things and other people within the productive process. If the former is called the technical division of labour, relations between people can be called the social division of labour. On the one hand it has been argued that a certain development of technology causes a corresponding division of social relations at work. This is often called 'technological determinism'. On the other hand it can be argued that the same set of tools might 'support' different sets of social relations, that is divisions of work, reward and power.

In Marx, both these readings can be found. On the one hand, Marx writes of how the advent of steam power was instrumental in the destruction of feudal relations and in promoting capitalist relations (that is the shift from small-scale peasant agriculture to a large-scale, wage-labour-based economy) (Bloch 1967):

> It is not the consciousness of men that determines their being, but on the contrary it is their social being that determines their consciousness. At a certain stage of their development, the material productive forces of society come into conflict with the existing relations of production or – what is merely a legal expression for the same thing – with the property relations within the framework of which they have hitherto operated. From forms of development of the productive forces these relations turn into their fetters. At that point an era of social revolution begins. (Marx 1976:3–4)

In this sense Marx's materialist conception of history sees technical change driving social change (including social relations of production). However, elsewhere, Marx places social relations of production within the 'material base' of society, and suggests that it is conflicts at this level that drive social change. In this latter sense Marx notes how capitalists use technology not only as a means of increasing production, but as a means of dealing with troublesome workers. Skilled workers can be replaced with less-skilled ones, while the division of work can be used to ensure that knowledge of the production process as a whole is denied to those who are actually doing the work:

> The instrument of labour strikes down the labourer. This direct antagonism between the two comes out most strongly, whenever newly introduced machinery competes with handicrafts or manufactures, handed down from former times. But even in Modern Industry the continual improvement of machinery, and the development of the automatic system, has an analogous effect. (Marx 1999:156)

As such technology is both a part of the forces of production (transforming nature) and a part of the social relations of production (a means of social control). Taking up this second line of argument, and once again drawing upon the work of Lukács and the Frankfurt school, the new Marxist perspectives distanced themselves from the technological determinist connotations found in orthodox Marxism.

# Reification

The theory of 'reification' seeks to explain why a society increasingly dominated by the application of science and technology may reinforce domination and inequality even by means of the very forces of truth and efficiency that offered such hope of setting humanity free. Georg Lukács (1971[1919]) used the term 'reification' to describe a state of consciousness in which human subjects are transformed into objects, and where the products of human subjective thought and action are transformed into things that appear as alien forces which act over humans and control their lives. This state of consciousness is both true and false at the same time within the reality of capitalism, both at work and in the marketplace. Lukács talks about false consciousness, but reification describes something real, even if that reality is so distorted as to make direct perception of it give rise to distorted ways of seeing. The division of labour within capitalism is said to place the worker in a position of subordination and fragmentation. The use of machines within production divides work in such a way as to make a clear perception of the overall process difficult to achieve. While Lukács was primarily describing factory work, his ideas drew upon both Marx and Weber, and the term reification can be applied as well to Weber's discussion of bureaucracy as it can to Marx's description of industrial production. Lukács' pre-Marxist attachments to existentialism and German idealism led orthodox Marxists to accuse him, and the later Frankfurt school that drew on his work, of being contaminated with 'bourgeois' ideas. However, it is a Marxism that, whether contaminated or enlivened, has outlived its orthodox rivals.

Reification also describes relations between the worker and the products of their work. Being party to only one fragment of the productive process, individual workers find it increasingly difficult to comprehend the overall logic of their work, or to relate to the finished product of their work. Equally, in the marketplace, all the products that circulate before ours eyes, in shops, advertisements and in the possession of other people, gain a charmed and magical character.

Lukács's account of reification sought to explain how the application of rational forms of technology and organization may lead to domination rather than liberation. These ideas were taken in a parallel direction by the Marxist writers of the Frankfurt School.

## Dialectic of Enlightenment

The work of the Frankfurt school covers a vast range of themes and materials. The most significant work produced by the first generation of its members addresses the relationship between science, technology and the idea of human progress. Theodor Adorno and Max Horkheimer's 1944 work *Dialectic of Enlightenment* (1979) is often the source of intense frustration and confusion. The book can be read as an exploration of the relationship between four key themes that thread through each other and throughout the book. These themes are: human progress; myth and reason; domination; alienation.

Each theme will be addressed in turn. Examples of contemporary Marxist research are boxed to provide the reader with illustrations of how such themes form the basis of an overall research agenda around the notion of 'critical theory'. The four themes themselves overlap, and each case-study can be seen to demonstrate this crossover. The teasing out of four themes should not lead the reader to assume that such themes are wholly separate in theory or in practical reality. They are arranged this way only for presentational simplicity.

### Human Progress

*Dialectic of Enlightenment* attempts to map the gains and the losses brought about by modernity. The tone of the book is dark. This was a reaction to the typical historical optimism associated with enlightenment and modernity, as well as to the specific historical conditions in which the book was composed (at the time of the Holocaust). As such it is important to realize that the authors do seek to defend the enlightenment from anti-rationalism, romanticism and conservative traditionalism. They write: 'We are wholly convinced that social freedom is inseparable from enlightenment thought' (1979: xiii). Yet at the same time they suggest: 'The fallen nature of modern man cannot be separated from social progress' (xiv). As its title suggests, *Dialectic of Enlightenment* seeks to outline the dialectical, or self-contradictory, nature of modern life. The very things that bring advancement also contain within themselves the possibility of great suffering and injustice. 'Even though the individual disappears before the apparatus which he [sic] serves, that apparatus provides for him [sic] as never before' (xiv). A great gift is also a great danger in that it may seduce its recipient and even render them dependent upon the giver.

The authors were well aware that it is only the legacy of enlightenment thinking that gave them the critical resources with which to launch an investigation into the dark side of enlightenment. It was only the advent of a 'public realm' of 'free expression' within modernity that allowed them to write and work as critical intellectuals challenging aspects of modernity. Yet, from the vantage of mid-twentieth-century experience, it is easy to see how the price paid for such seemingly puny opportunities might have seemed far higher than the benefits. It was very easy to see 'progress' at one level. The advances in the machineries of war, torture, death, propaganda and domination were all clear to see. The subsequent nuclear age, with its iconic mushroom cloud, made total human self-destruction a feasible possibility. It could not be doubted that humans had progressed in these things. Likewise, economic output, fuelled by wartime planning, had shown that progress in material production might easily satisfy all basic human needs. As such progress was manifest, if monstrous in its misdirection.

Yet what of progress in the ethical sense? War, bureaucracy and corporate power seemed to have rendered democracy a populist tool for greater manipulation even in those countries that had stood for democracy against fascism. Politics and social life seemed to have become adjuncts to the machinery of quantitative growth and power.

## From the Oven State to the Rocket State

Douglas Kellner's (2001) discussion of Thomas Pynchon's (1973) novel *Gravity's Rainbow* develops a theme within critical theory, the use of cultural artefacts as prisms through which to explore the dynamics of the society of which they are a part. Pynchon's novel explores the emergence of what he calls the 'Rocket State' in the aftermath of the Second World War and in the context of the cold war. The fusion of military competition and corporate global expansion created the conditions for the emergence of the 'Rocket State'. Nazi Germany exemplified the development of modern methods of scientific domination towards a particular logical extension. Totalitarian control over an occupied territory, and the concentration of enemies of that regime for the purpose of extermination, required the development and application of modern scientific methods of military control, administration and execution. Pynchon, drawing upon the work of Max Weber, refers to Nazi Germany as the 'Oven State'. The 'Rocket State' dispenses with the need for physical occupation of territory, instead developing the dual technologies of long-range nuclear missiles and global telecommunications. Such a state can effect extermination and propaganda on a global scale, by technical means that detach the host society of almost all manifest expressions of its totalitarian dominion. Dispensing with the need for an overtly militarized civil society, the Rocket State can threaten and enact huge acts of destruction and extermination (such as in Vietnam), while projecting, at home and abroad, the image of itself as a peace-loving, consumerist democracy. Kellner suggests that such a transition from the Oven State to the Rocket State represents the birth of a postmodern world. Such a civilization also expresses the mythic quality of science, wedded to the impression of civility, while stockpiling the means of ever more efficient barbarism.

All of this seemed to receive the seal of approval from the notion of progress itself. As things would always get better, whatever is around now must therefore be better than what went before and must also be the path to better things in the future. It was this sense of progress that led Adorno and Horkheimer to see science, as the most powerful expression of the ideal of human progress, as being an integral part of the 'ideology' of modernity.

## Medical Science as an Ideology of Progress

Vincente Navarro's Marxist account of medicine under capitalism (1976, 1985), and his Marxist critique of health care in the Soviet Union, seeks to show how medical science is tailored to the needs of social control, individualized responsibility and increased productivity. As Steven Rose (1997) points out, this tailoring can also be seen in the role played by pharmaceutical companies in the orientation of health care towards the use of expensive treatments rather than addressing the social and

(*cont'd*)

economic causes of illness. Rose also highlights how, for example, the tobacco industry prefers to fund research into cancer prevention by drug treatment than spend that money discouraging people from using their products in the first place. Health and health care are big business, and big business prefers profitable treatments to profit-squeezing environmental and workplace regulations that might better promote health. Moynihan *et al.* (2002) describe how pharmaceutical companies sponsor research that exaggerates the extent and seriousness of a range of conditions so as to increase sales of related drug treatments. They give a number of examples of what they call 'disease mongering'. They suggest (2002:886): 'Disease mongering can include turning ordinary ailments into medical problems, seeing mild symptoms as serious, treating personal problems as medical, seeing risks as diseases, and framing prevalence estimates to maximise potential markets.' They suggest this problem can only be solved if corporate funded information about disease is replaced by independent research. Ray Moynihan (2003) highlights the role played by the Pfizer Corporation in funding research into 'female sexual dysfunction'. The research highlighted that many women do not want sex as often as their partners do. Defining this as a dysfunction, paralleling male impotence, allows the condition to be seen as an illness, in need of treatment, and on a mass scale. Pfizer, the manufacturer of Viagra, has made vast profits in the male market, and would profit greatly from a female medical market 'curing' what might not best be described as a medical illness at all. Such 'disease mongering' is only the logical extension of capitalism to pharmaceutical research and manufacture. As Thomas Bodenheimer (1985) highlights, capitalist pharmaceutical companies are at the forefront of globalization, and have immense bargaining power with national governments in the developed world when it comes to developing health policy at home and aid policy to developing countries. The ideology of more science equals more progress equates current power with the human good, and diverts attention away from alternatives.

## Myth and Reason

One of the things enlightenment philosophers proposed was that human reason should be liberated from the dogmas of past thinking, free to think about and observe the world as it really is. The highest forms of dogma were the mythologies of organized religion and superstition. However, Adorno and Horkheimer suggest that reason and science have become mythical forms of thinking in their current manifestations.

If the classic myth reverses the relation of human to non-human, giving humans superhuman powers while also giving the non-human human powers (thought, intention, human emotion etc.), science supposedly eliminates such thinking. However, in a particular sense, this is exactly what science does.

On the one hand humans are treated like objects (in mechanistic medicine, reductionist biology and other deterministic forms of science applied to humans). If science is about determinant causation, then surely the future can be mapped out without regard for subjective opinion and lay consultation. There is no democracy or free will in mathematics. This can become a justification for domination and the use of 'science' as a substitute for democracy in politics. The sense that science can reveal human fate, irrespective of human will, recalls the mythic tales of prophecy in the words of oracles, witches and shamans in older forms of thinking.

On the other hand the non-human realm is reduced to human classifications and measures:

> From now on matter would at last be mastered, without any illusion of ruling or inherent powers, of hidden qualities. For the Enlightenment, whatever does not conform to the rule of computation and utility is suspect. (Adorno and Horkheimer 1979:6)

Because science asserts the possibility of mapping the universe, that which falls outside the map is deemed not to exist. Things are classified according to human criteria, coded by human systems of measurement, and this is then said to be what really exists. This is classical mythical thinking, to project human conceptions into the world and then suggest that you discovered these things in nature.

While the happy hunting ground is traded in for a mechanistic universe this is only the trading in of a mythic system suitable for one mode of economic and social life for a myth best suited to capitalism. Recall the earlier discussion of Newton. While it may be the case that Newton provided a powerful and in many ways accurate predictive model of the universe, his account was not free of 'ideological' baggage, and was certainly not immune to ideological abuse. Adorno and Horkheimer pay greater attention to Newton's forebear Sir Francis Bacon, but the same arguments apply.

Adorno and Horkheimer make reference to the rabbit in the scientific laboratory. Does this rabbit have an existence for the scientists as anything more than as an example of a particular class of thing within their scheme? No. If the rabbit belonged to their son or daughter they would no doubt give it a name and treat it as one of the family, but as a lab tool it has no existence outside its utility as an example. The reduction of real individual entities to mere examples of the scientist's abstract categories is classic mythic thinking (recall the biblical snake that is not a particular snake but is a mythic representation of 'evil' or loss of innocence). Regardless of whether one set of categories more accurately describes the world than another, such classification makes each individual simply one interchangeable example of a general type. Such thinking leads to the sense of impunity and indifference that can be expressed towards real sentient beings once they have been stripped of their uniqueness. The parallel with the gas chamber is just beneath the surface here.

## Domination

Science has been bound up with the domination of nature. Once it is taken for granted that nature is merely a set of things for humans to exploit it becomes easier to justify policies that make humans more efficient and productive, disciplined and easy to manage. Science becomes a justification for detachment and calculation of nature and other people. This can then be applied to the scientists themselves. Good rational scientists can be put to work for the purpose of social engineering. The role played by scientists and doctors in the Nazi Holocaust is highly illustrative of the dangers of science and technology as both an ideology and as a machine able to detach actors from the consequences of their own actions and from those whom they act upon (Bauman 1989, 1991, 1992; Arendt 1963; Milgram 1997). The race and eugenic theories propounded in Nazi Germany were no different from those commonly held within the medical and scientific community across Western Europe and the United States at the time. The distancing effected by science and technology between actors and those they act upon can be seen in many instances today. That the Nazi concentration camps, deportation programmes, execution units, gas chambers and sterilization campaigns are unique in the extent to which scientific principles and rational techniques of action and administration were applied, is one thing. However, Zygmunt Bauman's (1989) concludes that while different from Nazi Germany, the world today is not different enough.

### Science as Ideology: The Case of Eugenics

John Kurt Jacobsen's (2000) account of the history of eugenics draws together research from across the world (Kelves 1985; McLaren 1990; Stepan 1991; Kuhl 1994; Tucker 1995; Broberg and Roll-Hansen 1996; Thomson 1998). Jacobsen demonstrates that the use of science to legitimize racial, class and gender inequality, and to enforce its maintenance, was not confined to Nazi Germany. The term eugenics (eugenic meaning 'well born' or 'noble in heredity') was coined by Sir Francis Galton, cousin of Charles Darwin. Galton was distressed by the declining birth rates of those he considered to be naturally of superior intellect, and impressed by the high level of family ties among his undergraduate colleagues at Cambridge University (something he took to indicate the biological root of intelligence). He founded and bankrolled the eugenics movement in Great Britain from the 1860s on, leaving his estate to continue the work of promoting good breeding and restricting bad. Jews, southern Europeans, the working class, the Irish and those of African origin all became the object of eugenic designation as biologically

(*cont'd*)

inferior. The temptation to use science to legitimize social engineering was not confined to ruling elites. Middle-class social reformers, Fabian socialists, suffragettes and birth control advocates all sought to draw upon the language of science to justify their programmes (see also Petersen and Bunton 2002: chapter 2). Eugenics appealed to the educated middle classes as it sanctified their own self-image as an elite constituted by natural ability, caught between a degenerate aristocracy and the dangerous masses below.

Yet it was not in Great Britain that eugenic theories saw their most full application. Gentlemanly amateurism, an almost total lack of scientific training among the ruling elites of British state and economy, and a reluctance to engage in large-scale social reform inhibited 'scientific' programmes of social engineering. While eugenic theories were popular as an ideology of the educated classes in Britain, state intervention was less developed. It was in those societies where science, education and rational administration had been more fully embraced as a means of catching up with the then dominant British empire that eugenic theories were put most readily into practice. In the United States popular accounts of degenerate families (such as the Jukes in 1887 and the Kallikaks in 1912) presented 'decent folk' with the prospect of becoming overrun by the simpleminded and/or criminal. Degenerate traits were said to run in families and such people were assumed to breed more readily than 'respectable' folk. By the end of the First World War over half the states in the United States had adopted the practice of castration or vasectomy as a means of stemming the alleged tide of biological degeneration. '*Scientific American* advocated compulsory sterilization in five editorials between 1911 and 1914' (Jacobsen 2000:119). Scandinavian countries also adopted racial hygiene programmes to sterilize those whose offspring it was believed might be a burden to society. 'In France, in 1935, the Nobel prize-winner Alexis Carrel published a modest book calling for the "ideal solution" of "little economic gas chambers" for "all those with bad genes"' (Jacobsen 2000:123). These policies and the role of well-respected scientists in formulating, advocating and carrying them out were not an aberration, but mainstream science of its time. That the mainstream scientific community now reject such 'science' as an aberration in part reflects the Nazi extension of eugenics, but also reflects the attempt by science today to distance itself from what may be the most manifest example of science as ideology. Those seeking to deny that science can become ideology must seek to ignore this extended episode:

> Physicians on trial at Nuremberg for ghastly camp experiments embarrassingly cited American examples to prove that the ambition of eliminating 'inferior elements' was not unique to Germany. Nuremberg prosecutors, many of whom themselves were under sway of eugenicist notions, did not prosecute the Nazi doctors for the sterilizations, only for outright killings. As elsewhere in Germany, as the cold war revved up, many of these Nazi physicians returned to prominent posts. Reilly (1991:9) notes that 'international science critics failed to question the aim of race

*(cont'd)*

improvement in principle.' After World War II, renowned scientist Julian Huxley, brother of Aldous, insisted that eugenics 'has not been proved wrong, it had merely been wrongly applied'. The reductionist thrust of genetics research continued, and reductionism remained as liable as ever to be taken as the only legitimate view of science. (Jacobsen 2000:124)

Science, then, can become complicit in domination not merely in its application, but also in its form and content.

*Alienation*

Treating nature and other people as tools acts to distance the agent from the world, and so alienates them. This alienation goes deeper once the person fully disciplines himself or herself so as to avoid attachments to those they dominate. Once the person comes to see themselves as a tool for the conduct of business, politics, sex, sport etc., then the process of alienation is complete. Odysseus had himself bound to the mast of his ship while his crewmen had their ears plugged with beeswax so that he could hear the beautiful cries of the sirens without being dashed on the rocks. De Sade's Julliette seemed able to use her body as a tool to seduce powerful men without ever feeling remorse or suffering the consequences of her attachments without love. However, Adorno and Horkheimer suggest that treating others and ourselves as tools will always lead to alienation from the very person we were seeking to help in the first place. What is the point of being selfish if you lose yourself in the process?

# The Later Frankfurt Scholars: Marcuse and Habermas

Herbert Marcuse and Jürgen Habermas offer accounts of the lifeworld as the site of resistance to colonization by instrumental rationality. However, each offers a distinct conception of the lifeworld.

In the aftermath of the Second World War and the subsequent nuclear arms race of the cold war, Marcuse's version of a Marxist critical theory (1941, 1969a[1955], 1969b, 1972) drew upon a range of influences (including psychoanalysis, existentialism and aesthetics). Marcuse attempted to understand a world where science and technology offered great wealth and total destruction of the human race. In his most influential work, *One Dimensional Man* (1991/originally published in 1964), Marcuse identifies the link between science and domination. The key question for Marcuse lay in why grossly unequal and repressive social systems continued to exist. In part, he concluded that elites had come to cloak themselves in the language of technocratic efficiency and scientific management and/or social engineering. Marcuse went further than other Marxist critics did in questioning the ideological nature of science. For him, it is not simply the case that science is used badly in the interests of domination, or that modern science is partially biased in the models it draws upon to explain itself. Rather, Marcuse suggested that at a fundamental level modern physics, chemistry and biology are geared towards a form of knowledge driven by a need for control more than from a desire for understanding:

> The principles of modern science were a priori structured in such a way that they could serve as conceptual instruments for a universe of self-propelling, productive control; theoretical operationalism came to correspond to practical operationalism...the instrumentalities for the ever-more-effective domination of man by man through the domination of nature. (Marcuse 1991[1964]:158)

Marcuse was not suggesting that science is not a highly powerful system for investigating the world, nor that science was not highly successful at generating accurate predictions based upon the theories it generated. It is simply the case that the type of questions science is very successful at answering are the types of questions it asks, and these questions are geared towards certain kinds of control. In Marcuse's view modern science is naturally suited to the technological orientation of modern capitalism. Such an outlook lends itself to transfer from the natural to the social world, as it is from the social world in which modern science emerged that such an outlook was itself formed. Living in a particular social world leads to seeing the natural world in a certain way. This view of nature then makes the social world appear natural as it corresponds to nature (or at least the way one sees that nature):

> In this universe, technology also provides the great rationalization of the unfreedom of man and demonstrates the 'technical' impossibility of being autonomous, of determining one's own life. (Marcuse 1991[1964]:158)

Marcuse argued that not only was modern science well suited to being used as an ideological defence of social systems of domination. New forms of seeing the natural world would only emerge within new social conditions, or at least in the struggles to create such conditions and the struggles to overcome the present systems of social domination. Marcuse identified within ecological politics the seeds of a new scientific approach to nature. Rather than the reductionism and fragmentation of nature characteristic of the dominant Western model, the new ecology emphasized the integrated systemic nature of ecosystems, and the need to study nature accordingly. This was not anti-science, but a new science.

Jürgen Habermas's *Towards a Rational Society* (1971), an essay written to celebrate the seventieth birthday of Herbert Marcuse, focuses upon the danger of politics being reduced to technical administration (something Habermas (1979) accuses Marx of doing). Habermas's (1971) essays on science as politics present four aspects of the collapse of value-rational dialogue into instrumental management: (1) social questions become technical questions, (2) choice is reduced to 'scientific' strategies, (3) values are instrumentalized and (4) politics becomes scientific management. Habermas suggests that the basis for collective resistance and transformation is that human action is oriented towards understanding rather than just physical necessity. Habermas differs from Marcuse in arguing that it is not intrinsically problematic to explain events outside the social realm in terms of cause and control. For Habermas instrumental control of nature is not the problem, only the transfer of such models of explanation and problem-solving from nature to social life. Here they are both false and oppressive.

Marcuse sees the generative or creative capacities of both the social and natural lifeworlds as beyond the scope of reductionist models to explain. Habermas limits his critique to the misapplication of such accounts to the social lifeworld. The tension between these two positions within Marxism reflects the deeper divide between those (Marxists and others) who question the nature of scientific knowledge itself and those who restrict themselves to questioning the use and abuse of scientific knowledge, and scientific reductionism in addressing social questions.

## Marxism, Science and Anti-Science

While Marxists have provided much theoretical and empirical research that brings into question the political neutrality of scientific research and the application of science and technology in society, Marxists are, generally, supportive of a realist and materialist account of the natural world. Marxists are generally pro-science as such, and, as such, Marxists have been critical of forms of relativism that dismiss the value of science as a superior form of knowing the natural world. The most controversial recent example of this defence of science against 'postmodern' relativism came with the publication in the 1996 Spring–Summer special issue of the journal *Social Text* of an article by the Marxist physicist Alan Sokal. The article, 'Transgressing the Boundaries: Toward a Transformative Hermeneutics of Quantum Gravity' (Sokal 1996:217–52), appeared to defend discourse-analytic claims that quantum theory demonstrated that science was a social construction. The article was favourably reviewed by the journal's editors and published. The author then revealed the article to be a spoof, aimed at exposing the scientific illiteracy of the journal's editors. Sokal later defended his deception:

> Political progressives should seek to have that [scientific] knowledge distributed more democratically and to have it employed for socially useful ends. Indeed, the radical epistemological critique [the social constructivist/relativist position] fatally undermines the needed political critique, by removing its factual basis. After all, the only reason why nuclear weapons are a danger to anyone is that the theories of nuclear physics on which their design is based are, at least to a very high degree of approximation, objectively true... Science studies' epistemological conceits are a diversion from the important matters that motivated science studies in the first place: the social, economic and political roles of science and technology. (Sokal 2001:25)

Alongside other Marxists, Sokal is critical of the abuse of science and technology precisely because of its powerful capacity to understand the world and so control it (see Sokal and Bricmont 1998). Rose and Rose (1970:260, 1976a:xv–xvi) reserve at least some of their criticism for Luddites, romantic anti-science mystics and flower power hippies, even if the thrust of their work is critical of the technocratic elite who use science to effect and authorize their continued domination. Even Herbert Marcuse, who supported 1960s student radicalism, and who believed that social change would radically change science, was critical of romantic anti-science rhetoric among the flower power generation (see Kellner 1984). Marxists are realists and materialists first and foremost.

Stanley Aronowitz (1988, 1996), one of the editors of *Social Text* at the time of Sokal's article, and also a Marxist, rejects the claim that to question the objectivity of science is to abandon materialism for relativism. 'So the issue is not whether reality exists, but whether knowledge of it is "transparent"' (Aronowitz 1997:107). That the politics, culture and economics of society influence science does not render science pure fiction. 'What it means is that scientific knowledge is not immune from broad cultural or narrow political influence and its methods cannot function as a filter' (Aronowitz 1997:110). Aronowitz's materialism gives greater weight to social forces in the determination of ideas than does Sokal's, but while Sokal gives greater weight to the material world in shaping our ideas about it, he does not deny that social pressure also acts as a material factor in the knowledge production process. 'Who nowadays claims that culture has nothing to do with economic injustice, or that funding sources have no effect on scientific work? Who denies the value of sociological and political study of science and technology, or of the philosophical analysis of epistemological problems? My point is a modest one: that such investigations need to be conducted with due intellectual rigour' (Sokal 1997:111). Disputing the relative merits of each's comprehension of the other's field of material, and of the relative significance of each's material field in generating the best account of 'reality' may be the best route to such an intellectual rigour. It is also an interesting form of dialectical materialism in action.

Another interesting follow-up to Sokal's critique of social-constructivist accounts of science comes from the Marxist sociologist David Norman Smith (2001). Smith points out that while postmodern nihilism may be a dangerous and misguided irrationalism (at least from a Marxist perspective), it is not enough simply to dismiss such theory as feeblemindedness. Such thinking needs to be explained in terms of the social causes of its contemporary popularity. Smith draws the parallel with the 1920s in Germany. After the First World War many German intellectuals became disillusioned with the idea of social progress and with rational explanation in science. Oswald Spengler's (1926) critique of scientific and social progress resonated as much with scientists as with the wider society. Smith points out that this mood of anti-rationalism in part explains the popularity of the seemingly anti-causal Copenhagen Interpretation of quantum physics (developed by Niels Bohr and Werner Heisenberg). While Einstein was outraged by the uncertainty principle, and its apparent invitation to see the subatomic world in acausal terms, this interpretation became the accepted view at that time. That science is not immune to social influence or even the pull of irrationalism is Smith's conclusion. It is not enough to say that those who are not trained physicists are prone to read into physics their own social and political dispositions. The same can be seen in the actions and writings of leading experts in the very field of quantum physics Sokal is keen to defend from irrationalism, nihilism and anti-materialism. Sokal wants to defend science from infection by social bias, yet that bias may be there all the same. Smith is largely in agreement with Sokal over the dangers of irrationalism and the tone of anti-science evident in some postmodern writing, yet he seeks to point out that things are not as simple as Sokal would like them to be.

# Conclusions: Marxism – Critical and Realist Theory of Science

While Marx was to a great extent a celebrant of science and technology (to this extent he was realist), he was always a dialectical thinker. The meaning of critical in the Marxist sense refers to identifying the contradictions in reality, not just the ethical sense of criticism as opposition to what is not moral. For Marxists 'reality' does not simply assert its reality in the sense of forcing us to accept that things are the way they are, and therefore there is nothing to be done. Reality is full of tensions and pressures. The present bristles with alternative possibilities. This is as true of physical reality as social life. The study of 'reality' enables human beings to identify possibilities within reality, not just a set of fixed and frozen facts. Being always contains many possibilities for becoming. Technology and science are bound up within ongoing conflicts, even if their progressive nature may offer more than the sum of their original intentions or current applications. Marxists are critical by nature, but in the case of science this criticism is dialectical, challenging abuse and distortion precisely to defend science. As one of the most powerful achievements of human development, science is a double-edged sword. Some Marxists give greater attention to the realism, defending science from irrationalism. Others give greater attention to critique. Contemporary Marxist perspectives in the sociology of science are more attentive to the ideological nature of science than were previous generations. However, they still retain a general defence of science and rationality as positive forces in increasing understanding and human freedom, even while challenging science's ideological and material integration within systems of power and domination.

# 7

# Science and Patriarchy: Women as Subjects/Objects of Science

## Introduction

Feminist approaches to the study of science and its relationship to women have addressed a range of issues. The structure of this chapter will attempt to integrate this range within a four-point scheme. The first theme will be women's representation within science, the numbers of women practising science and their relative status within science. Second, the question of women's historical position in science will be addressed, in terms of both celebrated female scientists and those whose contribution has been hidden from history. The third theme will address feminist studies of scientific constructions of women and the impact of those constructions upon women's lives. The first three sections outline the range of empirical feminist research. These data have led to the question of whether evidence of bias and ideology within science is illustrative of 'a few bad apples' or of a deeper rot in the barrel. This issue leads to the fourth and final theme, that of whether feminism needs to propose a counter science to existing (masculine) science, or whether traditional science can best overcome its male-dominated legacy by encouraging more women into scientific careers. This question has led to the development of three feminist theoretical frameworks. These are 'feminist empiricism', 'feminist standpoint theory' and 'postmodern feminist theory'. In conclusion, it will be shown how feminist research has highlighted the need to question assertions of scientific authority, and also how this questioning has been applied to feminist research itself. This has led to a position where feminism appears to ask more questions than it has definitive answers to give. Nevertheless, the work of Hilary Rose and Sandra Harding in particular provide foundations for integrating the diverse range of questions posed by feminist research into a research programme. This not only represents a consistent critique of established scientific practice, but also poses the possibility of radically overcoming the links between established science, domination and misrepresentation.

## Splicing the Field

The range of issues addressed by feminist research has been summed up differently by different authors.

Sandra Harding (1986) gives one five-point scheme. She refers to these five points as five 'research programmes' within feminism. First, there have been studies of women's representation within science (what Harding and others call equity studies). How many women get in, get on and stay, in scientific careers? Second, Harding identifies studies that have looked at the 'misuse of science', where science is distorted to justify the subordination and exclusion of women. Third, there are studies that question the 'truth' claims of science, and assert that science is systematically distorted. Fourth, Harding identifies studies that analyse 'truth' itself as a textual strategy, a literary device. Such studies apply a sceptical literary theoretical perspective to truth claims in general. Finally, Harding outlines feminist debates on what has come to be called 'feminist epistemology' (whether there is a female way of knowing that differs from male knowledge-making). Should feminists work within the traditional scientific framework of value neutrality and objectivity, defend the view that women have a different and superior way of truth-seeking, or reject the idea of truth altogether?

Hilary Rose (1994) also presents a five-point scheme. For her the five questions that feminists have asked are:

1. Why are there so few women in science?

2. Who are the women scientists hidden from history?

3. How has science been tied up with the patriarchal domination and misrepresentation of women?

4. Can feminism generate an alternative epistemology?

5. How might feminist science fiction contribute to alternative ways thinking about women and science?

Jordanova (1995, cited in Maynard 1997) also sets out a five-point scheme:

1. Accounts of the lost women of scientific history.

2. Accounting for the numbers of women in science.

3. The representation of women in scientific work.

4. The critique of scientific claims to neutrality and objectivity.

5. The impact of science on women's lives.

# Equity

In science women are the minority at all the senior levels. The assumption that the numerical gap between women and men in science is the result of a deficit on the part of women is challenged by feminist research.

Victoria Stolte-Heiskanen brought together research from Austria, Bulgaria, Denmark, Finland, GDR, Greece, Hungary, the Netherlands, the Soviet Union, Spain, Turkey and Yugoslavia. She concludes (1991:5–6):

> With depressing uniformity, irrespective of the country, type of research organisation, scientific discipline, or degree of 'feminisation' of the field, the higher the status of the position held in the hierarchy, the fewer the women. Science represents no exception to this 'universal law' of women's fate.

Despite evidence that women are entering science in increased numbers throughout Europe, it is still the case that getting in is no guarantee of getting on or staying in. She writes (1991:7): 'Thus, nowhere has the conflict between the biological clock, the domestic clock and the clock of the research system been satisfactorily resolved.'

The report to the European Union, *Science Policies in the European Union: Promoting Excellence Through Mainstreaming Gender Equality* (2000), found that in six EU countries women represented less than 7 per cent of professors in science (including the social sciences). In all other EU states the figure was less than 5 per cent. While numbers entering science at undergraduate level had reached parity in some life sciences, this did not translate into equal career progression. Career progression appears like the blades of an open pair of scissors, with the percentage of men rising and women falling as movement from graduate student, through junior to senior academic positions, is mapped (2000:14).

---

### Degrees of Inequality

In the United States, women represented 25 per cent of those taking science and technology degrees in 1966. The figure was 47 per cent in 1995. This would appear to suggest imminent equality at 50 per cent, but the numbers going on to postgraduate study show that women are heavily concentrated in the social and life sciences, and that men are again the vast majority overall. Of those enrolled in US science graduate school, 35 per cent were women in 1995, and for PhDs 31 per cent. Most of these were in the life and social

(*cont'd*)

sciences. Figures for specific subject-areas tell an interesting story. 16 per cent of US biology graduate students in the 1960s were women. This rose to 40 per cent in 1995. Chemistry saw a rise from 7 per cent to 27 per cent, geosciences saw 3 to 22 per cent, maths 5 to 19 per cent, physics 2 to 12 per cent, and engineering 1 to 11 per cent (Etzkowitz *et al.* 2000:12). While the numbers of women are increasing, the gap is still huge, and movement on to career entry and promotion shows a similar thinning out of women scientists.

Judith Glover (2000) highlights the situation in Britain. At the pre-university entry level (A level or Highers) women's participation has shifted significantly (2000:38). Between 1966 and 1996, women's representation in biology moved from 48 to 58 per cent. In maths the shift was from 16 to 26 per cent, in chemistry from 20 to 35 per cent and in physics from 13 to 17 per cent. At first degree level the changes between 1973 and 1993 were from 3 to 14 per cent in engineering and technology subjects, from 14 to 18 per cent in physics, from 28 to 33 per cent in maths, from 17 to 37 per cent in chemistry, from 36 to 52 per cent in biochemistry, and from 44 to 60 per cent in the biosciences. Computing science saw a drop from 16 per cent in 1986 to 15 per cent in 1993 (2000:39). For higher degrees the figures between 1973 and 1994 changed in engineering and technology from 3 to 13 per cent, from 8 to 16 per cent in physics, from 9 to 30 per cent in chemistry, from 14 to 19 per cent in maths, from 19 to 45 per cent in biochemistry and from 24 to 42 per cent in the biosciences.

Nancy Lane (1997) presents the picture in the United Kingdom (that is Great Britain and Northern Ireland combined). In 1994, 59 per cent of undergraduates in biology were women, 51 per cent in veterinary studies and agriculture, 30 per cent maths, engineering 25 per cent, technology 14 per cent, physics 12 per cent. Postgraduates were equal in number between men and women in biology, while there was a female majority in medicine and medical sciences. Men vastly outnumbered women in all the 'physical sciences', and the number of women studying computer science had actually declined in percentage terms since the 1980s.

Harriet Zucherman and Jonathan Cole (1975, cited in Richards 1987:174) suggest, in their *Women in American Science*, that women carry a triple burden in attempts to enter the sciences; this consists of:

1.  cultural assumptions about science as a man's realm;

2.  dismissive attitudes towards those women who enter science;

3.  actual discrimination and organizational barriers in jobs, prizes, attention, publication and conferences.

However, Cole (1979) later distinguished social selection and self-selection. Cole argues that the former is nominal and largely illusory while the latter is the main issue. Science selects on the basis of merit. Self-selection goes on prior to entry or non-entry to the science establishment – it is determined by the prior culture and women's own choices. Cole argues (cited in Richards 1987:179) that 'sex discrimination within the science establishment is comparatively rare, for most women simply opt out of their own accord'. As such science is seen as gender-neutral but women are said to have been socialized into a non-neutral position. To be a man is to be normal, to be a woman is not. Cole assumes that women choose not to enter science for reasons that have nothing to do with science. This can be challenged on two fronts. First, the argument that women choose to drop science at school is not evidence that it is girls not science that are the problem. Second, there is overwhelming evidence that even those women who do choose to study and pursue a career in science experience discrimination in their development.

Sandra Hanson (1996) highlights the gender differences in socialization between boys and girls, in relation to not only parental expectations and support but also sibling and peer approval and disapproval, as well as school and/or teacher encouragement. It is the case that girls are still less likely to be socialized into thinking science is either attractive or for them, and this is in part the result of how science is taught and presented to them by those science graduates who teach them at school. It is not solely the result of science teaching, but this does play a part.

Flis Henwood *et al.* (2000:112–28) demonstrated that the way computing was taught radically altered the respective ways male and female students related to the subject. Henwood *et al.* argue that it is in part the masculine preconceptions about computing as a science that lead those teaching it in the conventional fashion to assume that what they are doing is gender-neutral. When female students find that style offputting and/or boring, this is explained in terms of a female inability to grasp the subject-matter, rather than a failure of the teaching methods.

Nancy Lane (1997) points out that women in the UK are more likely to gain upper second-class degree grades in their undergraduate studies, while men are more likely to get the very highest or the lower grades. This reflects the tendency of male students to take greater risks in assessment preparation, and the tendency of men to take subjects where answers are assumed either to be totally correct or totally wrong. Lane suggests women are thereby less likely to gain funding for postgraduate study, which is often based on gaining a first-class undergraduate degree grade.

Henry Etzkowitz, Carol Kemelger and Brian Uzzi (2000) argue that women entering science face the difficulty of being either honorary men or flawed women (2000:2). This is because the scientific community is so male-dominated that male members take it for granted that they are normal. As such, a woman in their midst is not only a rarity but also a challenge. Women are confronted with the taken-for-granted assumptions of a masculine scientific institution throughout the lifecourse, or at least for as long as they stay within it. Etzkowitz *et al.* question the currently popular assumption that as long as more women go into science, then more women will rise up within it. This 'pipeline thesis' (2000:5) assumes that the pipe does not leak, and that it is not blocked in many important places. Editorial boards of academic journals are overwhelmingly male-dominated and sexual harassment is frequently felt to occur with little opportunity for redress (Lane 1997:43).

Hilary Rose (1994:14) points out that work intensity is seen as a virtue in science. Working late into the night, with little regard for the routines of everyday life, is seen as part of the stereotypical image of the absent-minded or slightly mad male scientist. Given the assumption that women are the ones who will take primary responsibility for child-rearing and other domestic tasks, the role of scientist and the role of woman do not sit together easily. Women who wish to pursue a career in science are torn between these roles. Men, on the other hand, do not traditionally face this choice. As Sharon Traweek identified in her research with physicists (cited in Rose 1994:14), successful male physicists tended to be those who got married young, and whose wives took responsibility for arranging their domestic worlds. As such, these men were able to focus all their energy upon their careers. Highly educated women usually marry equally educated men whose career advancement is often easier (Lane 1997). The husband therefore has greater scope to earn more. As such, his career and relocation needs carry greater weight in family arrangements. Child-bearing and -rearing in the late twenties and early thirties sees many women scientists take a career break in the context of Britain's limited childcare services. This is something from which their career rarely fully recovers. Britain is not alone in this. Judith Glover (2000:61) points out that better state provision of childcare in France makes it easier for women there to stay on within a science-based career than in Britain, but it is still the case that women in France are heavily concentrated in the lower-status positions within the scientific realm.

In seeking to explain the situation in Britain, and elsewhere, Glover highlights a number of key factors in addition to assumptions about childcare and the effect of career breaks. Glover highlights an enduring misogyny (2000:118) within the mainly male scientific community. The professional identity of scientists is bound up with a legacy of what Glover calls a 'male, celibate, homo-social culture' (2000:120). This creates a male-friendly 'habitus'. Segmentalism, whereby men concentrate in those areas where most status and research funding is available (2000:123), also plays a part. Finally, she points to the fact that men have greater geographical mobility than women, something that allows them to pursue careers and to detach themselves from non-career-based commitments, such as to family, to friends and even to students. This higher geographical mobility is bound up with higher earnings and the lack of inhibiting cultural barriers to movement. Men are encouraged to think of their careers first and foremost.

## Positions, Promotions and Rewards

Lane points out (1997:41) that in 1995 only 3 per cent of the fellows of the British Royal Society (membership of which is bestowed on leading scientists) were women. Of 901 members of the Royal Academy of Engineers only 3 were women. Glover highlights research for the Royal Society and the Institute of Physics that showed how increased undergraduate numbers have not translated readily into career development. The ratio of women to men teaching physics in secondary school is 1:4, teaching undergraduates is 1:8, teaching at a postgraduate level is 1:10, while the ratio of women to men practising as science professionals outside academia is 1:20 (Glover 2000:41).

Women with science degrees still earn significantly less than men, and are more likely to work in the public rather than the more lucrative private sector (Glover 2000:44). Women are more likely to take career breaks than male colleagues and often the only way back into a scientific career after a break is to take a position as a lab technician rather than as an independent research leader. Glover cites Greenfield's (1996) observation that in science you have to publish or perish. A period of silence on the publishing front can spell career suicide for a research scientist, and women often find that after a career break they are unable to re-enter the field.

Female science graduates are more heavily concentrated in the lower-status, less-research-active positions within the education system (Glover 2000:51); see Table 7.1.

*Table 7.1*

### Science and engineering graduates in teaching, by sex and teaching sector in Britain

|                  | Women | Men  | All  |
|------------------|-------|------|------|
| Higher education | 23    | 44   | 37   |
| Secondary school | 58    | 53   | 55   |
| Primary school   | 18    | 3    | 9    |
| All              | 100%  | 100% | 100% |
| *n*              | 146   | 262  | 408  |

Adapted from Glover (2000:53).

*(cont'd)*

Within the higher-education sector, women are far more heavily concentrated in the more junior positions, with greater teaching responsibilities and so fewer opportunities to do research, to publish and thus to gain promotion; see Table 7.2.

*Table 7.2*

**Female (%) employment in higher education by scientific field and academic rank in Britain in 1994**

| Career status* | Biological sciences (excluding biochemistry) | Chemistry | Physics | Engineering/ technology |
|---|---|---|---|---|
| 1 | 3 | 0.4 | 0.4 | 0.5 |
| 2 | 8 | 2 | 2 | 1 |
| 3 | 31 | 9 | 11 | 9 |
| 4 | 48 | 28 | 16 | 14 |
| % of women in each field | 27 | 12 | 8 | 8 |
| *n* | 977 | 247 | 210 | 517 |

*1. Equals professor. 2. Equals reader/senior lecturer. 3. Lecturer. 4. Other (e.g. researcher)
Adapted from Glover (2000:54).

# Hidden Lives

Despite the immense barriers to entry, continuation and promotion experienced by women within science, it is not the case that women have played no part in the history of science. One danger of presenting the overall picture of exclusion given above is that such an account covers over the already neglected history of those women who did manage to get a foothold within science and whose participation has often been significant.

Anne Sayre's (2000[1975]) *Rosalind Franklin and DNA* gives an account of Franklin's contribution, as a crystallographer, to the 'discovery' of the structure of DNA. The fame and fortune for this 'discovery' was heaped upon the male researchers Watson and Crick, who played up their own role in the process and who belittled the contribution of Franklin. Sayre's book, published originally in 1975, caused a scandal and Franklin's contribution was given greater recognition. Sayre's text led others to investigate the role of hidden women in science.

Evelyn Fox Keller's experience as a physics student led her to research more generally the position of women within science. Keller's biography of Barbara McClintock, *A Feeling for the Organism* (1983), gives an account of the work of one female biological scientist. McClintock's research into maize corn led her to challenge many of the leading scientific assumptions of her day, and the corporate interests that drove most food-related research in the middle years of the twentieth century. McClintock showed that genes could transpose within chromosomes; that they could move around (the so-called 'jumping genes'). McClintock's career was blighted for decades both because she was a woman and because she challenged the dominant orthodoxy. Only late in life did she receive the recognition of the scientific community in the form of a Nobel prize in 1983.

Hilary Rose (1994:49) highlights the role played by the primatologist Jane Goodall in developing this field of biological science. Rose highlights the significance of 'empathy' within Goodall's approach to the study of primates. In the discussion of feminist epistemology below it will be pointed out that traditional male science has tended to associate good science with detachment while empathy is presented as irrational and female. Other primatologists have been studied by the feminist writer Donna Haraway (1990a, 1990b, 1991). Jeanne Altmann, Linda Fedigan, Adrienne Zihlman and Sarah Blaffer Hrdy all bring to light, in different ways, the political nature of interpreting animal behaviour. Each challenges in her own way the attempts by male researchers to naturalize their own vision of the natural gendered division of labour in humans, by analogy with the behaviour of other primates.

Kay McNulty Mauchly Antonelli is not a household name, but it was her work, leading a team of 75 women computers, that is, persons employed to make calculations in laboratories, that led to the development of ENIAC, the world's first electronic digital computer, in 1946. Search the internet for 'when women were computers'. Links recall women's role as the brains behind much scientific development attributed to men. Women, unable to gain full status as scientists, were often employed to do the calculations in laboratories, observatories and in the programming of early electronic computers. Hilary Rose points out (1994:15) that some women, on account of wealthy fathers or husbands, were able to pursue independent careers as researchers, being able to take unpaid positions to pursue their interests. However, far more women contributed to science in positions as human computers. For every Ada Lovelace, daughter of Lord Byron, and collaborator with Charles Babbage, there are many other forgotten or hidden female workers in the history of science. An interesting *4000 years of women in science* website can be found at: http://www.astr.ua.edu/4000WS/summary.shtml Of course, the women recorded in even feminist history are mainly from the elite classes and there were many more women who crunched numbers and mixed toxic chemicals in anonymity for want of the opportunity to break the barriers of gender and class.

While the biographical approach serves a useful purpose, the relationship between science and the lives of the majority of women must be told on a bigger sociological canvas.

# Science, Representation and the Control of Women's Lives

The part played by science in the construction and reinforcement of gender roles is a core field of feminist research. This research has concentrated on medical science and the biosciences (with an increasing emphasis upon the new genetics), but extends to studies of new information technology. Studies have identified historical continuities and contemporary innovations. The remainder of this section outlines eight studies and two collections of studies examining science's representation of and control over women.

In *Reading the Slender Body*, Susan Bordo (1990:83–112) examines contemporary medical representations of anorexia and the wider representation of female health and beauty. Bordo argues that medical science seeks to distinguish a pathological female self-image, where a person feels ugly and overweight even when unhealthily underweight, from a supposedly 'healthy' desire not to be 'fat'. In the context of a society that bombards women with images of thinness, and where perfectly healthy body size is consistently depicted as in need of slimming down, such a distinction is misleading. The separation between normal desire and pathological desire to be thin cannot be objectively made. The two are bound together in a society that places such routine pressure on women to lose weight. As such, medical attempts to make this distinction act to reinforce society's 'normal' expectation. By falsely separating the 'normal' from the 'pathological', medical science comes to naturalize a normality that is socially constructed, which subordinates women, and may itself best be described as 'pathologically' destructive.

Mary Jacobus, Evelyn Fox Keller and Sally Shuttleworth (1990) bring together a range of studies that identify the patriarchal assumptions underpinning nineteenth-century medical discourses on women. Mary Jacobus (1990:11–28) focuses upon the attempts made within medical science to maintain the assumed link between female sexual desire and the desire to be pregnant. The link between sexual desire, conception and maternal desire was assumed in women, even while it was not assumed that men were only interested in sex for the purposes of procreation. The desire to pacify female sexuality, and to naturalize female fidelity, even while excusing male sexual desire and promiscuity, structured the expectations of male medical researchers and directed their interpretation of evidence. Mary Poovey (1990:29–46) demonstrates how such male assumptions structured the medical establishment's attitude to syphilis in the 1840s. Women who engaged in prostitution were seen as medically abnormal, while the men who paid them were not seen as ill. 'Nymphomania', the term used to describe a woman with promiscuous sexual desires, was seen as a psychiatric condition, and the cause of the spread of syphilis. Male sexual desire was not seen as grounds for medical confinement. Emily Martin (1990:69–82) examines the representation of menstruation in medical discourses from the nineteenth century to the present. What is striking is the continued use of language that takes it for granted that a woman's body wants nothing more than to become pregnant. Even contemporary medical texts on menstruation view it 'in terms of a purpose that has failed' (1990:75). The assumption that women are wombs first, independent human actors second (if at all), pervades medical representation to this day.

Paula A. Treichler (1990:113–38) refers to the extensive literature on the shift in power from female midwives to male obstetricians in the control of childbirth (see also Newman 1985:128–43; Wajcman 1991). Treichler suggests that for all the benefits of modern medical intervention, it is still the case that the underlying assumption remains that giving birth is now an illness and that a pregnant woman is somehow sick. Pregnancy becomes unnatural even as medical control over it is made to appear natural. Combined with the findings of Jacobus and Martin, the medical construction of women suggests the female body is abnormal when pregnant and abnormal when not pregnant. Normality is rendered male.

Catherine Kohler Riessman (1992) suggests that women have been medicalized in all aspects where they are seen to deviate from men. This is a double-edged process, first in so far as false distinctions are made over such things as rationality and intelligence, and second with regard to substantial differences where the male is characterized as normal and the female as pathological.

Paula A. Treichler, Lisa Cartwright and Constance Penley (1998) bring together recent research on new medical imaging technologies. Far from providing science with a transparent image of reality, they conclude that new technologies 'reinforce what we have already learnt to see' (1998:2–3). In addition, what the editors of this collection find of particular significance is that such technologies encourage medical science to believe that they can understand what is going on 'inside' without asking the women they are examining. Technoscience believes it alone can gain truth about those it studies, and that detachment is superior to dialogue as a means of gaining understanding. This has allowed much of the scientific misrepresentation of women to go unchallenged, or meant at least that such challenges are not heard by experts who are trained not to listen. This will be discussed in the following section on feminist epistemology. Feminist standpoint theory suggests that listening and dialogue, rather than detached looking and examining, may transform science for the good, if given the opportunity.

Cynthia Eagle Russett's *Sexual Science: The Victorian Construction of Womanhood* (1991) catalogues the consequences of the Victorian obsession with racial and sexual difference, and the assumed biological basis of both. It was in the mid to late nineteenth century that natural history and physiology fused to create the foundations of modern biology (1991:4). Sexual and racial differences, already strong themes in Victorian thought, became 'the two great themes of nineteenth century science' (1991:7). The belief that inequality was naturally ordered structured the assumptions of scientists. Theories of intelligence, domesticity, aggression and dominance all poured forth from the pens of eminent male Victorian biologists, each structured within an unquestioned patriarchal mentality, and all used in various ways to reinforce the gendered division of power and responsibility that the Victorians had constructed in the industrial revolution. In such an era of radical social transformation, one which had seen significant changes in the nature of domestic and working lives, science played a crucial role in presenting the newly invented division of labour, of home and work, as natural.

Interestingly, as the position of women has changed over the last two hundred years, so too have the accounts of women in evolutionary terms. Each new account seeks to show that women today are the natural result of an evolution that orders the current state of affairs as a reflection of the state of nature. Despite the fact that these natural states of woman change on a regular basis, biology has always been on hand to suggest that today things are the way they have to be (Morris Fedigan 1992:103–22). As Linda Morris Fedigan (1992:122) concludes:

> People will not stop wanting to hear origin stories and scientists will not cease to write scholarly tales. But we can become aware of the symbolic content of our stories, for much as our theories are not independent of our beliefs, so our behaviour is not independent of our theories of human society. In these origin tales we try to coax the material evidence into telling us about the past, but the narrative we weave about the past also tells us about the present.

Lana Thompson's (1999) *The Wandering Womb: A Cultural History of Outrageous Beliefs about Women* parallels Cynthia Eagle Russett's account of science with a longer historical overview of male accounts of female difference. From ancient Greece to twentieth-century science, Thompson charts male anxiety and desire to control the female uterus. Ancient Greek beliefs about female hysteria being the result of the womb wandering about the body of a woman whose womb was not being productively used for the purpose of reproduction find striking echoes through the ages, not excluding the current era of medical science. Feminist studies of women and psychiatry demonstrate the continuity of many themes concerning female irrationality, emotionality and insanity as well as the association between these things and domesticity, maternal instinct and the assumed pathological nature of deviation from such roles and desires.

Elizabeth Ettorre and Elianna Riska, in their book *Gendered Moods: Psychotropics and Society* (1995), highlight the role played by the medical establishment, psychiatry and the pharmaceutical sciences and industry in representing pyschotropic drug use as a gender-neutral cure for personal problems, rather than a form of social control. This hides the deeper social pathologies that result in women more than men suffering from depression, anxiety and insomnia.

Society does not reward women equally with men. It expects women to take a greater responsibility for childcare. It confines them more often to the isolation and stress of domestic labour. It places contradictory expectations upon them to be both mother figure and sex object, strong and thin. Dispensing drugs to enable women to cope with such conditions is to use medical science to manage social problems. Ettorre and Riska refer to this process as 'medicalising everyday life' (1995:20). Using drugs to cover up the symptoms of injustice not only turns a social problem into a medical one but also avoids the need to ask the key question, namely 'why women more than men pursue lifestyles needing pharmacological supports' (1995:20). For example, while tranquillizer use becomes a problem in the eyes of the media, government and medical establishment, the causes of such dependence do not (1995:29). As long as the symptoms can be managed, pressure to solve the causes can be limited. Thus medical science becomes a vehicle for limiting the demands of the women's movement to overcome the inequalities and injustices experienced by women in society. Interestingly, Ettorre and Riska refer to Cooperstock's (1971) analysis of medical encounters with women, which showed that male doctors were more likely to label female emotional distress as evidence of a psychiatric condition than was the case when presented with male emotional distress. Ettorre and Riska suggest that while the number of women training to become doctors has increased dramatically since Cooperstock's research was carried out, evidence suggests that little has changed in the different interpretation given to displays of male and female emotion (Ettorre and Riska 1995:62). Ettorre and Riska conducted in-depth interviews with women using psychotropic drugs as a way of gaining understanding of the lives of the women concerned. This attention to the experience of women's lives is something that medical encounters rarely enable. This attention to women's experience and to their voices forms a key element in the suggestion that a feminist epistemology (or approach to knowledge gathering) may be superior to the current detachment encouraged by traditional science. Such detachment encourages the dispensing of drugs to keep women quiet, rather than the challenging of wider social processes.

Janet M. Stoppard (2000) develops a feminist social-constructionist approach to depression in a vein similar to the methods suggested by Ettorre and Riska. Rather than relying upon detached models of examination and medical interview, feminist researchers have sought to understand the experience of depression from women's own accounts of their lives.

There is considerable evidence that science has born the mark of a male bias in its representation of women, and that this bias has been placed at the service of a society that subordinates women. Does this mean that science is an ideology of male power? Alternatively, are these examples rather cases of bad science to be set against the true and worthy goal of a gender-neutral pursuit of knowledge? These questions form the basis of the 'feminist epistemology debate'.

# New Feminist Epistemologies

Evelyn Fox Keller's (1990, 1993) *From Secrets of Life to Secrets of Death* describes the parallel obsessions within science to control life, in both its creation and its destruction. The scientific spectrum from genetic research to weapons research can be characterized by a male desire to capture the secret of life, once seen as a secret held by women, and one from which men were excluded. Keller (1990:183–4) highlights the language of parenthood that has characterized male researchers when talking about their discoveries and their creations. She suggests that phallic and birth metaphors are particularly prominent in military research (1990:186). Is science essentially masculine, or can a masculine desire for dominance be overcome simply by the increased participation of women in science? This debate has led to heated discussion within feminist research, and thence to a number of distinct responses.

Sandra Harding (1986) distinguishes three 'feminist epistemologies', perspectives on the nature of knowledge generation and on the most appropriate response to the gendered nature of existing scientific knowledge production. These three perspectives are 'feminist empiricism', 'feminist standpoint theory' and 'feminist postmodernism'. Debates within and between feminist perspectives have raised serious and complex questions about the validity of scientific knowledge and the possibility of gaining unbiased accounts of the world.

## *Feminist Empiricism*

> [T]he feminist empiricist strategy argues that sexism and androcentrism [a view of the world from a taken-for-granted male perspective] are social biases, prejudices based on false beliefs (caused by superstitions, customs, ignorance, and mis-education) and on hostile attitudes. These prejudices enter research particularly at the stage of the identification and definition of scientific problems, but also in the design of research and in the collection and interpretation of evidence. According to this strategy such biases can be eliminated by stricter adherence to the existing norms of scientific inquiry. (Harding 1986:161)

From this point of view the most important strategic goal is to increase female participation within science and to enable more women to stay in and get on within scientific careers. Having more women in science will, it is argued, make it more difficult for male taken-for-granted assumptions to be introduced to the selection, design, conduct and analysis of scientific research. If the ideal of science is to be neutral and objective, then a more balanced composition of men and women in science will aid in that process. Feminist empiricist researchers in this tradition have devoted much effort to identifying the limited access and promotion of women in science and have sought to highlight the factors leading to this so that they can be best eliminated. Feminist empiricists, like liberal feminists in the political sphere, seek not to challenge the dominant model of rationality operating within the dominant institutions of society. Rather, they seek to challenge the view that women are somehow less capable of those characteristics most highly regarded, that is objectivity, neutrality and non-emotional detachment. Harding (1991:112–15) suggests that the virtues of such an approach are fourfold:

1. The call for more truth and more true knowledge conforms to prevailing values within existing science.

2. Feminist empiricism promises to improve the basic model of science without challenging the model; this makes it more persuasive to mainstream science and philosophy.

3. Such a stance does not weaken the position of women already inside science.

4. The model can make appeal to great female ancients in the scientific canon.

However, Harding argues, feminist empiricism, in highlighting the capacity of mainstream science to have systematically misrepresented women and nature, due to taken-for-granted male bias over hundreds of years, brings into question the fundamental premise of empiricism and the scientific models based upon empiricism. The basic premise of empiricism is that the world can best be understood through observation of it through the senses. If, however, the senses are influenced by the values of the beholder then how can such a model be supported? This has led to the development of a more radical feminist epistemological position: that of feminist standpoint theory.

## Feminist Standpoint Approaches

Feminist standpoint theory starts from the premise that there can be no pure and objective empirical standpoint, a view of the world from a neutral position. All perception is structured by preconceptions. Feminist standpoint theory builds upon the work of the Marxist theorist Georg Lukács (see Chapter 6). Lukács argued that dominant social groups have a vested interest in seeing the world as right and natural. Those in positions of power are unlikely to experience the tension between reality and dominant explanations of that reality. Those excluded from the benefits of the existing social order are more likely to experience such contradictions. A stranger is more likely to notice the things that the native takes for granted. Harding (1991:24) extends this logic to the position of women in science and in society more generally:

> Women are just such outsiders to the dominant institutions in our society, including the natural and social sciences. Men in the dominant groups are the 'natives' whose life patterns and ways of thinking fit all too closely the dominant institutions and conceptual schemes.

She goes on to suggest (1991:25): 'Women's oppression gives them fewer interests in ignorance.' The working classes in nineteenth-century Europe were the mainspring of radical challenges to a society that only in part included them. Workers' struggles to improve their lives led not only to consciousness-raising among workers themselves, but also created the conditions for intellectuals to address the issues that workers' struggles brought to attention. So, Harding argues, it is the case today that women's struggles for full inclusion in society generate a search for understanding both at the level of everyday women's experience, and at the level of intellectual reflection.

This creates an interesting tension within feminist standpoint theory, one that went to the heart of Lukács's thinking. We saw in the previous chapter how Lukács noted that while workers experienced the contradictions of capitalism most acutely, their experience was fragmented within the processes of production and domination. As such their everyday insights were often defused by mystification and reification. Lukács came to believe that it was only through the combination of workers' direct experience and the leadership of intellectual radicals (able to generate an overall perspective beyond reification) that social transformation could be successfully achieved. The same tension exists within feminist standpoint theory. Is it the case that women's direct experience of life enables higher understanding of themselves, and of reality more generally, than can be achieved within the confines of male-dominated science? Or is it the case that it is only through the mediation of feminist intellectual research that the struggles and experiences of women in everyday life can become the basis for a superior understanding of reality? Let us bring this highly abstract question down to earth.

Harding cites the work of Hilary Rose (1983, 1984) and Nancy Hartsock (1984), both advocates of a feminist standpoint epistemology. Harding notes that Rose's work gives a particular emphasis to women's experience in areas such as health care, fertility rights, abortion and childbirth. Experience of mainstream medical and scientific treatment of women has led to a number of counter-movements. These have been both political and cultural. Women have, individually and collectively, been able to resist male models of the female body and to generate counter-models, models based on direct experience and dialogue, rather than detached observation and experiment. In this way the women's movement has forced the medical and scientific establishment to pay closer attention to women's accounts and experiences and, in so doing, has challenged traditional research techniques and validated techniques that emphasize listening rather than simply detached looking.

Rose (1994) suggests that it is this validation of negotiation, attachment and listening that is key to the feminist epistemological challenge to traditional forms of research that validate detachment and observation. Such political challenges to mainstream knowledge formation create the spaces within science itself for new 'feminist' research forms. These spaces emerge in the life sciences and social sciences, and may even be seen in the physical sciences. While Rose argues that this transformation is only at the earliest stages, she argues that the feminist challenge to the separation of hand, brain and heart, characteristic of alienated patriarchal and capitalist technoscience, is both possible and underway. Harding notes that Nancy Hartsock's work gives greater emphasis to feminist work within science, and in theorizing science. However, Hartsock also concludes that it is only the combination of women's political feminism, women's everyday experiences and struggles, and the work of women within medical, social and life sciences, that can generate new forms of knowledge and of knowing. In answer to Lukács' conundrum, feminist standpoint theory seeks to strengthen the organic relationship between women's direct experience, feminist theory and the work of women in the institutions of science. Of course, this is no guarantee of success.

Feminist standpoint theory goes beyond the call for more women in science. Rather it challenges the very nature of scientific practice, and even the separation between science and other forms of experience and knowing. In particular, feminist standpoint theory argues that women's experience offers a route to a superior form of knowledge production. What does this mean? Sandra Harding puts forward a conception of 'strong objectivity' (1991: chapter 6). The standard defence of objectivity in science lies in the scope for truth claims to be tested by other researchers. Regardless of the source of a truth claim, objectivity lies in the ability of others in the scientific community to see if what is being claimed actually is the case. This is called the 'context of justification'. This assumes that the empirical findings of the original researchers are independent of the empirical findings of those testing them. What, however, if both sets of researchers share a set of taken-for-granted assumptions, and both teams interpret the evidence through the same value-laden theoretical perspective? Any similarity in their findings could be the result of their shared starting-point, or of the 'truth' of their conclusions. We cannot be sure. If the 'context of knowledge production' displays systematic one-sidedness, the 'context of justification' cannot be trusted as a source of objectivity. Harding's strong objectivity argument asserts that only where one-sidedness within the 'context of knowledge production' is eliminated can claims made in the 'context of justification' be trusted. Given the evidence of the intimate linkage between patriarchal politics and science, it is necessary to introduce feminist politics into the 'context of knowledge production'.

The question then arises, is feminist politics a counter-weight to rectify existing male bias or a pressure to prioritize a superior feminist form of knowing? While feminist empiricists argue the former, Harding, Rose and Hartsock provide evidence that a science based upon principles of listening and attachment over detachment and domination represents a superior science, or what they call a successor science. For these three writers, the basis upon which women have greater potential for insight lies in their location outside the male-dominated establishment. They have a lesser stake in seeing the world in terms of the desire to dominate, and are less likely to see detachment as a route to understanding. These characteristics are seen not as intrinsic female biological characteristics, but rather as the consequence of patriarchal social order.

### Eco-feminism

There is, however, a branch of feminist standpoint theory that does make the claim that it is women's biological makeup that renders them less vulnerable to the male desire for domination, detachment and control though abstraction. Eco-feminism interprets the history of Western science as a male quest to subdue nature and women through abstract, morally devoid, knowing. While the assertion that women are closer to nature is to be found in almost all attempts to justify the subordination of women, eco-feminists argue that this is the result of the prior subordination of nature to male domination. It is only a negative thing to be equated with nature if nature is viewed in a negative light to begin with. If nature received a more positive coverage then to be associated with it would be a positive thing.

Carolyn Merchant's (1980) *The Death of Nature: Women, Ecology and the Scientific Revolution* makes the case that the rise of western science was part of a denigration of the feminine, of human women and of a vision of nature as a maternal goddess figure. It is no accident that the rise of modern science occurred at the same time as the highpoint of European and North American persecution of witches. Bryan Turner (1987:87) cites the work of McLachlan and Swales (1980), who concluded that, between 1563 and 1727, 70 to 90 per cent of those accused of witchcraft in Europe were women. What these women were accused of was in effect that they knew too much and were organized. The systematic dismantling of female knowledge in areas of health and farming laid the foundations for the rise of a male-dominated, power-oriented, fragmenting and detached knowledge: western technoscience. Mies and Shiva therefore call eco-feminism 'a new term for an ancient wisdom' (1993:13). Eco-feminism has attracted a great deal of criticism from other feminist writers for its acceptance of the belief that women are closer to nature than men, and for the counter point, that women are not best suited for science. Feminists who want to transform science either from the inside or by means of a successor science reject such an essentialist view of science and women. This includes empirical feminists as well as those standpoint feminists like Rose, Harding and Hartsock who oppose essentialist accounts of masculinity and femininity. Postmodern feminists also reject such essentialist claims. They reject the unity of all such categories. Mies and Shiva argue that their motivation for writing as eco-feminists (1993:5) is that 'women, particularly urban, middle-class women, find it difficult to perceive commonality both between their own liberation and the liberation of nature, and between themselves and 'different' women in the world.

## Feminist Postmodernism

Postmodern feminists argue that any lack of a perceived commonality among women is because there is no natural unity. They also argue that there can be no single universal method of generating the truth. Postmodern feminists seek to be liberated from the myth of science. Sandra Harding (1986:151–6) cites the work of Jane Flax. Flax's psychoanalytic work initially highlighted the controlling nature of male knowledge seeking in science, something characteristic of what she called 'abstract masculinity', the product of a male socialization where sons are forced to adopt a far more detached relationship to their mothers than do daughters. Such a defensive and controlling approach to knowledge formation is seen as something pathological, and set against Flax's initial commitment to a feminist standpoint position, that is the argument for the superiority of a feminist science. Flax, however, came to believe that the advocacy of a female successor science retained too much of the male desire for an all-powerful and singular truth. In adopting a postmodern scepticism about all universal knowledge claims, Flax suggests that women and feminism attain a greater liberation. The work of Donna Haraway (1990a, 1990b, 1991, 1997) follows this transgressive line of critique. Rather than seeking to provide a single truth, from a singular perspective, for Haraway the role of the feminist theorist is to transgress. This means both to challenge the claims of science to produce unified accounts of reality and to challenge any attempt to define women as a unified and homogeneous category.

While eco-feminism and feminist postmodernism appear diametrically opposed to each other both in strategy and theory, Harding (1986, 1991) and Rose (1994) in particular have sought to identify the different tasks performed within feminism by empirical, standpoint and postmodern approaches. The postmodern resistance to essentialist classification is not incompatible with standpoint theory. Rose and Harding do not suggest women are united by their biology. They are united by the assumptions made about their biology. While it is not the primary objective of postmodern feminism to smooth the path for greater female participation in science as it currently operates, neither is this the goal of standpoint feminism. It is not contradictory to encourage women to enter science even while at the same time questioning the distortions within science and even the claim that science can ever be the whole truth. Haraway (1990a, 1990b, 1991) uses female primatology ironically. Different reductionist accounts of why women are the way they are, drawn from different researchers, are used to create a repertoire of subject positions from which to disrupt taken-for-granted assumptions about women. This can, at least strategically, be rendered compatible with Shiva's reconstruction of the feminine as a site of resistance to dominant values and institutions. While Haraway is more suspicious of the 'authenticity' of any attribution of 'organic' differences between men and women, such resistant female identity locations can still be positions from which to disrupt patriarchal society, whether they are natural or socially constructed.

It is possible to conclude that feminist debates over epistemology leave more questions than answers. This is no bad thing in a number of ways. The diversity of feminist approaches to science do not cancel each other out. Because it enables the addressing of different issues and audiences, as well as reflexive engagement with and support for diversity, the openness of the feminist agenda and research programme has proved both politically and intellectually challenging and fruitful. It is in many ways the most developed arena of 'reflexive epistemological diversity', the stance being advocated in this text.

# Conclusions

Feminist research has highlighted the position of women in science, the production of scientific knowledge about women, the use of science as an instrument of domination over women, and has also raised questions over the possibility of a science that does not reinforce patterns of male dominance, or domination in general. Feminist researchers have demonstrated that it is not enough simply to proclaim that women should be more involved in science. It is necessary to highlight the systematic difficulties and discriminations experienced by women within science, as well as the overwhelmingly male culture within science. This culture is characterised by not just the numbers of men, but also by a whole way of seeing the world. This shifting of the agenda is what Harding (1986) calls the shift from asking questions about women in science to asking deeper questions about science itself. Feminists agree that science has played a significant part in maintaining women's subordination, within both science and the wider society. Feminist researchers also agree that science has regularly generated false knowledge about women, and so is not a secure method of generating objective truth. Differences arise over the issue of whether science's historical association with domination and ideology can best be overcome by better science, by new science or by an escape from the dogmatic pursuit of a singular objective 'truth'. In this regard, the three new feminist epistemologies parallel the three other approaches to the sociology of science outlined in Chapters 4–6. Feminist empiricism focuses upon the internal dynamics of science and does not seek to debunk science, but it also wants to show how science is influenced by its social composition. Standpoint feminists adopt a Marxist framework and apply it to the liberation of women and the production of emancipatory knowledge against ideology and domination. The criticism made by standpoint theorists is that feminist empiricism makes a fetish out of the priorities and assumptions of 'malestream' science. This is precisely the criticism standpoint feminists also make against social-interests researchers (Rose 1994). Feminist postmodernism adopts a stance towards truth and freedom that is almost identical to that of ethnographic and discursive writers in the 'malestream' sociology of scientific knowledge. What is most positive about feminist research in the sociology of scientific knowledge is a degree of fluidity and openness, both within feminist perspectives and in adopting elements of other perspectives, that, while still relatively limited, generates more interesting connections that can be found between other schools.

# Part Three

## Case-Studies

# 8

# Second Nature: Genetic Modification and Commodification of the Non-Human

## General Introduction to Sociology and the New Genetics

Marxist, feminist, interest-based and ethnographic/discursive approaches to the new genetics display a degree of cross-fertilization that is more developed than is the case in other areas within the sociology of science. In part this is the result of the more developed and long-standing tradition of sociological research in the area of medicine and health. This field has received greater amounts of research funding than any other area of sociological research, so scope for crossover has been greater. More recent sociological research in the specific area of medical genetics has benefited from this already developed and dynamic intellectual environment. Another reason is that research focused upon genetically modified foods and cloning of non-humans feeds upon and feeds into longer-standing sociological research interests in environmentalism and environmental issues (Yearley 1991, 1996). While sociology established itself through opposition to and even neglect of the non-social or 'nature', in recent decades environmental sociology has become the largest single element of political sociology. Finally, sociology of science research that addresses 'scientific' attempts to account for human behaviour and social relations in terms of biological, evolutionary or hard-wired psychological programming resonates with the long-standing sociological theme of challenging 'biological reductionism'.

All three fields of interest – medical genetics, genetic modification of 'nature', and the genetics of human behaviour – link science to politics in a way that is more explicit than would be the case with lasers or with controversies over the spontaneous generation of life (see Chapter 4). While the development of new information and communication technologies has a direct relationship with day-to-day work and leisure, it is less typically seen as political. The developments in genetic science, however, appear to touch nerves within wide sections of society that link politics to everyday life in a very particular and significant fashion.

Health, the environment and the relative stability of inequality link the new genetics to central and long-standing themes within sociology and have generated significant levels of cross-fertilization in research. In addition health and medicine, environment and nature, and debates over biology as destiny, are areas central to the emergence of feminism within sociology.

As has been suggested, sociological research in relation to the 'new genetics' can be usefully divided into three sub-fields: medical, non-human and human behavioural genetics. These sub-fields are not entirely mutually exclusive. Debates over cloning cross over between the human and the non-human, as do many of the techniques involved in genetic modification. Genetic modification of animals and plants to develop pharmaceuticals relates medical and non-human genetics. The line between behaviour and health is not clear-cut, as certain behaviours and certain inabilities may be seen as medical conditions while others (or even the same behaviours and inabilities) in other circumstances may be seen as matters for the judicial system. However, in order to demonstrate the scope and value of the range of sociology-of-science perspectives and the potential for their fruitful cross-fertilization, Chapters 8, 9 and 10 will address each of the three sub-fields in turn rather than addressing each sociological perspective separately.

# Genetic Modification of the Non-Human

## Feminist Approaches

Vandana Shiva's (1998) discussion of agribusiness in the late twentieth century draws upon an eco-feminist version of feminist standpoint theory, but also upon discursive methods of analysis and approaches to commodification and the construction of nature that resonate with Marxist and social-interests approaches to the new genetics. Shiva's work seeks to demonstrate how a Western scientific mindset, what she calls a monoculture of the mind, reflects the dominant patriarchal and capitalist structures of a world dominated by male, Western capitalist elites. Writing five hundred years after the 'discovery' of the Americas by Columbus, Shiva suggests that in a period when the whole planet has been colonized by the West, attention has now turned to the colonization of inner space, and in particular the gene. Where older forms of Western patriarchal thinking saw the male seed as active and the supposed female earth as passive, the new biosciences allow for a reconception (1998:47–67). Now, the seed can be feminized as 'nature', and the male ordering principle is transferred to the scientist who seeks to control, map, own and modify this seed. Central to this reconceptualization is the attempt to map the genetic structure of DNA, and in so doing claim rights of ownership over what is then said to have been discovered. Just as women's knowledge regarding healing was discounted in the rise of modern bio-medicine, so now the indigenous knowledge of non-Western peoples is discounted in the attempt by Western pharmaceutical and agricultural corporations to claim ownership over products used by those peoples for generations. Genetic mapping of the inner structure of plant, animal and human products and processes is seen as giving a 'true' account of reality, and so a more valid 'discovery' than was available to those peoples who are seen only to understand the outcome, rather than the causes involved. In the same way that Western countries claimed land rights over colonized territories on the grounds that indigenous peoples had no maps or legal documentation of ownership, so now the new genetics is being used to overrule traditional conceptions of knowledge and use in favour of conceptions of ownership best suited to capitalist control.

While Shiva draws upon an eco-feminist standpoint, the work of Donna Haraway develops beyond a version of feminist standpoint theory in relation to the new genetics to a 'position' that is best characterized as postmodern. Haraway's discussion of the Flavr Savr tomato and the OncoMouse™ sets up a position from which to analyse the rise of the new genetic sciences that does not rely on any 'natural' position from which to critique the artificiality and manipulation characteristic of genetic modification. The Flavr Savr tomato was developed by Calgene Inc. of California using the transfer of genes from a fish into the DNA of a tomato to create a product that would last longer on supermarket shelves. Haraway is not interested in questioning the methods by which this is achieved or in evaluating its success in scientific terms. In this respect she is more of a realist than other sociologists of science who may have wished to research the process and its validity, rather than just the product arrived at. Haraway writes: 'In my view, constructivism is about contingency and specificity but not epistemological relativism' (1997:99). In as much as Haraway does not engage with the validity of scientific knowledge as such, her work simply addresses a different question to that being asked by those who investigate scientific epistemology. Haraway is interested to parallel the transgenic product of this corporate science with the transuranic elements created by nuclear science in fast-breeder reactors. Both processes create new nature, new entities and new elements that are both physically real and socially constructed. Nature can no longer be held as a regulative ideal. While questioning the motives and power relations that underpin such a corporate science, Haraway wishes to avoid outright critique of such 'unnatural' creations. 'I cannot help but hear in the biotechnology debates the unintended tones of fear of the alien and suspicion of the mixed' (1997:61). She has little sympathy with calls for the defence of purity, something she sees as uniting both eugenics and the defence of 'pure' nature. She is more interested in the abolition of nature itself as a mythic ideal by which women are so regularly constrained. OncoMouse™ is perhaps a more extreme case. Developed by DuPont (who were also at the heart of the development of plutonium and nylon), OncoMouse™ has been genetically modified to carry genes that will dispose it to breast cancer. OncoMouse™ was designed to be sold to researchers working to cure this condition in humans. As such this strain of mice has been designed with 'premature' death built in, and their design in this regard makes them open to be patented as intellectual property. Haraway foresees the day when many may come to owe their lives to this corporate rodent, and she suggests that OncoMouse™ stands as a position from which to witness the abolition of nature from the inside. While the new 'nature of no nature' (1997:103) is the vehicle for a new generation of techno-scientific capitalism, it is also the arena for new forms of resistance and protest. Shiva's focus is upon the defence of biodiversity, land rights and indigenous knowledge in developing countries. Haraway's constituencies are those living in the heart of the most affluent societies, in particular those whose sexuality or lifestyle is said to be unnatural.

## Marxist Approaches

R. C. Lewontin (1993) highlights the direct influence of capitalist economics upon contemporary agricultural science. The development of hybrid corn came to be seen as the most advanced and efficient method of increasing yields:

> The hybrid cross between the inbred lines has another quality, which is not much spoken about, a quality with a unique commercial value. If a farmer has a high-yielding variety of some crop, one that is resistant to disease and produces high commercial output as compared to the cost of inputs, his [*sic*] normal way of carrying on his business would be to save some seed of this high-yielding variety and plant it next year to again achieve high yields...Hybrid corn is different. Because it is the cross between two self-propagating homogeneous lines, one cannot plant the seed of hybrid corn and get new hybrid corn. Hybrids are not true breeding. (Lewontin 1993:53–4)

Lewontin cites those who developed the first lines of hybrid corn (1993:54) who directly reference this benefit to agribusiness, as it rendered farmers directly dependent upon corporate breeders for their seed. Lewontin points out that:

The nature of the genes responsible for influencing corn yield is such that the alternative method of simple direct selection of high-yielding plants in each generation and the propagation of seed from those selected plants would work. By the method of selection, plant breeders could, in fact, produce varieties of corn that yield quite as much as modern hybrids. The problem is that no commercial plant breeder will undertake such investigation and development because there is no money in it ... Once again, what appears to us in the mystical guise of pure science and objective knowledge about nature turns out, underneath, to be political, economic and social ideology. (1993:56–7)

## Capitalism and Genetically Modified Food

Recent controversies over genetically modified foods have raised very similar issues. Any quick scan of the Internet on the subject of terminator genes will generate hundreds of hits for pages devoted to the controversial topic of genetically modified organisms that cannot replicate, or that cannot do so unless specifically stimulated. Those who advocate such modification suggest that it represents a safety catch, one that would allow research into new genetically modified organisms without the fear that such organisms would spread out of control through cross-fertilization. Those who oppose the technology see it as a device to ensure corporate domination over farmers and nature. Such a technology would enable seed to become a product, centrally controlled, rather than something that retains its own generative capacity, a capacity that lies at the heart of many definitions of life itself, and which underpins autonomy from corporate domination.

Mark Harvey (1999) presents an account of genetic modification in agribusiness that demonstrates not only how current developments reflect capitalist priorities, but that different capitalist regimes produce different kinds of GM developments, in particular between US corporate agriculture and the smaller-scale capitalism of farming within the European Union. What Harvey is keen to demonstrate is that, from a Marxist perspective, it is not technology as such that is the threat, as can sometimes seem to be the case from the perspective of many anti-GM protestors and writers such as Shiva. Harvey highlights, using discourse-analytic techniques, how each side in the debate seeks to contrast the natural with the unnatural (1999: paragraph 2.8). Supporters seek to construct GM as a relatively small extension of a longstanding technique of plant and animal selection and breeding. Opponents seek to suggest that the shift to gene transplantation is a major shift that we cannot foresee the consequences of. For Harvey, it is not the technology that determines whether power will be centrally held, or widely distributed, yet the way GM technologies develop will reflect the struggle between global corporations, national and regional agricultural frameworks and alliances of consumers and producers in developed and developing countries alike. Fred Buttel's (1999) work goes on to outline the ongoing lines of conflict and power through which genetic modification of the non-human realm is being and will be filtered.

# Discursive Accounts

It is perhaps a reflection of the political sensitivity concerning genetically modified organisms that there are no ethnographic studies of working within a GM biotech company such that might parallel the work of Latour and Woolgar (1979, 1986). This may reflect the specifics of this particular branch of science, but may also reflect the increasingly politicized nature of science in contemporary society more generally. Discourse-analytic work has focused upon representations of GM science and the issue of public understanding of this branch of science.

Brigitte Nerlich, David Clarke and Robert Dingwall (Nerlich *et al.* 1999a and 1999b; see also Petersen 2002) discuss the representations of cloning technologies in relation to the discursive frames available to people to make sense of innovative technologies. In relation to the announcement of the cloning of Dolly the Sheep in 1997, this new possibility was digested by the media, scientists and non-scientists alike through metaphor and analogy. Nerlich *et al.* pay particular attention to the use of metaphors from science fiction in the way this new technology was described by a number of different social groups. It is not simply the case that non-scientists drew upon the language of science fiction to express or formulate their views. Scientists seeking to extrapolate a position favourable to the new technology also drew upon visions of the future based upon science fiction, to suggest that support needed to be given to the fledgling science. Parallels were drawn between the new techniques and older techniques, in particular *in vitro* fertilization (test-tube babies). While this technique had been controversial in the 1970s, it has now become 'taken for granted' and routine. Opponents of animal cloning sought to deploy negative frames drawn from science fiction, just as the supporters sought positive images. Both sides sought to infer that the other was embedded in the illusion of their respective science fictions while using the fictions most suited to making their own case. Nerlich *et al.* draw heavily on media coverage and secondary accounts of public and scientific debates. As such, their account gives particular emphasis to media representations and in particular science fiction 'frames', in explaining how non-scientists account for science. While suggesting that such an approach helps overcome the view that the public are simply ignorant about science, their approach does not allow for exploration of other sources of belief and knowledge. As will be seen in the discussion of medical genetics, ethnographic research has identified the complexity of non-expert knowledge formation (Edwards 2002). It is not enough to say that public understanding of science is mediated by media representations such as science fiction. Everyday workplace, family, friendship and community networks mediate and shape the reception and comprehension of media discourses.

# Social Interests

Reidar Almas (1999) locates current debates between supporters and protest groups over genetically modified foods in the context of the risk society. Almas suggests conflicting constructions of safety, risk and utility become increasingly manifest as experts from different academic fields, and working for different actors in the corporate, state and non-governmental arena, confront each other. Almas's account feeds directly into the social-interests approach to the analysis of scientific disputes. As Barnes (1999) suggests, without trust there can be no expertise. The conflicts of interest that underpin the contemporary risk society thesis thereby manifest themselves as conflicting scientific accounts of risk and safety in the field of food safety, production and consumption. Interestingly, Almas suggests that as different interest groups compete for influence in the genetically modified foods debate, each undermining the 'hard' science of their competitors by using their own scientific research to sway the public, so social science itself will take on a status as 'experts on peoples' concerns'. The attempt to constitute a new field of expertise to manage the failure of other fields of expertise in managing the public represents what Beck (1992) calls 'ongoing functional specialization'. However, such a move, while designed to manage nature and society more efficiently, has the reverse effect, generating increased conflict between interested parties. Beck (1995b:104) calls this 'involuntary institutional moonlighting'. Alison Shaw's (1999) research suggests the value of a social-interests account in explaining why government and corporately funded scientists believe (and want to believe) that the public are too ignorant for their opinions to be taken seriously on matters such as food safety. Dismissal is the standard approach, except when public opinion is treated as a 'serious' problem in need of 'managing', that is when public opinion is at odds with the scientists'. It is at this point that social scientists may be sought to investigate the social and/or cultural roots of resistance.

# Combining Social Interests with Discourse Analysis

Stuart Allan (2002) combines a discourse-analytic approach to the dispute over genetically modified foods in the UK with a social-interests perspective. Allan documents the development of coalitions, one in favour and one opposed to the development of GM crops. Each drew upon and funded its own scientific research and each sought to manage the media to its own ends. The UK government was largely on the side of the corporations keen to promote GM technologies in the agricultural sector, but, as Allan points out, the position of the government and of government scientists as experts and authorities was undermined in the debate over GM crops by the preceding controversy over BSE (or mad cow disease). Public trust in the government and its scientists was at what was then a record low in the aftermath of the BSE crisis and the statements of government scientists in favour of GM were ineffectual and often counterproductive. Controversy over the safety of GM foods came to a head in 1999 with the widespread media coverage given to the suggestion by Arpad Pusztai (a GM researcher with a long career as a pro-GM scientist) that eating genetically modified potatoes could be harmful to human health (see Chapter 6). Government attempts to silence Pusztai had the effect of further deepening public distrust. The Royal Society commission set up to investigate Pusztai's research, while unanimous in its dismissal of his work, had little effect in persuading a sceptical public, who were not convinced of the impartiality of the appointed experts. The Parliamentary Office for Science and Technology's recommendations that journalists follow the guidelines on reporting science set out by the Royal Society can be seen as an attempt to control the freedom of the press, or as a reflection of their failure to do so. Dissenting voices within the scientific community, allied with well-resourced protest groups and many well-known public figures, weakened the attempt to present opposition as irrational and anti-scientific.

Katherine Barrett and Elizabeth Abergel (2002) present an account of the scientific boundary work required to justify the introduction of GM crops in Canada in the mid-1990s:

> We are therefore interested in how regulators constructed and maintained boundaries around 'science' in the 'science based' assessment of GM canola, how these boundaries influenced the experimental design and interpretation of scientific data, and consequently, how these boundaries shaped the definition of a 'safe' GM organism. (2002:49)

Boundary work was undertaken in defining who was a legitimate expert, over the legitimate and illegitimate extension of expert status from one field into other fields, and by maintaining the impression of the 'autonomy' of the regulatory authorities from the commercial actors they were said to be in place to regulate, but whose mandate very much entwined their interests, resources and practices. Risk was defined in terms of direct risk to human health. This meant that toxicity tests were not carried out on non-mammalian species in the food chain. Data from limited field trials were taken to generate conclusions that could be generally applied. A variety of exclusions, exemptions and equivalents were adopted in such a way that the interests of commercial growers played a direct role in defining what the regulators had a legitimate right to be concerned about and so to research. Research was evaluated for the danger of false positives, where results might suggest an exaggerated threat based upon random fluctuations in a small sample, while the danger of false negatives stemming from the same small sampling techniques was not considered a problem. 'In establishing these types of boundaries, AAFC [the regulative agency] tended to restrict definitions of harm to short term, direct and relative impacts' (2002:54).

---

## The Disenchantment of the World

Mad cow disease (BSE), and the risk of cross-species infection, either from sheep (scrapie being the sheep equivalent of BSE) to cattle, or from cows to humans (in the form of Creutzfeldt–Jacob disease or CJD), highlighted the tangled web between government, science and the food industry (see Macnaghten and Urry 1998, cited in Jacobsen 2000). Whether the British government's scientific advisers changed their advice in line with the politicians' desire to play down public fears, or whether ministers used scientific advice selectively, the case of BSE severely weakened public faith in the impartiality of science and its role in informing policy. Whichever way one wanted to interpret the evidence, it appeared that politicians could always find a scientific perspective to add authority to their decisions.

The more recent case of the suspension and retirement of the researcher Arpad Pusztai from his post as head of a research team at Scotland's Rowett Institute in Aberdeen raised similar suspicions. Pusztai's research led him to conclude that feeding genetically modified potatoes to rats could lead to harmful effects on the animals' stomachs, bodies, metabolism and health generally. Towards the end of the research project, and after being told no further money would be available to develop the limited research, Pusztai appeared on television, with the support of his employers, to make the case for more research funding. He claimed, in a *World in Action* TV documentary in August 1998, that he would not eat genetically modified potatoes because doubts existed about their safety. He was suspended two days later and denied access to his own laboratory and research data. The claim made against Pusztai was that he had released his findings before they had been peer-reviewed. The Royal Society appointed six anonymous reviewers, who all condemned Pusztai's research, claiming it was 'flawed in many aspects of design, execution and analysis' (Radford 1999a, 1999b). Interestingly the Royal Society made a particular point of emphasizing that the six anonymous reviewers were 'independent' of industry. Yet it is hard to see how anyone with an established research career in this field would not have been in large part dependent upon either corporate or state funding, two sectors strongly committed to pushing ahead with what Pusztai's findings brought into question. The Royal Society's report was published in May 1999, and appeared to demolish Pusztai's research. Yet the uniformity of the Royal Society's findings was at odds with the subsequent peer-reviews given to Pusztai's work when it was submitted for publication in the medical journal *The Lancet*. One reviewer (the head of a research unit dependent upon government and private funding) openly condemned the journal for publishing what he felt to be an inadequate shambles. However, two other reviewers supported the research and its findings. The publication drew a wave of critical commentaries from the pro-GM researchers within the scientific establishment, all of which had financial links to the ongoing

(*cont'd*)

development of genetically modified foods. As Jacobsen (2000:158) points out, of the UK government's House of Lords select committee that approved the sale of GM foods just at the time the Pusztai affair was flaring up, 9 of its 12 members had a direct financial interest in the food industry. Of around 50 interested parties called before the select committee to give evidence, the overwhelming majority had a vested interest in promoting the technology. Scientists called to give evidence were prominent among those whose careers depended upon the ongoing development of genetically modified crops (see also Flynn *et al.* 1999; Gillard *et al.* 1999; *Guardian* 1999a, 1999b; McKie 1999; Evans 2002).

## Combining Marxist and Discursive Perspectives

Les Levidow (2001b) analysed the 'cognitive framing' of uncertainty concerning the environmental impact of genetically modified crops. The particular focus of his case-study was the regulatory disputes within the European Union over herbicide-tolerant oilseed rape and parasite-resistant maize. Over the course of the 1990s the shift in regulatory emphasis, induced by public protest, was from a primary concern for international market competitiveness and productive efficiency towards a precautionary concern over the negative implications of genetically modified crops for ecological diversity. This shift in emphasis led to a change in the criteria, focus and standard of scientific evidence required to settle disputes. 'When public protest and scientific disagreements intensified in the late 1990s, regulatory procedures broadened the relevant uncertainties' (2001b:865–6). A wider set of questions were seen as relevant, giving areas of uncertainty previously deemed unimportant a new significance, while established issues saw the balance of evidence change from a requirement to show harm to a requirement to show the absence of significant potential harm. Levidow concludes by demonstrating how a corporate agenda delegitimizing uncertainty came to be successfully challenged by a protest agenda of precaution that widened the scientific significance of uncertainty and the significance of scientific uncertainty.

This case-study extends earlier work (2001a) in which Levidow locates corporate models of science within a broader fetishization of market models of science and technology. Such a market model defines efficiency strictly by criteria of profitability and assumes the superiority of commodifiable knowledge over shared knowledge. It is always assumed that the problems of developing societies lie in there not having enough corporate science, and problems that arise with such science are always assumed to result from the misapplication of such knowledge, rather than from the market model itself. Any criticism of maximum yields and short-term profitability is dismissed as irrational and anti-scientific. Those within the 'cognitive frame' of market fetishism cannot help but to see the world this way.

Chaia Heller (2002) extends Levidow's fusion of Marxist and discursive approaches in her analysis of the counter-hegemonic rise of 'peasant expertise' in the debate on GM crops in France and globally. Heller suggests that early debates in the 1990s over GM crops were framed around a discourse of scientific risk assessment. Such a frame yielded authority only to scientists in defining the issues, the necessary evidence, its analysis and the appropriate conclusions and courses of subsequent action. The rise of peasant expertise as a counter-discourse placed emphasis on food 'quality' and good taste as the fusion of local culture and practical experience. Heller draws upon the actor network approach in highlighting the significance of symbolic objects such as land, burger bars, farm machinery and Roquefort cheese in the construction of networks and framing devices by which the GM agenda was transformed and successful alliances were forged between local activists from around the world within a global anti-capitalist movement.

# 9

# Human Nature? Human Behaviour and Genetic Determinism

Attempts to explain human behaviour in biological terms are not new. Conflicts over biological and social explanations of such things as aggression, alcoholism, criminality, family form, sexuality, masculinity and femininity, intelligence, racism, poverty and career-mindedness have been central to sociology since its inception, often misleadingly described in terms of 'nature versus nurture'. Recent developments in genetics have raised anew the question of whether human behaviour, in terms of individual action and social inequalities, are programmed into our genes. This chapter addresses a selection of studies from the range of sociology of science perspectives. These studies address the scope and limits of biological science in explaining human behaviour. From within a social-interests perspective, Barry Barnes's work addresses responsibility and action. From an ethnographic perspective, Tim Ingold focuses on the learning involved in acquiring supposedly 'universal' human characteristics. From a discourse analytic perspective, the work of Alan Petersen, Peter Conrad and David Miller traces the attempt to identify a 'gay gene'. Feminist researchers such as Donna Haraway and Dorethy Nelkin highlight the social preconceptions that structure much of what is assumed to be neutral research and interpretation of evidence 'explaining' why women are less powerful in society than men. Writers combining Marxist and feminist perspectives have drawn attention to the parallels between genetic claims made about women and those put forward to explain and/or justify ethnic and supposedly 'racial' inequalities. These themes are very much in line with those of Marxist writers such as Peter Dickens, Stephen Jay Gould, R. C. Lewontin, Steven Rose and others. My own work on the limits of evolutionary psychology (EP), a contemporary attempt to explain human behaviour in terms of hard-wired behavioural modules in the brain, combines attention to language, academic and cognitive interests as well as to wider social relations of power.

# Social Interests

Barry Barnes (2000, 2002) highlights a misconception when dealing with claims of biological explanation or reduction. This is the assumption that biological claims relating to causal explanation somehow override human 'free' choice and responsibility. Barnes gives the example of the XYY chromosome, where some males have two rather than the usual one Y (male) sex-specific chromosome. For a time it was generally believed, and in some circles still is, that this extra male chromosome 'caused' a greater disposition towards violent behaviour. Court cases have dismissed possession of an extra Y chromosome as a defence in cases of violence. The logic of a biological reductionist explanation suggests that biological causation undermines personal responsibility for choosing or not choosing to behave in a violent fashion. What Barnes points out is that reductionism only appears as a powerful explanation as long as one holds to free choice as the alternative. Barnes suggests that what makes humans unique is the extent to which they are capable of being 'affected' by each other through social and linguistic 'influence'. The ability to resist or interpret biological characteristics lies in our socialization, not in some abstract conception of free will. Social influence is a causal process, just as much as any biological processes. When we call upon people to act responsibly, we use the notion of free will as a causal device to affect those other people, because to claim that they have a choice when acting warrants the use of punishments and rewards if they break social rules. Punishments and rewards have causal effects, as does the language of choice and responsibility in as much as such language warrants the social distribution of pain and pleasure. Genetic reductionism and a non-social account of human action (as based on free choice) feed off each other and can be seen as two sides of the same, anti-sociological, coin.

# Ethnographic and Discursive Approaches

Tim Ingold surveys anthropological explorations regarding the development of 'universal' human behaviours (2000). While such things as learning to walk occur in all cultures, the suggestion that walking is a 'hard-wired' programme in the human brain, one that simply expresses itself when the body develops to a sufficient level, is misleading. Such behaviour has to be learnt, just as riding a bicycle or juggling does. Just because the former appears universal while the latter is culturally specific does not escape the fact that each has to be learnt, and that different cultures walk in slightly different ways. Ingold suggests the phrase 'soft assembly' is better than the term 'hard-wired', when describing such developmental processes.

Peter Conrad (1997) presents research into mass media coverage of genetic science 'findings' on topics such as alcoholism, intelligence and homosexuality. From a discourse-analytic perspective, Conrad seeks to identify the representational devices at work in media coverage, devices that eliminate ambiguity and complexity in favour of simplistic and deterministic 'causal' accounts of the relationship between genes and human behaviour. The case of homosexuality and the so-called 'gay gene' will be taken here to illustrate this approach. In July 1993 Dean Hamer, a neurogeneticist from the United States' National Institute of Health, announced in the journal *Science* (Hamer *et al.* 1993: 321):

> DNA linkage analysis of a selected group of 40 families in which there were two gay brothers and no indication of nonmaternal transmission revealed a correlation between homosexual orientation and the inheritance of polymorphic markers on the X chromosome in approximately 64 percent of the sib-pairs tested.

While Hamer referred to his findings as correlations rather than direct proof of causation, mass media coverage of his work, in the United States at least, according to Conrad (1997:147), soon popularized the idea that what had been discovered was a 'gay gene'.

In Conrad's work the act of social construction by which a correlation was turned into a causal agent, the so-called 'gay gene', occurred in the mass media, rather than in the biological sciences themselves. However, research by Alan Petersen (1999a) suggests that the scientific community was not immune to the process of escalation, by which a correlation gets turned into a causal explanation. Petersen conducted a discourse analysis of coverage given to Hamer's research in a number of popular science journals, primarily aimed at a scientifically literate audience. These journals were *Nature, Science, New Scientist, Scientific American* and *Science News*. Petersen identifies a number of implicit assumptions within the 'scientific' discourse:

> In the overwhelming majority of the articles examined, the unquestioned premise is that homosexuality is a deviation from normative heterosexuality and that this deviation can be mostly explained by biology. In the main, authors have neglected to ask why there should have been no research on the genetic basis of heterosexuality or why work should focus predominantly on male homosexuality rather than female homosexuality. Furthermore, I could find only one article that questioned the assumption that sexual orientation is dimorphic: that men are 'programmed' for attraction to women, that women are generally programmed for attraction to men, that male homosexuals have female programming, that lesbians have male programming (see Byne 1994). The homo/hetero-sexual distinction, with its implied vision of mutually exclusive and relatively fixed sexual identities (that is opposite-sex and same-sex pairs), is taken as a given (see Sedgwick 1994). (Petersen 1999a:172–3)

Petersen's work highlights two fundamental points. First, the escalation from correlation to causation was something that occurred within the scientific community itself, and not simply in the hands of a scientifically illiterate mass media. Second, a series of highly dubious, and empirically unjustified, assumptions about human sexuality had been imported, largely without question, into the 'scientific' analysis of Hamer's work.

One further step can be added to this process. If it was not simply the mass media that imported simplistic causal models and rhetorical devices, neither was it simply the wider scientific community that did so in responding to Hamer's work (Miller 1995). Hamer *et al.* (1993) in the original *Science* article suggest that in 40 pairs of gay brothers, two thirds carried the particular cluster of genetic markers. While they admit the distinction between correlation and causation, they go on to claim that their research demonstrates that at least one form of homosexuality is transmitted through the maternal line. Miller (1995:279) points out that such a term as 'transmission' imports the language of causation back into the argument. Miller also points out that Hamer *et al.* do not draw attention to the remaining pairs of brothers that did not carry the same cluster, nor to the necessary counterfactual possibility that the same set of markers may be equally present in heterosexual twins. The belief that an individual's sexuality is fixed across time and singular in orientation, observed in popular science journals by Petersen, can also be seen in Hamer.

As Alison Anderson (2002:335) notes, the 'struggle among news sources to define the issues' in the area of human genetics requires detailed attention to particular disputes.

# Feminist Approaches and Its Links to Other Approaches

Research into attempts to naturalize women's position in society by recourse to biological determinism represents a core theme in feminist sociology. Recent feminist research into the use of genetic discourses to naturalize women's position in society is particularly interesting in its diversity, and in its linkages with other research traditions.

Dorethy Nelkin (2000) suggests that contemporary evolutionary psychology contains within its logic a desire not simply to reject religious models of the natural order between men and women, but to replace religious forms of patriarchal thinking with a new patriarchal theory of everything. Once its claim to be only applying the principles of neutral science are shown to be an ideological illusion, so the whole edifice can be seen as little more than the latest attempt to put women in their place, and not just women. Feminist writers such as Donna Haraway, Barbara Katz Rothman and Hilary Rose have highlighted the parallels between biological arguments that seek to naturalize gender inequalities and those used to justify inequalities between so-called 'races'.

As was pointed out in Chapter 7, Donna Haraway's writings on the subject of primatology (1990a, 1990b, 1991) engage in a strategy of playing one supposed set of empirical findings about the natural order of male and female relations off against another, and another and so on. In so doing Haraway seeks to effect a self-undoing of such projections of human social relations onto other primates. In these works Haraway also points to the on-going and similarly self-contradicting use of biological reductionism in the naturalization of 'race', 'racism' and 'racial' inequality.

Hilary Rose (2000a, 2000b) combines feminist with Marxist frameworks in her analysis of what she calls the 'rhetoric of arrival' deployed by the latest generation of biological reductionists. Evolutionary psychologists (discussed above) usually begin any attempt to apply their 'hard-wiring' theory of human behaviour with reference to what they set their work against, that is what they call the 'standard social science model' or the theory of the blank slate. In so doing their work is presented as the latest thing, the cutting edge; the introduction of something new to a supposedly longstanding consensus that human behaviour is entirely socially constructed. Rose points out that this 'rhetoric of arrival' (2000a:114) conceals the long-standing tradition in which EP stands. EP represents only a modification of a tradition of fixing human character in biology, in particular differences between men and women, rich and poor and between 'white' people and other 'races'. Rose highlights the parallels between contemporary EP and the attempts by previous generations of biological reductionists to distance the work of Charles Darwin from its intellectual and political context. Rose points out that Darwin imported assumptions about race, class and sex from the work of Thomas Malthus and from the Victorian upper-middle-class society of which he was a part. Earlier forms of reductionism, such as Herbert Spencer's social Darwinism (and the survival of the fittest), Nazi eugenics, Konrad Lorenz's ethology theories of race and aggression, and more recently the sociobiology of E. O. Wilson, all foundered in their attempts to legitimize social inequalities by recourse to 'scientific' explanation. As societies change, so each attempt to fix the present as 'biological destiny' foundered. EP is only the latest in a long line of such thinking. Rose points to the backlash against feminism and the rise of neo-liberal politics as creating the 'perfect ecological niche of a new wave of biology-as-destiny' (2000a:107). Rose takes the example of Daly and Wilson (1998) to highlight the weakness of EP thinking. Martin Daly and Margo Wilson point to evidence that step-parents are 100 times more likely to kill their stepchildren than are biological parents. This evidence is then taken to demonstrate that the bond of love between parent and child is biologically 'hard-wired' into human beings. Rose makes two points. First, the vast majority of step-parents do not abuse or kill the children they raise, something that cannot be explained in biological reductionist terms. Second, and perhaps more significantly, Rose points to the dismissing of evidence about adoption in Daly and Wilson's work. Daly and Wilson point out that the rate of child murder by adoptive parents is the same as that for biological parents, but downplay this evidence as only a recent phenomenon. Yet this evidence undermines their whole argument. If biological and adoptive parents are the same in this regard, the difference between both and step-parents must lie in the social relationships between parents and children, not in their biological relations. Rose dismisses the EP claim, that the only alternative to their reductionism is acceptance of an untenable blank-slate thesis, as a politically motivated rhetorical device. Rose concludes that stripped of politically motivated rhetorical devices there is very little left to engage with. Rose dismisses Kingsley Browne in passing (2000a:114). Browne suggests (1998a, 1998b) the 'fact' that a man could have a near infinite number of babies if he had the resources to 'seduce' enough women, while a woman can only have as many babies as she can have herself, leads men to be more motivated by material success.

In her discussion of the new genetics Barbara Katz Rothman (1998, 2001) characterizes contemporary attempts to show that intelligence is distributed unevenly according to 'race' as 'the macroeugenics of race' (1998:43). This runs in parallel with what she calls 'the microeugenics of procreation' (1998:171), the attempt to manage women's bodies within regimes of reproductive genetic 'fitness'. The most controversial recent attempt to ground intelligence in genetics and by race has been Richard Herrnstein and Charles Murrey's (1994) book *The Bell Curve*. This 800-page text claimed the results from IQ tests showing that 'black' Americans scored on average 15 percent lower than 'white' Americans were both an objective measure of intelligence and the result of genetic differences between 'races'. In her discussion of *The Bell Curve* Rothman points to the selective use of evidence by which Herrnstein and Murrey build their case for racially based and fixed intelligence. For example, citing the Minnesota study of transracial adoption, Herrnstein and Murrey note that by the age of 10 'black' children adopted by 'white' parents show IQ scores significantly lower than 'white' children adopted by 'white' parents. The authors suggest that this represents the effect of genetic 'race' over social conditions. Rothman points out what Herrnstein and Murrey fail to mention about the Minnesota study. This is that, at the age of 7, there is no significant difference between 'black' and 'white' adoptees. If IQ is fixed and innate, this should not be the case at all. If a child's intellectual confidence and success is significantly influenced by social environment then a 'black' child in a racist society is likely to be relatively sheltered in earlier years, but as time progresses their exposure to the prejudices of the wider society is likely to increase. Rothman concludes (1998:81) that, while the Minnesota study can be read to suggest the power of social influence, Herrnstein and Murrey deliberately select only those elements that support their intellectual and ideological interests. Rothman shows how different conceptions of 'race' have always reflected the brand of racism popular at the time. 'When race was solid, it stood. When race was liquid, it flowed. When it is crystal [its current molecular genetic construction], it twinkles, on and off, bit by bit, fragmenting' (1998:71).

Hilary Rose and Barbara Katz Rothman's combination of feminist and Marxist approaches links directly with work by other Marxist critics of the 'science' of intelligence, heredity and inequality.

# Marxist Research

Stephen Jay Gould's (1996[1981]) *The Mismeasure of Man* provides a systematic account of the founding figures of intelligence testing and the argument that intelligence is both singular and inherited. Writing as a Marxist it is interesting that Gould refers to himself as an 'internalist' when it comes to writing about such matters. His account is focused upon the emergence of mathematical models and statistical tests designed to enable the inference of an underlying, unified and fixed thing, to be called 'general intelligence', beneath the surface variety of human talents and abilities. This primary focus upon the history of statistical methods is set against an account of the goals to which such methods were applied, and the political and ideological motives that framed and drove both.

Alfred Binet developed the IQ (intelligence quotient) test in France at the end of the nineteenth century. Binet rejected the view that intelligence was innate, and his tests were designed to identify those who might be falling behind so that they might be given added support. Transplanted to the United States by Goddard, Terman and Yertes, the IQ test was incorporated into a model of innate intelligence, a model and a measure used systematically to justify forced sterilization, unequal education and discrimination in recruitment on the basis of class and race. In parallel, the English psychologist and statistician Charles Spearman developed the statistical technique of factor analysis in the early years of the twentieth century as a method of identifying patterns in the results of multiple tests. Spearman already held to the view that beneath the variety of results from different tests of intelligence there lay an underlying 'general intelligence' ($g$). The method of factor analysis plots axes through complex data, lines of correlation within data across multiple dimensions (results from different tests in this case). These lines can then be seen as scales along which results can be predictively plotted with a specified degree of accuracy. While Spearman was sceptical of the inherited character of $g$, his successor, Sir Cyril Burt, was a passionate advocate of the view that intelligence was innate. Burt's work, and the application of his work in the form of variations of the IQ test, consigned millions of British children to an intellectual destiny based upon tests at the age of 11, while the combination of Spearman's method and Burt's hereditarian interpretation has become the foundation of successive attempts to justify 'racial' inequality in genetic terms.

Gould suggests that others have focused attention upon the evidence that Burt falsified his own data, or at least turned a blind eye to the practice by his researchers. That Burt's data set of identical twins somehow tripled in size over time with no change in the statistical results even to three decimal places raised alarm bells (Kamin, 1974). Rose *et al.* (1984) point out that all documented studies of identical twins, supposedly separated at birth, and which have formed the basis of claims as to the relative innateness of intelligence, carry methodological flaws that should lead their conclusions to be dismissed. However, Gould argues, an even more significant error exists in Burt's work. This, Gould claims, lies in the reliance upon factor analysis to substantiate the choice of axes of correlation. No single axis will provide a line of correlation that ties together the results of all available tests of intelligence. The choice remains between adopting a single intelligence quotient model, or, alternatively, assuming a multi-dimensional model with many axes of ability. In the case of the former, one line can be selected (referred to as the 'first principle component'), and all deviation from it can be attributed to other factors. In the case of the latter, many axes of correlation can be plotted, each acting to 'plot' some of the observed results. The technique of factor analysis does not answer the question as to which model to adopt, and the ability to generate correlations does not allow the inference of causal processes in the way Spearman did in claiming to have discovered *g*, or in the way Burt did in claiming to have demonstrated the innate character of intellectual ability:

> The first principle component is a mathematical abstraction that can be calculated for any matrix of correlation coefficients; it is not a 'thing' with physical reality. Factorists have often fallen prey to a temptation for reification – for awarding physical meaning to all strong principal components. Sometimes this is justified; I believe that I can make a good case for interpreting my first pelycosaurian [Gould was a palaeontologist] axis as a size factor. But such a claim can never arise from the mathematics alone, only from additional knowledge of the physical nature of the measures themselves. (Gould 1996:280)

Gould points out that no evidence has ever been produced to empirically demonstrate the physical reality of *g*. Correlations in statistical tests between results from a variety of IQ tests suggest the existence of an underlying causal process or set of processes, but this is not enough to infer the truth of one particular construction of what that process might be. Gould points out (1996:282) that other models may be applied to the data and that other interpretations work equally well, if not better (he discusses L. L. Thurstone's work on the foundations of multiple-intelligence models (1996:326–46)). The choices made by Spearman and by Burt reflect preference, not evidence, and these preferences are better understood in a political and ideological frame, than as neutral theoretical models.

To sum up, there is no evidence to prove the existence of a single unified and unalterable general intelligence, and consequently arguments that such a general intelligence is innate are equally unfounded. Gould demonstrates that the desire for both of the above things to be true is a better explanation for why so many are willing to believe it, and that the progression of psychology to a position of prestige in Western societies was largely the result of selling this unfounded view to government and corporations, themselves keen to believe it. Biology as destiny is preferable to elites over redressing the injustices that might otherwise be highlighted in explaining inequality.

Gould's first edition of *The Mismeasure of Man* was motivated by the attempts by Arthur Jensen (1969) and others to rekindle the 'race' and IQ link in the late 1960s and early 1970s. The 1996 revised edition was a response to the publication of Herrnstein and Murrey's (1994) *The Bell Curve*. Gould contends that Jensen, Herrnstein and Murrey do nothing other than reiterate the observation that those from less advantaged backgrounds do less well in IQ tests than those from more advantaged ones, while seeking to explain these results by means of Spearman and Burt's spurious inferences from statistical models.

Steven Rose, R. C. Lewontin and Leon Kamin (1984) provide a more wide-ranging survey of the ideological foundations of reductionist biology in relation to questions of capitalism, racism and patriarchy. They also discuss the use of biology-as-destiny arguments as means of detaching mental illness from the social relations that intensify and often cause human psychological distress. Their book was written as a response to sociobiology, the dominant biology-as-destiny school at the time. Rose *et al.* highlight the presupposition within sociobiology that humans, and other living things, evolved and/or continue to evolve on the basis of relative adaptation to their external environments. Individual organisms, or individual genes within organisms, pitted against each other in a hostile world, fight it out to see who will survive and who will perish. Rose *et al.* point out that genes and organisms do not just adapt to their environments; they actively engage in the collaborative transformation of their environments. The simple and atomized adaptationist view of nature, evolution and humanity (the struggle of all against all) is not a neutral reflection upon nature. It is a neo-liberal political and economic outlook projecting itself onto nature so as to naturalize its existing vision of how society ought to be. Peter Dickens (1996, 2000, 2001, and 2004) provides a similarly provocative and insightful Marxist analysis of a range of claims concerning social and biological evolution, inequality and political ideology.

R. C. Lewontin's (1993) *The Doctrine of DNA* develops a number of the points already made, plus some useful additions. First, Lewontin highlights the misleading nature of the term 'innate capacity' as distinct from the older and cruder term 'innate ability'. 'Innate capacity' is what Lewontin calls 'the empty bucket metaphor' (1993:27). While the idea that ability is a direct outcome of genes is impossible to sustain, the idea that each person has an innate capacity, that may or may not be fulfilled, still retains a notion of the separation of a primary biology and its social expression. Lewontin asserts that 'when an environment changes, all bets are off' (1993:30). In one environment the genes that dispose a person to shortsightedness may lead to a very early death, while in an environment where spectacles are readily available, this genetic difference is rendered insignificant. As such the extent to which many genetic differences lead to significant or non-significant positive or negative outcomes is itself entirely environmentally dependent. Attempts to measure variation within a population are often used (misleadingly) to infer mathematical measures of relative influence between environment and genes in individuals. Classically this takes the form of claims such that $X$ per cent of intelligence is genetic while $Y$ per cent is acquired, but Lewontin (1993:30) asserts:

> Environmental variation and genetic variation are not independent causal pathways. Genes affect how sensitive one is to environment, and environment affects how relevant one's genetic differences may be. The interaction between them is indissoluble... The contrast between genetic and environmental, between nature and nurture, is not a contrast between fixed and changeable. It is a fallacy of biological determinism to say that if differences are in the genes, no change can occur.

If pale skin increases likelihood of skin cancer then sun tan lotion is recommended. Pocket calculators, pencils and paper, clothes, iron pills, sunglasses and aeroplanes all fly in the face of the rather perverse reductionist preoccupation with something called 'naked ability' as a true test of human individual value and/or performance. Even athletes train, eat well and use the latest technologies. Every practical measure of ability defines parameters where movement beyond these is treated as cheating. Genetic accounts of intelligence seek to suggest that any 'intervention', practice or support constitutes such a violation. However, IQ tests are no different from any other ability. If you practice, you get better. If you have a positive and supportive environment, you get better. Different rules and conditions change the parameters by which fitness would be defined in any case. Naked ability is an illusion, comforting for those who would like to pass off the environmental conditions that suit them best as being no environmental conditions at all, while seeking to depict any intervention in the environments of those less well off as outrageous special treatment, positive discrimination and 'cheating'. Marxists seek to point out that such ideology is not new, and that science has not been immune from servicing such elite-serving untruths.

## Combining Sociological Approaches in the Critique of Evolutionary Psychology

Evolutionary psychology seeks to explain human behaviour with reference to our adaptation to Stone Age life (David 2002b). The method of 'reverse engineering' is applied. Reverse engineering infers the ancestral conditions that would have made certain genetically inherited behaviours increase their bearers' reproductive success. EP posits the existence of a range of 'hard-wired mental "modules"', each designed (adapted) to elicit a particular programmed response when presented with the relevant stimulus.

The concept of the modularity of mind forms a central plank of the work of EP (for example Barkow *et al.* 1992; Gigerenzer *et al.* 1999; and Pinker 1995, 1999, 2002). For EP, the notion of modularity allows natural selection principles to be applied to psychological phenomena. The module, by analogy with the gene, becomes the unit of selection. Jerry Fodor's (1983, 2000) original formulation of modularity assumes a dual processor model. A general processor for higher-order problem-solving complements specific modules. EP adopts a mass modularity approach. EP's general programme extends the logic of 'hard-wired' mass modularity to every aspect of human behaviour, however complex. The common metaphor given for this notion of mass modularity is the Swiss army knife (Barkow *et al.* 1992). Here the brain/mind is a multitude of relatively independent blades, each one built to carry out a specific task.

Such an account seems to be a purpose-built intellectual module serving a singular function, that of denying the possibility that humans could be other than they are. EP advocates suggest rationality cannot be defined outside its reproductive functionality. If a way of 'thinking' helps an organism survive and reproduce it is said to be rational. Given the political environment in which EP seeks to spread, EP seems relatively well adapted. In its own terms EP therefore displays evolutionary rationality. As EP denies the possibility of a higher general rationality above functional rationality (adaptiveness), it renders itself immune to critique, at least from within its own logic. However it is not necessary to accept such an account of the mind/brain. Research in human brain function in the fields of child development and in 'cognitive archaeology'; demonstrate the weakness of mass modularity, in terms of both 'hard wiring' and the fragmentation of intelligence.

Annette Karmiloff-Smith (1992, 2000) demonstrates that 'hard wiring' fails to account for child development. There is plenty of evidence that the mind/brain is 'environment-expectant', seeking out certain stimuli and having preprogrammed developmental tendencies – such as for language acquisition. However, it is also 'environment-dependent': different environments produce different patterns of neural wiring within set boundaries. Studies of brain damage that EP researchers take to demonstrate modularity (specific brain area damage leading to relatively discrete loss of function), according to Karmiloff-Smith, demonstrate the 'plasticity' of the brain. Damaged brains display forms of *wiring* that differ from non-damaged brains not only in the dysfunctional areas. The brain appears to compensate for damaged regions by creating alternative neural connections.

(*cont'd*)

Steven Mithen's (1996) 'cognitive archaeology' presents an account of evolutionary development in which modularity plays its part, but in which it is far from the definitive last move in the evolution of modern humans. In brief, he suggests that if mass modularity were all there was to the mind it would be impossible to explain the development of art, religion and science. He argues these developments demonstrate the capacity of the human mind to transcend modular intelligence and to work across specific intellectual domains. He points out that were mass modularity a full account of the human mind then we would hardly be capable of using metaphor and analogy, faculties that emerge from the ability to work across boundaries between specific intellectual capacities, or what EP would call modules. If we were unable to use metaphor and analogy, Cosmides (in Barkow *et al.* 1992) would not have been able to invent the Swiss-army-knife metaphor for the brain. That she did undermines the argument the metaphor is supposed to convey. This is a classic example of performative contradiction (Habermas 1984 and 1987) – the making of claims the premises of which undermine the very possibility of making such claims, or which undermine the possibility that such claims could or should be taken seriously. In short, EP cannot justify its claims in terms of either evidence (it prefers speculative inferences about pre-history) or rational argument (its claims are self-contradictory). Explanation therefore might better be found in terms of the career and ideological interests that are served in adopting the language of evolution, adaptation and 'hard wiring' in the current intellectual and political climate (David 2002b; see also Benton 2000).

# 10
# Medical Genetics and Human Health

This chapter begins with a discussion of the work of Barry Barnes, who addresses different aspects of the biotechnology knowledge generation and application process from a social-interests vantage-point. Issues concerning neutrality in the interpretation of genetic diagnoses and/or markers as 'illnesses' and/or as 'disabilities', and the questionable construction of 'non-directiveness' in the process of counselling, have been addressed by discourse-analytic researchers and feminist researchers using forms of discourse and conversation analysis (Petersen, Shakespeare, Pilnick). Michael Mulkay and Paul Martin combine interest-based work with discourse-analytic methods. Jeanette Edwards' combination of feminist and ethnographic approaches challenges the deficit model of public understanding of science, something often used to dismiss as unimportant or irrelevant the questioning of experts by non-scientific 'laypersons'. Michael Fortun and Paul Rabinow provide two very different fusions of ethnographic and discursive approaches to the new genetics. Fortun seeks to parallel the socially constructed nature of trust in venture-capital markets with the often inflated claims being made by corporate scientists about genetic conditions and cures. Rabinow seeks to suggest that a discourse-analytic questioning of any essential human nature makes it appropriate for us to embrace the potential to modify our genes. Elizabeth Ettorre's research examines how genetic technologies have been applied to regulate women's lives. Hilary Rose and Barbara Katz Rothman's Marxist and feminist work raises questions about the commercial interests at work in the global rush to privatize genetic knowledge and to encourage reproductive 'fitness'. R. C. Lewontin and Robin Bunton provide evidence, at a number of different levels, concerning the capitalist interests driving the direction of research in the new genetics. Jürgen Habermas develops a critical-theoretical framework to locate recent debates over the application of genetic engineering to human beings.

# Social Interests

Barry Barnes (1999) suggests:

> Just as there is no indefeasible method for establishing the superiority of one expert technical analysis over another conflicting one, so there is no method for determining the best account of where a purely technical analysis is appropriate and where it is not. (1999:59)

Where priests once claimed general intellectual authority, this domain has been gradually eroded in the modern era. Where doctors were once deemed guardians of a moral and physical conception of 'health', they are now, in some cases, and in the eyes of some people, best seen as technicians of the body. For some, medical expertise extends to questions such as whether it is right to terminate a foetus with a particular genetic condition or predisposition. For others medical expertise does not warrant that extension of jurisdiction. Barnes gives the example of the 14-day rule for embryo research set down in UK legislation (the Human Fertilisation and Embryology Act 1990). This prohibits continued experimentation on an embryo after 14 days from the initial collection of the fertilized egg. This deadline acts to constitute a profane object prior to the 14th day and a morally significant object after that date. This boundary is an arbitrary compromise established through the clash of interest groups (as discussed in Mulkay 1997; see the box on p. 160–1), not a morally or empirically objective position. Established boundaries, within and between which groups claim and limit the claims of others to jurisdiction, are based upon convention, trust and interest. With ongoing differentiation of expert roles, there has been increased scope for questioning the authority and legitimacy of any one set of experts and roles. Here Barnes is close in his conclusions to those of Ulrich Beck (1992), though closer to Mary Douglas (see Barnes 1972b:252). The new biotechnology can expect the validity and scope of its authority to be continually in question in an age of ongoing differentiation of expertise. So too will the new biotechnology come to challenge the validity and scope of other arenas of socially legitimized authority (for example the roles or mothers, fathers, siblings, families, etc.):

> Biotechnological innovations will in due course permit a number of presently undifferentiated concerns to be addressed and evaluated separately as so many distinct technical tasks; these may include genetic mapping and selection including sex selection, the fusing of egg and sperm, the management and growth of embryo and foetus independent of the parent's body, the social structuring of childrearing, the involvement in sexual activity purely as pleasurable recreation. Many existing social roles and institutions will be altered out of recognition if even just some of these possibilities become actual. (Barnes 1999:66)

# Discourse Analysis

Many significant debates about the scope of scientific authority hinge around the way genetic information is passed to those being examined, and how this information is communicated in the context of discussions of 'what to do next'. Work in this area has been carried out by discourse and conversation analysts, feminists and disability researchers using similar methods. Petersen (1999b; Petersen and Bunton 2002) examines the professional and practitioner literature on genetic counselling, and in particular the rise of the discourse of 'non-directiveness' within this work. The discourse of non-directiveness serves, Petersen suggests, to distance the new genetics from what is described as the old eugenics. Eugenics is characterized in terms of coercive restraint upon reproduction by those deemed unfit. To avoid the implication that science is once again engaged in such practices, genetic counselling promotes the view that it does and should give the patient the choice to act on any genetic information they are given in the way they see fit, rather than in line with what the 'experts' deem appropriate. Petersen suggests that such a construction of genetic counselling seeks to promote the view that more information means more choice and more freedom for those informed. However, Petersen suggests, this view is highly problematic, for two main reasons. First, the practice of genetic counselling does not always live up to this ideal, especially in the context of limited health budgets and pressure to follow up genetic tests (particularly during pregnancy) with what is considered either as 'appropriate' or 'typical' responses. Second, the counsellor's position as expert often means they are asked what counsellees should do, and even answers framed in terms of what other people typically do can be seen to suggest what is deemed correct. Petersen points out that expert literature is often limited on this subject. What he points out is the rhetorical work being done by the discourse of non-directiveness, in creating a rhetorical distance from eugenics, irrespective of whether such an approach is achieved in practice.

Using interviews with women who had undergone genetic testing and counselling with regard to breast and ovarian cancer, Nina Hallowell (1999) identified an underlying moral economy of responsibility underpinning the information women deemed 'at risk' received as well as the way they felt it was appropriate to act upon that information. Far from giving these women greater freedom, genetic information framed within a discourse of responsible action, both in seeking to be tested and acting appropriately once tested, generated a greater sense of constraint. While genetic screening may appear the only logical thing to do for women in 'at risk' groups, this logic is questionable, and positioning oneself in the category 'at risk' has many negative emotional and psychological risks in itself. Only 5 to 10 per cent of breast and ovarian cancers can be predicted genetically and there is little evidence that medical science can significantly improve life expectancy for those individuals if the cancer predisposition actually develops. As such, the medical focus is geared more to the responsibility of such a woman towards others (relatives and future offspring) than towards herself. As the majority of breast and ovarian cancer sufferers do not carry the predisposing gene, an 'all clear' from a genetic test is far less than it might appear (see also Rothman 1998:143–9). Genetic testing is primarily beneficial to others.

Alison Pilnick (2002) used conversation analysis of interactions between genetic counsellors and counsellees to investigate the issue of 'non-directiveness' in practice. What she highlights is that conversation often involves 'competing interactional contingencies'. In other words, the counsellor may seek to provide only neutral information while the counsellee asks specifically for advice about what they should do with the news they have been given. In other situations, the counsellor, in seeking to make sense of large amounts of complex information, gives examples and explanations that may be considered directive where they appear to judge that the counsellee has not fully grasped the information in 'neutral' form. Pilnick concludes (2002:349) that the discourse of non-directiveness might best be suspended altogether, as it is unworkable as a general principle in the complex and contingent practice of counselling. This may open the new genetics more fully to the accusation of eugenic management by experts. However, to open the new genetics to such an accusation may only be to expose the truth.

The assertion that the new genetics retains a eugenic logic, one of promoting genetic fitness through the elimination of the genetically 'unfit', is taken up most vigorously by disability activists and theorists. Tom Shakespeare (1999), using a discourse-analytic approach to medical and scientific journals, first of all identifies a universal disclaimer in contemporary medical and scientific discourses. This is to always assert that the new genetics is not eugenic in its intent or in its practice. Shakespeare argues that debates over what is and what is not eugenic can never be fully resolved. The use of the term as a counter-point acts to immunize whatever is being advocated at any particular time from the accusation that it is or could be coercive. This rhetorical device is then commonly followed by a second dualism, that between narratives of tragedy (the condition of being disabled attributed to faulty genes) and narratives of hope (the condition of being saved from such a life attributed to advances in genetic science). Shakespeare suggests that such narratives and rhetorical devices conceal two fundamental gaps in the scientific and medical discourse. First, there is no recognition of the validity of the lives and experience of those people classified as 'disabled'. Silenced by the narrative of tragedy these lives become seen as lives not worth living. This is both dangerous and offensive to all those so defined, and is often accompanied by overt or covert assertions that such persons are a burden and of no use to society. Second, such accounts equate disability with the biological characteristics of bodies and minds, and with the genes that are assumed to have coded for such characteristics, rather than to the social conditions in which such minds and bodies find themselves disadvantaged, constrained, discriminated against and/or excluded. Shakespeare distinguishes biological impairments from the disabling consequences of social arrangements in which such impairments are not catered for. Making the distinction between impairment and disability allows attention to be given to physical and mental conditions that require non-conventional medical and/or social considerations without ignoring the social factors that turn impairment into disability.

Radical disability activists suggest that defining a life as biologically not worth living on the grounds that, in this society, that life would be miserable and unfulfilled is no different morally from the termination of female foetuses in societies that highly prize male offspring (Bailey 1996). While genetic and medical expertise may enable predictions about life expectancy and degree of impairment, does this give such experts the authority to judge where, on either continuum, a cutoff point is reached, beyond which a life is not worthy of being lived? Rejecting the jurisdiction of genetic and/or medical experts to decide what constitutes a life worth living raises the question of whether such decisions should be left to parents or individual women, or to the state, or to no one. Once impairment and disability are distinguished, scientific knowledge and moral judgement cannot be simply equated. In both cases it is often assumed that both terms in each pair refer to the same thing, and that decisions concerning each should best be made by the same technical or scientific experts. As Barry Barnes points out (above) this is not by any necessity the case. While experts have an interest in expanding (and in some cases restricting) their claims to authority, disability activists combine discourse- and interest-based approaches to challenge the construction of 'invalid' identities, and the rights of experts to make such judgements (Morris 1991; Oliver 1995; Shakespeare 1995, 1998; Hubbard 1997).

---

### Combining Social Interests and Discursive Approaches

Michael Mulkay (1997) presents an account of the passing of the Human Fertilisation and Embryology Act 1990 in the United Kingdom. Mulkay examines the interaction of interest groups and their attempts to present the issue of embryo research in either a positive or a negative light. This combination of social-interests and discursive analyses allows Mulkay to plot the course of a scientific and political dispute and develop an explanatory account of its outcome. In the early stages of the dispute much of the media coverage focused upon moral objections to embryo research. The success of the pro-embryo-research lobby was to present such research as being medically and commercially valuable, thus recruiting powerful allies in their campaign. Attempts by critics to challenge the likely benefits of such research were unsuccessful, largely because politicians were prepared to accept the word of those in the scientific community who advocated the research. Critics were

*(cont'd)*

characterized (1997:113) as religious and dogmatic. Mulkay however challenges this one-sided characterization and points out that claims on both sides displayed a dogmatic faith in the morality and truth of their positions. While critics drew upon the discourse of 'Frankenstein's monster', advocates drew upon the counter-discourse of science being persecuted by the church ('Galileo versus the inquisition'). The success of the latter framing of the debate over the former, at least in the minds of those politicians who voted on the matter, lay not simply in rhetoric, though this was important. Rhetoric resonated with and helped construct an alliance of interested parties, in the scientific and medical community, in business and in government, an alliance that came to see its interests best represented in the acceptance of embryo research, and whose economic and political resources were sufficient to win the vote.

Paul Martin (1999) similarly combines aspects of a social-interests approach with that of a more discourse analytic (actor network) method in his research into the social shaping of gene therapy and the reconstruction of genetic disease. Martin highlights the way genetic research and medical models of disease were gradually brought into line with each other, or at least have been in a number of crucial areas and respects, though this is still ongoing. In addition, the development of gene therapies required the development of new biochemical and information technologies. The need was to align the practices and interests of significant groups of medical practitioners, genetic researchers and commercial actors (in pharmaceuticals and computing). This has involved a significant shift of resources and effort towards the identification of genetic predispositions towards certain diseases and to the development of genetics-based therapies. The movement of research funding in one direction rather than another is as much the cause of increased success in those areas as it is the consequence.

# Combining Feminist and Ethnographic Approaches

Jeanette Edwards's (2002) ethnographic/feminist work focuses attention upon the frames of reference used by working-class female non-scientists in their evaluations of genetic technologies and the choices and constraints such technologies may be used to generate. Edwards highlights that while most people are not experts in the new genetics, they are capable of drawing upon a wide range of everyday knowledge and insight when making sense of new technologies. New information is viewed and contextualized in relation to 'issues of personhood and dignity, of family and community, of social identity and stigma, of social class and economics, or appropriate and inappropriate relationships, of expertise and trust in experts' (2002:323). In this sense at least, lay understanding is not too dissimilar to expert knowledge construction.

While the expertise involved in conducting genetic tests is different from that of managing family relations, it is essential that one does not assume the invalid status of the other. This links directly with feminist concerns over the reconstruction of science towards listening and dialogue in data collection and analysis rather than sole reliance upon detached observation (see Chapter 7).

### Combining Ethnography and Discourse Analysis: Divergent Conclusions about the Social Construction of Communities and Bodies in the Case of Iceland/DeCODE genetics

The combination of ethnographic and discursive methods can generate provocative conclusions. As part of an ethnographic research project examining the establishment of legislation enabling the construction of a genetic database for the entire population of Iceland by DeCODE genetics, Michael Fortun (2001) encountered persistent rumours concerning financial payments made by commercial interests to Icelandic politicians. Commenting upon these rumours to journalists made Fortun party to a conflict over the social construction of commercial trust. Fortun observes that speculation over the truth of such accusations paralleled investor speculation in the future of this commercial enterprise. This future was itself premised upon trust in both the speculations made by scientists over the medical value of their future research and the claims made by DeCODE genetics' managers concerning the viability of its commercial future. To this extent science, capitalism and law are social constructions, built upon rhetorical strategies and dependant upon trust in the honesty and ability of experts, trust that can never be fully justified. Paul Rabinow's ethnographic and discourse analytic work around the DeCODE genetics project in Iceland generated very different conclusions. For Rabinow (1999), the development of genetic therapies offer the chance to move beyond a sociobiological debate, about the reduction of humans to some essential nature, to a biosociality debate over the choice to remake our nature in the absence of any necessary essential nature. Rabinow's discursive approach builds upon the same questioning of essentialism and reductionism that is characteristic of most feminist and disability activists' use of discourse analysis, but Rabinow's conclusion is that we should therefore embrace diversity and use genetics to promote this potential. Rabinow's position parallels the practical steps taken by some in the disability movement to use genetic tests to actively choose offspring with conditions commonly labelled as 'disabilities' (such as profound deafness – Orr 2002). As has been mentioned above, identifying the limits of expertise does not necessary leave scope for unquestionable authoritative judgements of any kind as to what should and should not be permitted, or who should be allowed to decide.

## Combining a Feminist Standpoint and Discourse-Analytic Research

Elizabeth Ettorre's work (1999, 2000, 2001, 2002) addresses the tension between choice and oppressive expectation contained within the social relations of new predictive genetic technologies in the field of reproduction. Early feminist writing on reproductive technology (Firestone 1970) identified women's exclusion from equality in the public realm with their being bound to domestic responsibilities, not least that of pregnancy and childcare. Such writers hoped that new technologies would liberate women from reproductive burdens in the same way it was hoped that washing machines and vacuum cleaners would liberate women from housework. Such a view assumed that more technical possibilities would translate into more freedom for women. Regarding choices over the genetic testing and selection or termination of embryos on the basis of 'genetic health', the following statement may appear to sum up such a view:

> My principle here is pretty simple: Just have most of the decisions made by women as opposed to men. They're the ones who bear children, and men, as you know, often sneak away from children that aren't healthy. We're going to have to feel more responsible for the next generation. I think women should be allowed to make the decisions, and as far as I'm concerned, keep these male doctor committees out of action. (James Watson, cited in Fukuyama 2002:186)

The essence of Watson's argument is that the bond between mother and embryo-foetus-child is the strongest. As such, it is the mother's judgement concerning the best interests of that embryo-foetus-child which should be given priority, given the inability of the embryo-foetus-child to formulate or express any opinion on the matter. Watson's advocacy of a mother's embodied relationship with her child as a foundation for ethical judgement in relation to the abstraction and detachment of genetic science is rather ironic given his own position as one of the abstractors. Individual women in an age of reproductive consumerism will be more likely to choose genetic interventions for their child, especially if others are doing the same thing, than would ethics committees seeking to take account of a supposed wider community interest. The pain and shame experienced by women labelled as 'bad reproducers' in an age of 'designer babies' may render embodied experience and individual choice far more powerful tools in the enforcement of conformity than state regulation. This is the conclusion of Ettorre's research into women's experience and expert discourses in a range of different national settings. While embodied experience and the ability to relate to others is a foundation for both ethical judgement and action based upon such judgement, such experience is also the means by which individuals are controlled (whether by means of manipulation, persuasion or coercion). Embodied experience is a necessary condition, but it is not a sufficient condition for making moral decisions. Ettorre's feminist critique, of the unquestioned assumption that 'choice' to attempt perfection is less oppressive than the acceptance of diversity, parallels the work of Petersen, Pilnick, Hallowell and Shakespeare discussed above. Other feminist researchers have researched parallel dimensions of genetic choice or eugenic pressure (Kerr and Cunnungham-Burley 2000; Kerr *et al.* 1997, 1998a and 1998b; Wajcman 1991; Steinberg 1997).

The question 'Who decides?' still remains. Without the illusion that such decisions can be made on technical criteria, we might conclude that all such choices should be prohibited (the view of many religious groups, as well as some disability activists and feminists). Alternatively we may decide that individuals should be allowed to choose the genes of their offspring as individual consumers (the view of Watson, Rabinow 1999 and Lee Silver 1998). Sociological research cannot tell us what to do, even if it can expose the dubious claims made by those who would persuade us that science and/or medicine can make ethical decisions for us. Ettorre's research, and that of other feminists, forces us to adopt a highly sceptical attitude towards any model by which some embryos are selected and others rejected. However, such research cannot tell us where to draw the line or whether we should have no line and instead go for all or nothing. In this sense sociologists are experts in questioning expertise.

# The Fusion of Marxist and Feminist Approaches

Hilary Rose's account of the new genetics in relation to risk and investment highlights the relationship between the management of women's lives (discussed above) and corporate interests:

> The new genetics is central to today's techno-economic project. Thus while the leading scientific ideologues of the Human Genome Project (HGP), as its international institutional expression, claim its potential contribution to medicine and to knowledge, most have shares in biotechnology companies. Not only does the HGP mark the moment when the life sciences entered Big, that is industrialized, Science (De Solla Price 1963), it is also the moment when they made a new relationship to capital. (Rose 2000b:67)

Huge corporate investment in genetic research demands the private accumulation of any value derived from such work, while also seeking to offset any liability for financial or human losses. When a technology is deemed successful, huge profits stand to be made. When such technologies generate risks it is likely that citizens and the state will be asked to foot the bill (Rose 2000b:73). The promise of large state and venture-capitalist investment generates pressure for exaggerated claims concerning the role of genes in all manner of social and medical problems, from alcoholism and homelessness to cancer and schizophrenia. The ideology of reductionism is fertile ground for researchers looking for funding, and for neo-liberal ideologues seeking to individualize responsibility for human suffering. Rose refers to the rise of a new 'cultural terror', the fear of faulty genes, genes that imprint failure and personal responsibility for that failure. Rose suggests that it is no coincidence that the rise of such a genetic reductionism has coincided with the resurgence of neo-fascism across the developed world, a politics that feeds upon hereditary accounts of degeneracy and upon the social dislocation wrought by neo-liberalism at both the national and global levels. Those that have the means will feel the pressure to give their children 'the edge' in an individualistic and competitive society, while able then to blame the social disadvantage of others on their failure so to do.

## Marxist Approaches

R. C. Lewontin claims (1993:74):

> No prominent molecular biologist of my acquaintance is without a financial stake in the biotechnology business. As a result, serious conflicts of interest have emerged in universities and in government service. In some cases graduate students working under entrepreneurial professors are restricted in their scientific interchanges, in case they might give away potential trade secrets.

The commercial imperative not only drives science in the direction of commercially profitable end products, rather than more basic research or socially useful goals; it also inhibits the very core of scientific creativity, the sharing of results and the cross-fertilization of ideas. Intellectual property and what Merton (see Chapter 1) called intellectual 'communism' are pulling in opposite directions. Robin Bunton (in Petersen and Bunton 2002) documents the fusion of new genetic research with corporate interests in the emergence of a new global capitalist framework of property rights. The mapping of the human genome itself became a race between the state-funded Human Genome Project and the commercially sponsored Celera Genomics (Davies 2001). While the former sought to place its findings in the public realm, Celera sought to patent each gene it was able to sequence to enable these patents to be sold or licensed for use to commercial or academic research in the future. The fear that this basic genetic information would be generally available to anyone and for free, what Merton would view as the very foundation of scientific research, allowed Celera to draw in large quantities of venture capital. This flood of funding occurred just as large pharmaceutical companies in the West, pleading fear of financial ruin, paid millions of dollars in legal fees to fight attempts by the South African government to purchase cheaper derivative copies of patented AIDS-inhibiting drugs from India and Brazil (*Independent* 2000). Unable to pay the tens of thousands of dollars per person per year that Western corporations demand for the cocktail of three AIDS-inhibiting drugs, millions face premature death. The corporations finally backed away from the prospect of an embarrassing legal defeat (the primary research for two of the three drugs having been developed by a charity and a publicly funded university team, and only privatized afterwards). Such actions parallel the practices of global agribusiness corporations discussed in Chapter 8 (see Shiva, 1998).

Jürgen Habermas (2003) challenges the paralleling of parental influence by socialization and by genetic modification. He also rejects the gradual fusing of the clinical orientation towards 'healing' and the technical orientation towards genetic 'enhancement'. He argues (2003:21): 'What seems to be returning today, against a background of globalizing neoliberalism, is the explosive alliance of Darwinism and free trade ideology'. Liberal eugenics starts from the acceptance of pre-implantation genetic diagnosis for 'severe' heritable diseases, and then proclaims that, as no objective line can be drawn around the category 'severe', the best criteria for determining what is socially desirable is what parents themselves desire for their child. Habermas argues that the 'ethical self-understanding of language using agents' (2003:11) requires the separation of instrumental rationality, as the legitimate governing principle in certain domains, from the principles of 'symmetrical relations between free and equal people' (2003:23) in the realm of communicative interaction. Modern science, in alliance with liberal market instrumentalism (2003:24), dedifferentiates theoretical, technical and practical (ethical) criteria in measuring the value of a human life only in terms of nutrition, physical health and a long lifespan, rather than in terms of reflexivity, autonomy and intersubjective communication. Habermas addresses the potential consequence of planned genetic interventions for the 'produced' person, in terms of their self-identity. To have specific characteristics of one's makeup selected 'for' you, by conscious, identifiable and therefore 'responsible' others, may alienate personhood in ways distinct from the experience of a body that has no 'designer'. Certain forms of socialization, or lack of it, at key, and non-repeatable, stages of early childhood, may lead to irreversible physical, emotional or mental characteristics (2003:83). However, socialization is, in the main, at least in principle, open to reflexive challenge and change in the course of an individual's development as a responsible actor (2003:62). It is this possibility for change and reflexive self-possession that forms the basis for modern ethical indignation towards forms of social and psychological ascription (2003:63). The prospect of genetic intervention for the purpose of deliberate design therefore transgresses the ethical foundations of modern legal and social systems of responsibility, as well as the foundations of individual identity and social solidarity (see Barnes 2000 – but from a very different vantage). In critical theoretical terms this is a colonization of the lifeworld orientation towards understanding others as ends in themselves, by forms of instrumental reduction that equate generative processes with manufacture, and of human subjects with objects. Liberal eugenicists might say 'So what?'. After Copernicus and Darwin, this. Is the latest decentring of human beings (from the centre of the universe, from the centre of nature, and now from their own self-identity) not just another truth that we will take in our stride as a species? Habermas rejects this equation. We are not at the centre of the universe, nor the animal kingdom, but, through reflexive, intersubjective communicative action, language-using agents can assert a responsibility and a self-possession at the centre of our own individual and collective lives. The conditions experienced within instrumentally rational economic and political systems should not be reified into an account of our intrinsic condition. To do so is to fall victim to the negative dialectic of enlightenment, to empower our selves by instrumentalizing ourselves, only to thereby enslave ourselves. 'We' are not totally decentred objects, no different from other instrumentally manipulable means to other ends, even if that is a common experience under capitalism.

It should be noted here that no difference of intrinsic significance arises within the above argument whether one chooses to understand a 'self-reflexive language-using species' in terms of causal influence (as Barry Barnes (2000) does), or in terms of non-instrumental 'reasons', agreed upon by intersubjective communication (as Habermas does).

# Part Four

## Conclusions

# 11

# Reflexive Epistemological Diversity (RED)

## Reflections upon Sociological Approaches to the New Genetics

Sociological research in the area of new genetic technologies is characterized by a high degree of cross-fertilization between theoretical perspectives and methodological approaches. This has led to a wide range of insights, much of which is complementary, but at the same time generating a degree of critical reflexivity about the limits not only of genetic science but also of singular sociological models. Marxists and feminists have highlighted the relationship between genetic science and established social relations of power. Such relations are also manifest in the findings of discourse analytical research, ethnographic work, feminist research and the discourse analytic research carried out by researchers from within the disability movement. However, these researchers have also pointed to forms of resistance and forms of counter-expertise that challenge the dominance of established expertise and institutional power. Work from within an interest-based perspective has highlighted that it is precisely where many expert groups compete for influence and prestige that scope emerges for critical dissent and the emergence of counter-experts. Such claims to counter-expertise include those made by groups seeking to valorize the expertise of experience (Collins and Evans 2002), whether that is the experience of women, parents, or those categorized as genetically 'unfit'. 'Externalist' researchers give greater attention to the influence of wider social relations of power and challenge in opening up the parameters of 'expertise' and of what is considered significant and acceptable evidence. Conflicts over the boundaries of expertise also generate growing scope for the claims of expert status made by social researchers in the realm of new genetic science and technology. However, the claim of social scientists to expertise is as much in terms of questioning the authority of experts as it is in asserting their own authority to know or decide.

171

Important differences exist between sociological perspectives, such as between Marxists and feminists over the nature of social relations of power and domination, and between both Marxists and feminists and those forms of discourse analysis that emphasize the contingent nature of class and gender identities. While ongoing, these have not prevented fruitful research based upon combining approaches, and in many ways the confrontation of approaches adds validity and challenges preconceptions. While ethnographic research complements work carried out upon expert discourses (academic texts, legal debates and media coverage of genetic science), ethnographic work is also important in that it limits the temptation to make causal inferences about the formation of public attitudes and beliefs from media and expert coverage. Similarly, interest-based work, while able to link with both macro-structural sociological approaches to power and to micro-sociological approaches to inter-action and language, is also able to temper both approaches and the tendency in each to attribute central importance to the realm of social action their method is most suited to addressing.

Sociological research identifies a significant difference in social reaction and interpretation to genetic research in the areas of human health and food production. Bound up within the discourses and institutions of health and medicine, genetic research focused upon human disease prevention and cure has tended to receive a far more positive reception than has research into genetically modified food and cloning (Conrad 1999; Gofton and Haimes 1999; Petersen 2001). This can be explained in relation to the existence of an already established environmental movement, complete with well-funded counter-experts on hand to challenge the science of corporations and states. Where mechanistic forms of biology have been radically challenged in relation to the external environment, they remain strong in relation to biomedicine, at least in Western societies. This distinction is as sociologically significant as it is indicative of the value of a sociological approach when analysing the authority and direction of science in society. As has been pointed out in relation to medical, behavioural and non-human genetic science, the power and direction of science is politically and economically shaped. Differences in the development and reception of new genetic science in different regions of the world and over time need to be accounted for in this way also.

The examination of genetics from a sociological perspective highlights the limits of scientific expertise at two levels. First, the epistemological certainty claimed by science is challenged. How successfully can genetic research predict cancer? Is cloning safe? Will genetically modified organisms spread out of control through cross-fertilization? Is IQ a legitimate measure of innate and general intelligence? Second, with regard to the generalization of authority from technical knowledge to moral and evaluative judgements, the reduction of social groupings into genetically defined units is also placed in question. When, if ever, does the genetic predisposition to impairment make a life not worth living? Before what point, if any, is it legitimate to experiment upon a human embryo? When does a genetic difference constitute a deficiency? Should human clones be allowed? Where does the new genetic desire to make people better cross over into the old eugenic desire to make better people? Where do we draw the line? Sociological research highlights the misconception that all these questions are merely technical issues. Second, the reflexive function of a diverse range of sociological approaches also has the self-limiting effect of forcing us to recognize that in questioning the ability of genetic experts to take decisions on behalf of society, sociologists cannot then insert themselves into the newly emptied role of moral 'expert'. One consequence of 'reflexive epistemological diversity' is the awareness that no singular community of knowledge (whether they be biologists, feminists, discourse analysts, lawyers, trade unionists or indigenous peoples) can claim to capture the whole truth from within their own realm of 'expertise'. In some things we must respect the voices of many forms of expertise. In some things there may be no authorities.

# Reflexive Epistemological Diversity

The sociology of scientific knowledge offers a range of epistemological perspectives on the questions of whether science offers universal truth or partial knowledge, and of whether science promotes human emancipation or facilitates domination. Interest theory focuses attention upon institutional and career competition within science and in relation to wider social interests. While questioning the purity of scientific knowledge and identifying links with dominant interests, this approach retains a degree of neutrality, suggesting that science is neither one thing nor the other with regard to either key question. Ethnographic and discursive approaches (EDA) focus upon interaction and language within scientific practice. While more sceptical on the question of 'truth', such an approach suspends judgement over questions of power and domination. EDA have raised as many questions about the validity of externalist accounts of science (Marxists and feminists), in particular the danger or imposing 'a priori' assumptions about power and domination, phenomena that are not immediately observable in the kinds of micro and internalist data collection favoured by ethnographers and discourse analysts. Marxist and feminist researchers suggest that such invisibility is the consequence of such a narrow epistemological focus of attention. Marxists focus upon economic and political power and its reflections in the practice and outcomes of scientific research and application, while feminists focus upon gender relations and their manifestations within science, and in its impact on women's lives.

This epistemological diversity, this range of different foci of attention and methods of data collection, generates differing accounts of science. To the extent that data collected by different means, and within differing theoretical frameworks, leads to conflicting representations of science in society, the sociology of science field, as a whole, benefits in two ways. First, through reflexivity comes the recognition that any singular account, using a limited range of methods and research questions, cannot hope to provide a full account of scientific knowledge. Reflexivity is two-dimensional, at the level of questioning over-generalization, and second, in raising questions about the validity of any singular aspect of an account. However, second, in addition to reflexivity, multiple accounts provide grounds for complementarity. The range of studies discussed in Chapters 8, 9 and 10 draw upon mixed methods to generate data that is more detailed and more general, even if no account should even be assumed to provide a full picture. 'Reflexive epistemological diversity' is neither a theory of naïve complementary pluralism nor a defence of ontological relativism.

Harry Collins and Robert Evans (2002 and 2003) seek to move science studies towards recognition of multiple forms of expertise, rather than simply questioning the authority claims of science. Scientific and non-scientific expertise are said to be based upon forms of experience. Collins and Evans suggest such 'Studies of Expertise and Experience' (SEE) avoid debunking expertise, even while avoiding blanket deference to science, and avoiding undiscriminating relativism between all knowledge claims. Scientists are narrow specialists. Science, as a whole, has no general expertise. Those with specific expertise are always small subgroups with a narrow jurisdiction.

Critics have questioned Collins and Evans's account. Sheila Jasanoff questions whether it is either useful or sociologically valid to assert the reality of established and challenger expertise (2003:389–400). Jasanoff holds to the more relativistic stance of questioning all attributions of authority. Any attempt to confer expertise will only be appropriated differentially, depending upon the distribution of power in any conflict. Collins and Evans (2003:444–7) suggest that a balanced judgement between realism and relativism is simply the most valid way of accounting for the 'truth' of 'expertise', and that uncertainty should not be taken as grounds for paralysis, even if asserting such a view is no guarantee that its contents will be heeded.

Brian Wynne (2003:401–17) suggests Collins and Evans equate all questions of expertise with those questions that can be answered with a singular 'true' answer, even if such an answer might best be arrived at sometimes through the collaboration of many sets of experts. Such 'propositionalism' or 'decisionism', Wynne claims, neglects the cultural context that gives events multiple meanings that cannot be reduced to a single correct answer. Collins and Evans (2003:437) suggest that while many issues cannot be resolved in terms of finding the one correct answer, it is the case that there are questions where a right answer is what everyone concerned is looking for, even if there are social and cultural reasons why different groups might or might not be willing to believe a conclusion. Realism and relativism are put to work differently in this single response.

Arie Rip (2003) suggests that Collins and Evans's primary extrapolation from the characteristics of esoteric sciences when defining their ideal typical contributory expert belies a primary orientation to, and reverence for, Western science. Rip suggests such an approach fails to question the wider social influences that allow such fields of inquiry to dominate and claim higher status. This is said to be a generic weakness of internalist approaches to the sociology of scientific knowledge. Collins and Evans (2003:440) accept that their account does defend certain realist claims in the physical sciences, even if expertise is still narrowly defined. For them science is both culture and resource.

This debate highlights tensions between relativism and realism, between ethnographers and discourse analysts who emphasize the fundamentally irreducible nature of culture and/or meaning and the more limited claims of those who suggest a better account of reality may be possible by overcoming the one-sidedness of currently dominant approaches. The debate also highlights the tension between an internalist approach to science and more critical and/or suspicious externalist accounts that do not believe a highlighting of plural expertises will overcome the dominance of those with the most power. While Collins and Evans move towards 'reflexive epistemological diversity', the debate with their critics comes closer still.

'Reflexive epistemological diversity' combines multiple dimensions of realism with multiple dimensions of relativism. Each perspective within the sociology of science contains both. Critical realists defend forms of realism against ideological distortions, while critical theorists place greater emphasis upon challenging the domination and distortion contained in currently prevalent forms of realism in contemporary manifestations of science. Marxism (in the science wars and beyond) displays the tension between realism and relativism within itself. Feminism, similarly, contains a tension between forms of standpoint theory that defend the epistemological value of forms of listening and attachment because they are seen to give a more valid approach to 'reality', while postmodern feminists adopt a more critical and relativistic stance in relation to existing scientific practice (recall the tension between embodied experience and the construction of gendered identity in Ettorre's work on pregnancy and motherhood; see Chapter 10). Interest theory displays even more clearly, and sometimes playfully, this tension between realism and relativism. Social interests are seen as both ambiguous (Barnes 1974) and causally explanatory (Bloor 1976; Collins 1985). Explanation in physical science is at once permanently vulnerable to 'experimenter's regress' (Collins 1985), and yet in places drawn upon in accounts (for example in Collins and Pinch 1998a: chapter 4). This same tension is less explicitly recognized in the work of ethnographers and discourse analysts, who at once seek to suspend causal realism, while forced to draw upon it in accounts of the significance of language and interaction in the formation and presentation of scientific authority. Steve Woolgar's (1988) critique of realism is both valuable and self-limiting.

The consequence of this tension between realism and relativism (between a defence of epistemological authority and scepticism towards any universal authority claims) is not the debunking of all knowledge claims. The consequence of the experimenter's regress, of the critique of causal realism, and of the demonstration of ideological interests (linked to career, class or gender) is not outright rejection of science, or at least it should not be. Rather it should lead to recognition of the self-limiting character of multiple expertises.

The question then arises as to the nature of the sociologist of science's expertise. Can the sociologist of science provide only an expertise in critically evaluating the authority claims of other experts, in particular those of natural scientists, and of other social scientists? Here again, the tension between realism and relativism becomes apparent. The realist tendency within each perspective tends towards epistemological reduction of explanation to their particular level of analysis and therefore authority. This is no less true than in the natural sciences. The relativist tendency within each perspective tends towards a questioning of authority claims in general. This is something more developed in the social sciences than in the natural sciences. This is in large part because different perspectives in the social sciences have failed to establish the strong disciplinary and field-specifying boundaries characteristic of the natural sciences. However, this is not so say that such boundary-setting is not prevalent, damaging and significant in the social sciences. The development of the sociology of scientific knowledge moves along this line of tension between realism (prone to epistemological reductionism) and reflexive relativism (prone to epistemological chicken). Sociologists have something to say about how things are the way they are, if at the same time they have as much to say about why things are unlikely to be quite the way experts (including themselves) say they are.

A 'context of knowledge production' more open to 'reflexive epistemological diversity' comes closer to what Harding (1991) calls the condition most conducive to 'strong objectivity'. However, this 'context' is never fully achievable, and to believe such a standpoint could ever be fully achieved would be naïve. Mannheim criticized Marx for believing he had achieved such a standpoint, Barnes criticizes Mannheim for believing he had identified it. Woolgar criticizes Barnes for believing it. Rose and Harding criticize malestream science for failing to achieve it, while Flax questions Rose and Harding for believing in the possibility and desirability of such a position. Rather like the 'ideal speech situation' proposed as a pragmatic universal in the work of Jürgen Habermas (1984, 1987), 'reflexive epistemological diversity' is unachievable in ideal form, even while acting as a framework and benchmark in approaching disputes between forms of epistemological reduction and chicken.

The human condition, as 'language-using agents' (Habermas, 2003), resists instrumental and biological reduction. What makes us capable of social interaction is also what makes us through social interaction. It is this 'standpoint' that renders reductionism ethically and ontologically flawed. It is also the position from which resistance to such reduction emerges. In fact, it is this 'standpoint' as 'language-using agents' that forms the common point of departure for Marxists, critical of reification and alienation, and feminists, critical of the exclusion of women from the category of rational actor, and of the equating of rationality with instrumental rationality in male-dominated science. The 'standpoint' of 'language-using agents' is also the point of departure for social-interests theories attending to relations of social influence, cognitive and career interests, whether in terms of Harry Collins's use of Wittgenstein's language games, 'polymorphic action' and Polanyi's 'tacit knowledge', or in terms of Barry Barnes's attributions of responsibility as features of causal social influence among linguistic animals. Linguistic interaction is of course the central characteristic focused upon in the work of ethnographers and discourse analysts. All perspectives in the contemporary sociology of scientific knowledge agree that it the position of 'language-using agent' that makes human beings different from other animals and objects in ontological, epistemological and ethical terms.

It is this 'standpoint' as 'language-using agents' that enables and requires movement beyond the sociological reductionism of Mary Douglas, and the combination of sociological reduction and individualized adaptation found in Ulrich Beck. In today's so-called 'risk society', Ulrich Beck and Mary Douglas agree on one thing at least. Social specialization of institutional functions and personal roles has bred a differentiation of epistemological standpoints, throughout society and not just at the level of designated 'expert authorities'. While Douglas seeks to rekindle a centring authority, the return to deference by traditional means, this route seems permanently barred. In this respect Beck is right to suggest that recognition of epistemological diversity is unavoidable and necessary in the creation of a democratic, participatory and sustainable future society. However, his calls for a new 'reflexive modernity' lack clarity and substance with regard to the means of achieving it (see David and Wilkinson 2002). Reflexivity alone represents little more than an invitation to adapt to the range of existing authorities, even if we are witnessing the emergence of a greater number of competing elites. Delanty (2002) is correct to criticize the advocacy of such 'reflexivity' as is found in the work of advocates of 'the third way'. It is important to distinguish between the reflexivity of adjustment and a reflexivity that seeks to challenge the hierarchy of knowledge and authority more fundamentally, even while challenge to the exclusive and general validity of scientific knowledge should not be taken to represent and absolute rejection of the value of expertise, science and authoritative knowledge. A careful examination of competing authority claims, from within science, from within the sociology of science, and from the voices of those whose expertise comes from non-authoritative experience (exploitation, parenting, experiencing impairment, discrimination etc.) allows for something more than elite pluralism. Douglas and Beck offer differing accounts of sociological determinism, even if Beck goes on to suggest how best to adapt individually, while Douglas wishes for a return. Attention to the intersubjective achievement of social life requires that researchers bring together work upon social life at all levels of abstraction, from language in one-to-one interaction to wider relations of power and social interests. Attention to the intersubjective achievement of social life also requires abandoning the binary distinction of agency and structure, as well as the insularity of attention only to micro-interaction or macro-structures. In the sociology of science this means a move beyond the separation of 'internalist' and 'externalist' approaches.

The ongoing scientification of technology should not blind us to the fact that science remains a sub-field of technology, of knowledge geared towards a form of understanding oriented towards 'grasping' reality in ways that cannot be detached from particular forms of social interest, constructions of power and instrumental control. While complex and multi-dimensional, science looks from a location that is social. It has a social standpoint as it were. The history of science (and its facts), alongside the wider history of technology (and its artefacts), is a history of power, but power is contradictory and witness to many conflicts. Facts and artefacts have interpretations and affordances, scope for reflexivity in thought and action. As Gernot Böhme points out (Chapter 3), there can be no 'good' science (in the ethical sense) outside a good society. Science can only answer the questions it is resourced to ask, and answer in ways influenced by the orientations established in those questions and by those asking. As science will change to reflect the priorities of the society it is a part of, so it will reflect, and be a part of, the conflicts within any society (see David 1996):

> When we open our atlases, we find a number of diverse maps of the world. They analyse that world in different ways and answer different kinds of questions about it. These maps do not need to compete for the prize of being called the most fundamental. It is just as true to say that 'the world consists' of lands and oceans, or of climatic zones, as that it consists of the territories of different nations, and so on. It is also as true to say any of these things as to say that it consists of physical particles in fields of force ... There is no bottom line. Our choice of terms depends on the purpose for which we want to analyse the world at the time. (Midgley 1996:512)

Midgley provides a compelling argument for abandoning reductionism and idealism/relativism, in favour of a form of 'epistemological diversity'. While the world may be unified in a fundamental ontological sense, this is not to say either that we have a single best method for accessing all aspects of such a reality, or that there will ever be such a singular best approach. However, by itself, Midgley's account goes only as far as 'epistemological diversity'. The 'purposes for which we want to analyse the world' are not questioned, and so the validity of each page in the atlas is not critically reflected upon. 'Reflexive epistemological diversity' moves beyond complementary pluralism towards a more critical engagement between accounts.

It is not enough to stack up accounts of why the frog jumped into the pond, or of pages in an atlas. The four traditions in the contemporary sociology of scientific knowledge provide insights, but considerable insularity has inhibited developments. Chapters 8, 9 and 10 demonstrated the value of multiple approaches to specific issues, and of the value of combining approaches. However, tensions and limits are equally important to note, both in the production of definitive 'truth' and in defining the meaning of 'domination', 'freedom' and 'ethical action'. 'Reflexive epistemological diversity' (RED) combines forms of relativism and realism. RED allows many voices, values dialogue and respects competing epistemologies, even while encouraging a sceptical questioning of all such standpoints. Nevertheless, 'reflexive epistemological diversity' cannot say what is true and false, or decide what is right and wrong. We will have to do that for ourselves, together. 'Reflexive epistemological diversity' builds upon and highlights the intersubjective condition of 'language using agents'. Frogs can't exercise 'reflexive epistemological diversity'. If they could, they might get together and give the snake a different answer.

# References

Adorno, Theodor and Horkheimer, Max (1979[original 1944]) *Dialectic of Enlightenment*, London, Verso.

Allan, Stuart (2002), *Media, Risk and Science*, Buckingham, Open University Press.

Almas, Reidar (1999), 'Food Trust, Ethics and Safety in Risk Society', *Sociological Research Online*, 4, no. 3, http://www.socresonline.org.uk/socresonline/4/3/almas.html accessed 10 April 2003.

Anderson, Alison (1997), *Media, Culture and the Environment*, University College London Press.

Anderson, Alison (2002), 'In Search of the Holy Grail: Media Discourse and the New Human Genetics', *New Genetics and Society*, 21 (3), 327–37.

Arendt, Hannah (1963), *Eichmann in Jerusalem: A Report on the Banality of Evil*, New York, Viking.

Aronowitz, Stanley (1988), *Science as Power*, Minneapolis, University of Minnesota Press.

Aronowitz, Stanley (1996), 'The Politics of the Science Wars', in Ross, Andrew (ed.) *Science Wars*, Durham, Duke University Press, 202–25.

Aronowitz, Stanley (1997), 'Alan Sokal's "Transgression"', *Dissent*, Winter, 107–10.

Ashman, Keith M. and Baringer, Philip S. (eds) (2001), *After the Science Wars*, London, Routledge.

Bailey, R. (1996), 'Prenatal Testing and the Prevention of Impairment: A Woman's Right to Choose?', in Morris, J. (ed.), *Encounters with Strangers: Feminism and Disability*, London, Women's Press, 143–67.

Barber, Bernard (1961), 'Resistance by scientists to scientific discovery', *Science*, 134 (3479), 596–602.

Barkow, J. H., Cosmides L. and Tooby J. (1992), *The Adapted Mind: Evolutionary Psychology and the Generation of Culture*, Oxford University Press.

Barnes, Barry (ed.) (1972a), *Sociology of Science*, London, Penguin.

Barnes, Barry (1972b), 'On the Reception of Scientific Beliefs', in Barnes (1972a), 269–91.

Barnes, Barry (1974), *Scientific Knowledge and Sociological Theory*, London, Routledge & Kegan Paul.

Barnes, Barry (1977), *Interests and the Growth of Knowledge*, London, Routledge.

Barnes, Barry (1999), 'Biotechnology as Expertise', in O'Mahony, Patrick (ed.), *Nature, Risk and Responsibility: Discourses of Biotechnology*, London, Macmillan, 52–66.

Barnes, Barry (2000), *Understanding Agency: Social Theory and Responsible Action*, London, Sage.

Barnes, Barry (2002), 'Genes, Agents and the Institution of Responsible Action', *New Genetics and Society*, 21 (3), 291–302.

Barnes, Barry, Bloor, David and Henry, John (1996), *Scientific Knowledge: A Sociological Analysis*, London, Athlone.

Barnes, Barry and MacKenzie, Donald (1979), 'On the Role of Interests in Scientific Change', in Wallis, R. (ed.), *On the Margins of Science: The Social Construction of Rejected Knowledge*, University of Keele, *Sociological Review Monograph*, no. 27, 49–66.

Barnes, Barry and Shapin, Steven (1979), *Natural Order: Historical Studies of Scientific Culture*, London, Sage.

Barrett, Katherine and Abergel, Elisabeth (2002), 'Defining a Safe Genetically Modified Organism: Boundaries of Scientific Risk Assessment', *Science and Public Policy*, 29 (1), 47–58.

Bauman, Zygmunt (1989), *Modernity and the Holocaust*, Cambridge, Polity.

Bauman, Zygmunt (1991), *Modernity and Ambivalence*, Cambridge, Polity.

Bauman, Zygmunt (1992), *Mortality, Immortality and Other Life Strategies*, Cambridge, Polity.

Bauman, Zygmunt (1993), *Postmodern Ethics*, Oxford, Blackwell.

Beck, Ulrich (1992), *Risk Society: Towards a New Modernity*, London, Sage.

Beck, Ulrich (1995a), *Ecological Enlightenment*, Atlantic Highlands, NJ, Humanities Press International.

Beck, Ulrich (1995b), *Ecological Politics in an Age of Risk*, Cambridge, Polity.

Beck, Ulrich (1996), 'Risk Society and the Provident State', in Lash, Scott, Szerszynski, Bronislaw and Wynne, Brian (eds), *Risk, Environment and Modernity: Towards a New Ecology*, London, Sage, 27–43.

Beck, Ulrich (1997), *The Reinvention of Politics*, Cambridge, Polity.

Beck, Ulrich (1998), *Democracy without Enemies*, Cambridge, Polity.

Beck, Ulrich, Giddens, Anthony and Lash, Scott (1994) *Reflexive Modernization*, Cambridge, Polity.

Ben-David, Joseph and Collins, Randall (1966), 'Social Factors in the Origins of a New Science: The Case of Psychology', *American Sociological Review*, XXXI, 451–65.

Benton, Ted (2000), 'Evolutionary Psychology and Social Science', *Advances in Human Ecology*, 8, 65–98.

Bernal, John Desmond (1964 [original 1939]), *The Social Function of Science*, Cambridge, MA, MIT Press.

Bijker, Wiebe E., Hughes, Thomas P. and Pinch, Trevor (eds) (1989), *The Social Construction of Technological Systems: New Directions in the Sociology and History of Technology*, Cambridge, MA, MIT Press.

Bloch, Marc (1967), *Land and Work in Medieval Europe*, London, Routledge & Kegan Paul.

Bloor, David (1976) *Knowledge and Social Imagery*, London, Routledge & Kegan Paul.

Bodenheimer, Thomas (1985), 'The Transnational Pharmaceutical Industry and the Health of the World's People', in McKinlay, John B. (ed.), *Issues in the Political Economy of Health Care*, London, Tavistock, 187–216.

Böhme, Gernot (1977), 'Cognitive Norms, Knowledge-Interests and the Construction of the Scientific Object: A Case Study in the Functioning of Rules of Experimentation', in Mendelsohn *et al.* 129–42.

Böhme, Gernot (1979), 'Alternatives in Science – Alternatives to Science?', in Nowotny and Rose, 105–25.

Böhme, Gernot and Stehr, Nico (1986), 'The Growing Impact of Scientific Knowledge on Social Relations', in Böhme, Gernot and Stehr, Nico (eds), *The Knowledge Society: The Growing Impact of Scientific Knowledge on Social Relations*, Sociology of the Sciences Yearbook X, Boston, Reidel, 7–29.

Böhme, Gernot, Van Den Daele, Wolfgang and Krohn, Wolfgang (1978), 'The Scientification of Technology', in Krohn *et al.*, 219–50.

Bordo, Susan (1990) 'Reading the Slender Body', in Jacobus *et al.* 83–112.

Broberg, Gunnar and Roll-Hansen, Nils (eds) (1996), *Eugenics and the Welfare State: Sterilization Policy in Denmark, Sweden, Norway and Finland*, East Lansing, Michigan State University Press.

Browne, Kingsley (1998a), *Divided Labours: An Evolutionary View of Women at Work*, London, Weidenfeld & Nicolson.

Browne, Kingsley (1998b), 'Segregation of the Sexes is Here to Stay', in *The Financial Times*, Weekend FT iv, 10/11 October.

Buttel, Fred (1999), 'Agricultural Biotechnology: Its Recent Evolution and Implications for Agrofood Political Economy', *Sociological Research Online*, 4, 3, http://www.socresonline.org.uk/socresonline/4/3/buttel.html accessed 10 April 2003.

Byne, William (1994), 'The Biological Evidence Challenged', in *Scientific American*, 270 (May), 50–5.

Callon, Michel (1989), 'Society in the Making: The Study of Technology as a Tool for Sociological Analysis', in Bijker *et al.*, 83–103.

Chalmers, Alan (1982), *What Is This Thing Called Science?*, 2nd edn, Milton Keynes, Open University Press.

Chalmers, Alan (1990), *Science and Its Fabrication*, Milton Keynes, Open University Press.

Cole, Jonathan (1979), *Fair Science: Women in the Scientific Community*, New York, Free Press.

Collins, Harry (1981), 'What is TRASP? The Radical Programme in the Sociology of Scientific Knowledge', *Philosophy of the Social Sciences*, 11, 215–24.

Collins, Harry (1985), *Changing Order*, London, Sage.

Collins, Harry and Evans, Robert (2002), 'The Third Wave of Science Studies: Studies of Expertise and Experience', *Social Studies of Science*, 32 (2), 235–96.

Collins, Harry and Evans, Robert (2003), 'King Canute Meets the Beach Boys', *Social Studies of Science*, 33 (3), 435–52.

Collins, Harry and Pinch, Trevor (1993), *The Golem: What Everyone Should Know About Science*, Cambridge University Press.

Collins, Harry and Pinch, Trevor (1998a), *The Golem: What You Should Know About Science*, 2nd edn, Cambridge University Press.

Collins, Harry and Pinch, Trevor (1998b), *The Golem at Large: What You Should Know About Technology*, Cambridge University Press.

Collins, Harry and Yearley, Stephen (1992), 'Epistemological Chicken', in Pickering, Andrew (ed.), *Science as Practice and Culture*, University of Chicago Press, 17–46.

Conrad, Peter (1997), 'Public Eyes and Private Genes: Historical Frames, News Constructions, and Social Problems', *Social Problems*, 44 (2), 139–54.

Conrad, Peter (1999), 'A Mirage of Genes', *Sociology of Health and Illness*, 21 (2), 228–41.

Cooperstock, R. (1971), 'Sex Differences in the Use of Mood-modifying Drugs: An Explanatory Model', *Journal of Health and Social Behaviour*, 12, 238–44.

Cowan, Ruth Schwartz (1968), 'Sir Francis Galton and the Continuity of Germ Plasm: A Biological Idea with Political Roots', *Actes du XII Congrès International d'Histoire des Sciences*, 8, 181–6.

Cowan, Ruth Schwartz (1972), 'Francis Galton's Statistical Ideas: The Influence of Eugenics', *Isis*, 63, 509–28.

Dake, K. (1992), 'Characterizing the Public: Myths of Nature: Culture and the Social Construction of Risk', *Journal of Social Issues*, 48 (4), 21–39.

Daly, Martin and Wilson, Margo (1998), *The Truth About Cinderella: A Darwinian View of Parental Love*, London, Weidenfeld & Nicolson.

David, Matthew (1996), 'Information: Culture or Capital?', *Radical Philosophy*, 79 (Sept.–Oct.), 56.

David, Matthew (2002a), 'Problems of Participation: The Limits of Action Research', *International Journal of Social Research Methods: Theory and Practice*, 5 (1), 11–17.

David, Matthew (2002b), 'The Sociological Critique of Evolutionary Psychology: Beyond Mass Modularity', *New Genetics and Society*, 21 (3), 303–13.

David, Matthew (2003), 'The Politics of Communication: Information Technology, Local Knowledge and Social Exclusion', *Telematics and Informatics*, 20 (3), 235–53.

David, Matthew and Wilkinson, Iain (2002), 'Critical Theory or Self-Critical Society', *Critical Horizons*, 3 (1), 131–58.

David, Matthew and Zeitlyn, David (1996), 'What Are They Doing? Dilemmas in Analysing Bibliographic Searching: Cultural and Technical Networks in Academic Life', *Sociological Research Online*, 1, 4 http://www.socresonline.org.uk/socresonline/1/4/2.html accessed 31 October 2003.

Davies, Kevin (2001), *The Sequence: Inside the Race for the Human Genome*, London, Phoenix.

Delanty, Gerard (1999), 'Biopolitics in the Risk Society: The Possibility of a Global Ethic of Societal Responsibility', in O'Mahony, Patrick (ed.), *Nature, Risk and Responsibility: Discourses of Biotechnology*, London, Macmillan, 37–51.

Delanty, Gerard (2001), *Challenging Knowledge: The University in the Knowledge Society*, Buckingham, Open University Press.

Delanty, Gerard (2002), 'Constructivism, Sociology and the New Genetics', *New Genetics and Society*, 21 (3), 279–89.

De Solla Price (1963) *See* Price (1963).

Dickens, Peter (1996), *Reconstructing Nature: Alienation, Emancipation and the Division of Labour*, London, Routledge.

Dickens, Peter (2000), *Social Darwinism*, Milton Keynes, Open University Press.

Dickens, Peter (2001), 'Linking the Social and Natural Sciences: Is Capital Modifying Human Biology in its Own Image?', *Sociology*, 35 (1), 93–110.

Dickens, Peter (2004), *Society and Nature*, Cambridge, Polity.

Douglas, Jack (1967), *The Social Meaning of Suicide*, Princeton University Press.

Douglas, Mary (1978), *Cultural Bias*, London, Royal Anthropological Institute, Occasional Paper no. 35.

Douglas, Mary (1991[original 1966]), *Purity and Danger: An Analysis of the Concepts of Pollution and Taboo*, London, Routledge.

Douglas, Mary (1994), *Risk and Blame: Essays in Cultural Theory*, London, Routledge.

Douglas, Mary (1996), *Thought Styles*, London, Sage.

Douglas, Mary and Wildavsky, Aaron (1982), *Risk and Culture: An Essay on the Selection of Technical and Environmental Dangers*, Berkeley, University of California Press.

Durkheim, Emile (1982[original 1895]), *The Rules of Sociological Method*, London, Macmillan.

Durkheim, Emile (1989[original 1897]), *Suicide*, London, Routledge.

Durkheim, Emile (1995[original 1912]), *The Elementary Forms of Religious Life*, New York, Free Press.

Dutton, William H. (ed.) (1999), *Society on the Line: Information Politics in the Digital Age*, Oxford University Press.

Eagle Russett, Cynthia (1991), *Sexual Science: The Victorian Construction of Womanhood*, Boston, MA, Harvard University Press.

Edwards, Jeanette (2002), 'Taking "Public Understanding" Seriously', *New Genetics and Society*, 21 (3), 315–27.

Engels, Frederick (1940), *Dialectics of Nature*, London, Lawrence & Wishart.

Engels, Frederick (1988), 'Socialism: Utopian and Scientific', in McLellan, David (ed.), *Marxism: Essential Writings*, Oxford University Press, 62–9.

Ettorre, Elizabeth (1999), 'Experts as Genetic Storytellers: Exploring Key Issues', *Sociology of Health and Illness*, 21 (5), 539–59.

Ettorre, Elizabeth (2000), 'Reproductive Genetics, Gender and the Body: "Please Doctor, May I Have a Normal Baby?"', *Sociology*, 34 (3), 403–20.

Ettorre, Elizabeth (ed.) (2001), *Before Birth: Understanding Prenatal Screening*, London, Ashgate.

Ettorre, Elizabeth (2002), *Reproductive Genetics: Gender and the Body*, London, Routledge.

Ettorre, Elizabeth and Riska, Elianna (1995), *Gendered Moods: Psychotropics and Society*, London, Routledge.

Etzkowitz, Henry, Kemelger, Carol and Uzzi, Brian (2000) *Athena Unbound: The Advancement of Women in Science and Technology*, Cambridge University Press.

EU Report (2000) *Science Policies in the European Union: Promoting Excellence through Mainstreaming Gender Equality*, Brussels, European Commission.

Evans, Rob (2002), 'Whitehall Admits GM Foe was "Martyred"', *The Guardian*, 22 June.

Eyerman, Ron and Jamison, Andrew (1991), *Social Movements: A Cognitive Approach*, Cambridge, Polity.

Firestone, Shulamith (1970), *The Dialectic of Sex*, New York, Morrow.

Flynn, Laurie, Gillard, Michael and Rowell, Andy (1999), 'Ousted Scientist and the Damning Research into Food Safety', *The Guardian*, 12 February.

Fodor, Jerry (1983), *The Modularity of Mind*, Cambridge, MA, MIT Press.

Fodor, Jerry (2000), *In Critical Condition*, Cambridge, MA, MIT Press.

Forman, Paul (1971), 'Weimar Culture, Causality and Quantum Theory, 1918–1927: Adaptation of German Physicists and Mathematicians to a Hostile Environment', *Historical Studies in the Physical Sciences*, 3, 1–115.

Fortun, Michael (2001), 'Mediated Speculations in the Genomics Futures Markets', *New Genetics and Society*, 20 (2), 139–56.

Franck, Robert (1979), 'Knowledge and Opinions', in Nowotny and Rose, 39–56.

Freeman, Chris (1999), 'The Social Function of Science', in Swann and Aprahamian, 101–31.

Freudenthal, Gideon (1986), *Atom and Individual in the Age of Newton: On the Genesis of the Mechanistic World View*, New York, Kluwer.

Fukuyama, Francis (2002), *Our Posthuman Future: Consequences of the Biotechnology Revolution*, London, Profile.

Fuller, Steve (1997), *Science*, Milton Keynes, Open University Press.

Fuller, Steve (2000), *Thomas Kuhn: A Philosophical History for our Times*, University of Chicago Press.

Garfinkel, Harold (1967), *Studies in Ethnomethodology*, Englewood Cliffs, NJ, Prentice-Hall.

Gerth, H. H. and Mills, C. Wright (eds) (1991), *From Max Weber: Essays in Sociology*, London, Routledge.

Gigerenzer G., Todd P. M. and the ABC Research Group (1999), *Simple Heuristics that Make Us Smart*, Oxford University Press.

Gilbert, Nigel and Mulkay, Michael (1984), *Opening Pandora's Box: A Sociological Analysis of Scientist's Discourse*, Cambridge University Press.

Gillard, Michael Sean, Flynn, Laurie and Rowell, Andy (1999), 'Food Scandal Exposed', *The Guardian*, 12 February.

Glover, Judith (2000), *Women and Scientific Employment*, Basingstoke, Macmillan.

Gofton, Les and Haimes, Erica (1999), 'Necessary Evil? Opening Up Closings in Sociology and Biotechnology', *Sociological Research Online*, 4, 3, http://www.socresonline.org.uk/socresonline/4/3/gofton.html accessed 10 April 2003.

Goldsmith, Maurice (1980), *Sage: A Life of J. D. Bernal*, London, Hutchinson.

Gould, Steven Jay (1996[original 1981]), *The Mismeasure of Man*, London, Penguin.

Gouldner, Alvin (1976), *The Dialectic of Ideology and Technology: The Origins, Grammar and Future of Ideology*, London, Macmillan.

Gouldner, Alvin (1979), *The Future of Intellectuals and the Rise of the New Class*, New York, Macmillan.

Greenfield, Susan (1996) 'Comment', *The Independent on Sunday*, 26 May.

*Guardian, The* (1999a), 'Food Scandal: Chronology', 12 February.

*Guardian, The* (1999b), 'Pusztai "To Be Vindicated"', 12 October.

Habermas, Jürgen (1971) *Towards a Rational Society*, London, Heinemann Educational.

Habermas, Jürgen (1972), *Knowledge and Human Interests*, London, Heinemann Educational.

Habermas, Jürgen (1979), *Communication and the Evolution of Society*, London, Heinemann Educational.

Habermas, Jürgen (1984), *The Theory of Communicative Action* (volume one), Cambridge, Polity.

Habermas, Jürgen (1987), *The Theory of Communicative Action* (volume two), Cambridge, Polity.

Habermas, Jürgen (2003), *The Future of Human Nature*, Cambridge, Polity.

Hagstrom, W. O. (1965), *The Scientific Community*, New York, Basic.

Hagstrom, W. O. (1972a), 'Gift-Giving as an Organizing Principle in Science', in Barnes, 105–20.

Hagstrom, W. O. (1972b), 'The Differentiation of Disciplines', in Barnes, 121–25.

Hallowell, Nina (1999), 'Doing the Right Thing: Genetic Risk and Responsibility', in Conrad, Peter and Gabe, Jonathan (eds), *Sociological Perspectives on the New Genetics*, Oxford, Blackwell, 97–120.

Hamer, D. H., Hu, S., Magnuson, V. L. and Pattatucci, A. M. L. (1993), 'The Linkage Between DNA Markers on the X Chromosome and Male Sexual Orientation', *Science*, 261 (16 July), 321–7.

Hanson, Sandra (1996) *Lost Talent: Women in the Sciences*, Philadelphia, Temple University Press.

Haraway, Donna (1990a), 'Investment Strategies for the Evolving Portfolio of Primate Females', in Jacobus *et al.*, 139–62.

Haraway, Donna (1990b), *Primate Visions: Gender, Race, and Nature in the World of Modern Science*, London, Routledge.

Haraway, Donna J. (1991) *Simians, Cyborgs and Women: The Reinvention of Nature*, London, Free Association.

Haraway, Donna (1997), *Modest Witness @ Second Millennium FemaleMan Meets Onco Mouse: Feminism and Technoscience*, London, Routledge.

Harding, Sandra (1986), *The Science Question in Feminism*, Buckingham, Open University Press.

Harding, Sandra (1991) *Whose Science? Whose Knowledge? Thinking from Women's Experience*, Buckingham, Open University Press.

Hartsock, Nancy (1984), *Money, Sex and Power*, Boston, MA, Northeastern University Press.

Harvey, Mark (1999), 'Cultivation and Comprehension: How Genetic Modification Irreversibly Alters the Human Engagement with Nature', in *Sociological Research Online*, 4, 3, http://www.socresonline.org.uk/socresonline/4/3/harvey.html accessed 10 April 2003.

Heidegger, Martin (1978), *Basic Writings* (ed. David Farell Krell), London, Routledge, Kegan & Paul.

Heller, Chiai (2002), 'From Scientific Risk to Paysan Savoir-Faire: Peasant Expertise in the French and Global Debate over GM Crops', *Science as Culture*, 11 (1), 5–38.

Henwood, Flis, Plumeridge, Sarah and Stepulevage, Linda (2000), 'A Tale of Two Cultures? Gender and Inequality in Computer Education', in Wyatt, Sally, Henwood, Flis, Miller, Nod and Senker, Peter (eds) *Technology and In/equality: Questioning the Information Society*, London, Routledge, 111–28.

Herrnstein, Richard and Murrey, Charles (1994), *The Bell Curve: The Reshaping of American Life by Difference in Intelligence*, New York, Free Press.

Hessen, Boris (1931[reprinted 1971]), 'The Social and Economic Roots of Newton's Principia', in Bukharin, Nikolai *et al.* (eds), *Science at the Crossroads*, London, Cass, 146–212.

Hobsbawm, Eric (1999) 'Preface', in Swann and Aprahamian, ix–xx.

Hubbard, Ruth (1997), 'Abortion and Disability: Who Should and Who Should not Inhabit the World?', in Davis, Lennard (ed.), *The Disability Studies Reader*, New York, Routledge, 187–200.

Independent, The (2000), 'Europe and UK Hampering Third World's Fight on Aids', 5 December, 3.

Ingold, Tim (2000), 'Evolving Skills', in Rose and Rose, 225–46.

Irwin, Alan (2001), *Sociology and the Environment*, Cambridge, Polity.

Jacobsen, John Kurt (2000), *Technical Fouls: Democratic Dilemmas and Technological Change*, Oxford, Westview.

Jacobus, Mary (1990), 'In Parenthesis: Immaculate Conceptions and Feminine Desire', in Jacobus *et al.*, 11–28.

Jacobus, Mary, Keller, Evelyn Fox and Shuttleworth, Sally (eds) (1990), *Body/Politics: Women and the Discourses of Science*, London, Routledge.

Jasanoff, Sheila (2003), 'Breaking the Waves in Science Studies', *Social Studies of Science*, 33 (3), 389–400.

Jensen, Arthur (1969), 'How Much Can We Boost IQ and Scholastic Achievement?', *Harvard Educational Review*, 39 (1), 1–123.

Jevons, F. R. (1969), *The Teaching of Science*, London, Allen & Unwin.

Jordanova, Ludmilla (1995), 'Women and Science – What Does History Have to Offer?', public lecture in the series 'Women and Science', University of York, 26 January.

Kamin, Leon (1974), *The Science and Politics of IQ*, Potomac, MD, Erlbaum.

Karmiloff-Smith, Annette (1992), *Beyond Modularity: A Developmental Perspective on Cognitive Science*, Cambridge, MA, MIT Press.

Karmiloff-Smith, Annette (2000), 'Why Babies' Brains Are Not Swiss Army Knives', in Rose and Rose, 129–43.

Keller, Evelyn Fox (1983) *A Feeling for the Organism: The Life and Work of Barbara McClintock*, San Francisco, CA, Freeman.

Keller, Evelyn Fox (1990) 'From Secrets of Life to Secrets of Death', in Jacobus *et al.*, 177–91.

Keller, Evelyn Fox (1993), *Secrets of Life, Secrets of Death: Essays on Gender, Language and Science*, London, Routledge.

Kellner, Douglas (1984), *Herbert Marcuse and the Crisis of Marxism*, London, Macmillan.

Kellner, Douglas (2001), *The Postmodern Adventure: Science, Technology and Cultural Studies at the Third Millennium*, London, Routledge.

Kelves, Daniel (1985), *In the Name of Eugenics: Genetics and the Uses of Human Heredity*, New York, Knopf.

Kerr, Anne and Cunningham-Burley, Sarah (2000), 'On Ambivalence and Risk: Reflexive Modernity and the New Human Genetics', *Sociology*, 34 (2), 283–304.

Kerr, Anne, Cunningham-Burley, Sarah and Amos, Amanda (1997), 'The New Genetics: Professionals' Discourse Boundaries', *Sociological Review*, 45 (2), 279–303.

Kerr, Anne, Cunningham-Burley, Sarah and Amos, Amanda (1998a), 'The New Genetics and Health: Mobilising Lay Expertise', *Public Understanding of Science*, 7, 41–60.

Kerr, Anne, Cunningham-Burley, Sarah and Amos, Amanda (1998b), 'Eugenics and the New Genetics in Britain: Examining Contemporary Professionals' Accounts in Science', *Technology and Human Values*, 23 (2), 175–98.

Kirkup, Gill and Smith Keller, Laurie (eds) (1992), *Inventing Women – Science, Technology and Gender*, Buckingham, Open University Press.

Kohler Riessman, Catherine (1992) 'Women and Medicalization', in Kirkup and Smith Keller, 123–44.

Krohn, Wolfgang, Layton, Edwin T., Jr and Weingart, Peter (eds) (1978), *The Dynamics of Science and Technology*, Sociology of the Sciences Yearbook II, Dordrecht, Reidel.

Kuhl, Steven (1994), *The Nazi Connection: Eugenics, American Racism and German National Socialism*, New York, Open University Press.

Kuhn, Thomas (1962), *The Structure of Scientific Revolutions*, University of Chicago Press.

Kuhn, Thomas (1970), *The Structure of Scientific Revolutions*, 2nd enlarged edn, University of Chicago Press.

Küppers, Gunter (1978), 'On the Relation Between Technology and Science – Goals of Knowledge and Dynamics of Theories. The Example of Combustion Technology, Thermodynamics, and Fluidmechanics', in Krohn *et al.*, 112–33.

Lane, Nancy (1997), 'Women in Science, Engineering and Technology: The Rising Tide Report and Beyond', in Maynard, 37–54.

Latour, Bruno (1999), 'On Recalling ANT', in Law, John and Hassard, John (eds), *Actor Network Theory and After*, Oxford, Blackwell, 15–25.

Latour, Bruno and Woolgar, Steve (1979), *Laboratory Life: The Social Construction of Scientific Facts*, London, Sage.

Latour, Bruno and Woolgar, Steve (1986), *Laboratory Life: The Construction of Scientific Facts*, 2nd edn, London, Sage.

Law, John (1999), 'After ANT: Complexity, Naming and Topology', in Law, John and Hassard, John (eds), *Actor Network Theory and After*, Oxford, Blackwell, 1–14.

Levidow, Les (2001a), 'Utilitarian Bioethics? Market Fetishism in the GM Crops Debate', *New Genetics and Society*, 20 (1), 75–84.

Levidow, Les (2001b), 'Precautionary Uncertainty: Regulating GM Crops in Europe', *Social Studies of Science*, 31 (6), 842–74.

Lewontin, R. C. (1993), *The Doctrine of DNA: Biology as Ideology*, London, Penguin.

Lewontin, Richard and Levins, Richard (1976), 'The Problem of Lysenkoism', in Rose and Rose (1976d), 32–64.

Lukács, Georg (1971[original 1919]), *History and Class Consciousness*, London, Merlin.

Lupton, Deborah (1999a), *Risk*, London, Routledge.

Lupton, Deborah (1999b), *Risk and Sociocultural Theory: New Directions and Perspectives*, Cambridge University Press.

Lyotard, Jean-François (1986[original 1979]), *The Postmodern Condition: A Report on Knowledge*, Manchester University Press.

MacKenzie, Donald (1978), 'Statistical Theory and Social Interests: A Case Study', *Social Studies of Science*, 8, 35–83.

MacKenzie, Donald (1988), 'Stellar-Intertial Guidance: A Study in the Sociology of Military Technology', in Mendelsohn, Everett, Roe Smith, Merritt and Weingart, Peter (eds), *Science, Technology and the Military*, Sociology of the Sciences Yearbook XII, Boston, Klewer, 187–241.

MacKenzie, Donald and Wajcman, Judy (eds) (1999), *The Social Shaping of Technology* (2nd edn), Buckingham, Open University Press.

McKie, Robin (1999), 'Why Britain's Scientific Establishment Got so Ratty with a Gentle Boffin', *The Observer*, 17 October.

McLachlan, H. and Swales, J. K. (1980), 'Witchcraft and Anti-feminism', *The Scottish Journal of Sociology*, 4 (2), 141–66.

McLaren, Angus (1990), *Our Own Master Race: Eugenics in Canada 1885–1945*, Toronto, McClelland & Stewart.

Macnaghten, Phil and Urry, John (1998), *Contested Natures*, London, Sage.

Malecki, Ignacy and Olszewski, Eugeniusz (1972), 'Regularities in the Development of Contemporary Science', in Barnes, 147–65.

Mannheim, Karl (1960 [original 1928]), *Ideology and Utopia: An Introduction to the Sociology of Knowledge*, London, Routledge & Kegan Paul.

Marcuse, Herbert (1941), *Reason and Revolution: Hegel and the Rise of Social Theory*, London, Oxford University Press.

Marcuse, Herbert (1969a[original 1955]), *Eros and Civilisation*, London, Abacus.

Marcuse, Herbert (1969b), *An Essay on Liberation*, Boston, MA, Beacon Press.

Marcuse, Herbert (1972), *Counterrevolution and Revolt*, Boston, MA, Beacon Press.

Marcuse, Herbert (1991 [originally published in 1964]), *One Dimensional Man*, London, Routledge.

Martin, Emily (1990) 'Science and Women's Bodies: Forms of Anthropological Knowledge', in Jacobus *et al.*, 69–82.

Martin, Paul (1999), 'Genes as Drugs: The Social Shaping of Gene Therapy and the Reconstruction of Genetic Disease', in Conrad, Peter and Gabe, Jonathan (eds), *Sociological Perspectives on the New Genetics*, Oxford, Blackwell, 15–35.

Marx, Karl (1976), *Preface and Introduction to a Contribution to the Critique of Political Economy*, Peking, Foreign Languages Press.

Marx, Karl (1978), *The Eighteenth Brumaire of Louis Bonaparte*, Peking, Foreign Languages Press.

Marx, Karl (1999), 'The Machine versus the Worker', in MacKenzie and Wajcman, 156–7.

Marx, Karl and Engels, Fredrick (1970), *The German Ideology*, student edn, London, Lawrence & Wishart.

Marx, Karl and Engels, Fredrick (1971[original 1948]), *Manifesto of the Communist Party*, Moscow, Progress.

Mason, David, Button, Graham, Lankshear, Gloria and Coates, Sally (2002a), 'Getting Real about Surveillance and Privacy at Work', in Woolgar, 137–52.

Mason, David, Button, Graham, Lankshear, Gloria, Coates, Sally and Sharrock, Wes (2002b), 'On the Poverty of Apriorism: Technology, Surveillance in the Workplace and Employee Responses', *Information, Communication and Society*, 5 (4), 555–72.

Mason, Peter (1999), 'Science in History', in Swann and Aprahamian, 255–67.

Maynard, Mary (ed.) (1997), *Science and the Construction of Women*, University College London Press, 1997.

Mendelsohn, Everett, Weingart, Peter and Whitley, Richard (eds) (1977) *The Social Production of Scientific Knowledge*, Sociology of the Sciences Yearbook I, Dordrecht, Reidel.

Merchant, Carolyn (1980), *The Death of Nature: Women, Ecology and the Scientific Revolution*, New York, Harper & Row.

Merton, Robert (1970[original 1938]), *Science, Technology and Society in Seventeenth Century England*, New York, Harper & Row.

Merton, Robert (1972[original 1942]), 'The Institutional Imperatives of Science', in Barnes, 65–79.

Midgley, Mary (1996), 'One World, But a Big One', *Journal of Consciousness Studies*, 3 (5–6), 500–14.

Mies, Maria and Shiva, Vandana (1993) *Ecofeminism*, London, Zed.

Milgram, Stanley (1997/original 1974), *Obedience to Authority: An Experimental View*, London, Pinter & Martin.

Miller, David (1995), 'Introducing the "Gay Gene": Media and Scientific Representations', *Public Understanding of Science*, 4, 269–84.

Mills, C. Wright (1959), *The Sociological Imagination*, New York, Oxford University Press.

Mithen, Steven (1996), *The Prehistory of the Mind*, London, Pheonix.

Morris, Jenny (ed.) (1991), *Pride against Prejudice: Transforming Attitudes Towards Disability*, London, Women's Press.

Morris Fedigan, Linda (1992), 'The Changing Role of Women in Models of Human Evolution', in Kirkup, Gill and Smith Keller, Laurie (eds), *Inventing Women – Science, Technology and Gender*, Milton Keynes, Open University Press, 103–22.

Moynihan, Ray (2003), 'The Making of a Disease: Female Sexual Dysfunction', *British Medical Journal*, 326 (4 January), 45–7.

Moynihan, Ray, Heath, Iona and Henry, David (2002), 'Selling Sickness: The Pharmaceutical Industry and Disease Mongering', *British Medical Journal*, 324 (13 April), 886–91.

Mulkay, Michael (1969), 'Some Aspects of Cultural Growth in the Natural Sciences', *Social Research*, 36, 1, 22–52 (abridged in Barnes 1972, 126–42).

Mulkay, Michael (1972), *The Social Process of Innovation*, London, Papermac.

Mulkay, Michael (1997), *The Embryo Research Debate: Science and the Politics of Reproduction*, Cambridge University Press.

Navarro, Vincente (1976), *Medicine Under Capitalism*, London, Croom Helm.

Navarro, Vincente (1985) 'The Crisis of the International Capitalist Order and Its Implications on the Welfare State', in McKinlay, John, B. (ed.), *Issues in the Political Economy of Health Care*, London, Tavistock, 107–40.

Nelkin, Dorethy (2000), 'Less Selfish than Sacred? Genes and the Religious Impulse in Evolutionary Psychology', in Rose and Rose 14–27.

Nerlich, Brigitte, Clarke, David D. and Dingwall, Robert (1999a), 'The Influence of Popular Cultural Imagery on Public Attitudes Towards Cloning', *Sociological Research Online*, 4, 3, http://www.socresonline.org.uk/socresonline/4/3/nerlich.html accessed 10 April 2003.

Nerlich, Brigitte, Dingwall, Robert and Clarke, David D. (1999b), 'The Book of Life: How the Completion of the Human Genome Project was Revealed to the Public', *Health: An Interdisciplinary Journal for the Social Study of Health, Illness and Medicine*, 6 (4), 445–69.

Newman, Elkie (1985), 'Who Controls Birth Control?', in Faulkner, Wendy and Arnold, Erik (eds), *Smothered By Invention; Technology in Women's Lives*, London, Pluto, 128–43.

Noble, David (1984), *Forces of Production: A Social History of Industrial Automation*, New York, Knopf.

Nowotny, Helga (1977), 'Scientific Purity and Nuclear Danger: The Case of Risk Assessment', in Mendelsohn *et al.*, 243–62.

Nowotny, Helga (1979), 'Science and its Critics: Reflections on Anti-Science', in Nowotny and Rose, 1–25.

Nowotny, Helga and Rose, Hilary (eds) (1979), *Countermovements in the Sciences*, Sociology of the Sciences Yearbook III, Dordrecht, Reidel.

Oliver, Michael (1995), *Understanding Disability*, London, Palgrave.

Orr, Deborah (2002), 'The Moral Consequences of This Baby Hunger', *The Independent*, 15 May, 5.

Peel, J. D. Y. (1969), 'Understanding Alien Belief Systems', *British Journal of Sociology*, 20, 69–84.

Petersen, Alan (1999a), 'The Portrayal of Research into Genetic-Based Differences of Sex and Sexual Orientation: A Study of "Popular" Science Journals, 1980–1997', *Journal of Communication Inquiry*, 23 (2), 163–82.

Petersen, Alan (1999b), 'Counselling the Genetically "At Risk": the Poetics and Politics of "Non-directiveness"', *Health, Risk and Society*, 1 (3), 253–65.

Petersen, Alan (2001), 'Biofantasies: Genetics and Medicine in the Print News Media', *Social Science and Medicine*, 52, 1255–68.

Petersen, Alan (2002), 'Replicating Our Bodies, Losing Our Selves: News Media Portrayals of Human Cloning in the Wake of Dolly', *Body and Society*, 8 (4), 71–90.

Petersen, Alan and Bunton, Robin (2002), *The New Genetics and the Public's Health*, London, Routledge.

Pilnick, Alison (2002), 'What "Most People" Do: Exploring the Ethical Implications of Genetic Counselling', *New Genetics and Society*, 21 (3), 339–50.

Pinch, Trevor and Bijker, Wiebe E. (1989), 'The Social Construction of Facts and Artifacts: Or How the Sociology of Science and the Sociology of Technology Might Benefit Each Other', in Bijker, Hughes and Pinch, 17–50.

Pinker Steven (1995), *The Language Instinct*, London, Penguin.

Pinker, Steven (1999), *How the Mind Works*, London, Penguin.

Pinker, Steven (2002), *The Blank Slate: The Modern Denial of Human Nature*, London, Penguin/Allen Lane.

Polanyi, M. (1957), *Personal Knowledge*, University of Chicago Press.

Poovey, M. (1990), 'Speaking of the Body: Mid-Victorian Constructions of Female Desire', in Jacobus *et al.*, 29–46.

Popper, Karl (1972), *Conjectures and Refutations*, London, Routledge & Kegan Paul.

Potter, Jonathan (1996), *Representing Reality: Discourse, Rhetoric and Social Construction*, London, Sage.

Price, Derek J. de Solla (1963), *Big Science, Little Science*, London, Macmillan.

Price, Derek J. de Solla (1972), 'Science and Technology: Distinctions and Interrelationships', in Barnes, 166–80.

Pynchon, Thomas (1973), *Gravity's Rainbow*, New York, Viking Compass.

Rabinow, Paul (1999), 'Artificiality and Enlightenment: From Sociobiology to Biosociality', in Biagioli, Mario (ed.), *The Science Studies Reader*, London, Routledge, 407–16.

Radford, Tim (1999a), 'Scientists Doubt GM Food Research', *The Guardian*, 19 May.

Radford, Tim (1999b), 'GM Research "Flawed in Design and Analysis"', *The Guardian*, 19 May.

Ravetz , Jerome (1973), *Scientific Knowledge and its Social Problems*, London, Penguin.

Reilly, Phillip R. (1991), *The Surgical Solution: A History of Involuntary Sterilization in the United States*, Baltimore, Johns Hopkins University Press.

Richards, Stewart (1987), *Philosophy and Sociology of Science: An Introduction*, Oxford, Blackwell.

Rip, Arie (2003), 'Constructing Expertise', *Social Studies of Science*, 33 (3), 419–34.

Rose, Hilary (1983), 'Hand, Brain and Heart: A Feminist Epistemology for the Natural Sciences', *Signs: Journal of Women in Culture and Society*, 9 (1), 73–90.

Rose, Hilary (1984), 'Is a Feminist Science Possible?', paper presented to MIT Women's Studies Program, April 1984.

Rose, Hilary (1994) *Love, Power and Knowledge: Towards a Feminist Transformation of the Sciences*, Cambridge, Polity Press.

Rose, Hilary (2000a), 'Colonising the Social Sciences?', in Rose and Rose, 106–28.

Rose, Hilary (2000b), 'Risk, Trust and Scepticism in the Age of the New Genetics', in Adam, Barbara Beck, Ulrich and Van Loon, Joost (eds), *The Risk Society and Beyond: Critical Issues for Social Theory*, London, Sage, 63–77.

Rose, Hilary and Rose, Steven (1970[original 1969]), *Science and Society*, London, Pelican.

Rose, Hilary and Rose, Steven (eds) (1976a), *The Political Economy of the Natural Sciences*, London, Macmillan.

Rose, Hilary and Rose, Steven (1976b), 'The Problematic Inheritance: Marx and Engels on the Natural Sciences', in Rose and Rose (1976a), 1–13.

Rose, Hilary and Rose, Steven (1976c), 'The Incorporation of Science', in Rose and Rose (1976a), 14–31.

Rose, Hilary and Rose, Steven (eds) (1976d), *The Radicalisation of Science*, London, Macmillan.

Rose, Hilary and Rose, Steven (1976e[original 1972]), 'The Radicalisation of Science', in Rose and Rose (1976d), 1–31.

Rose, Hilary and Rose, Steven (1999), 'Red Scientist: Two Strands from a Life in Three Colours', in Swann and Aprahamian, 132–59.

Rose, Hilary and Rose, Steven (2000), *Alas, Poor Darwin: Arguments against Evolutionary Psychology*, London, Cape.

Rose, Steven (1997), *Lifelines*, London, Penguin.

Rose, Steven, Lewontin, R. C. and Kamin, Leon (1984), *Not in Our Genes: Biology, Ideology and Human Nature*, London, Pelican.

Rothman, Barbara Katz (1998), *Genetic Maps and Human Imaginations: The Limits of Science in Understanding Who We Are*, New York, Norton.

Rothman, Barbara Katz (2001), *The Book of Life: A Personal and Ethical Guide to Race, Normality, and the Implications of the Human Genome Project*, London, Beacon Press.

Rozek, Theodore (1996), 'Dumbing Us Down', *New Internationalist*, 286, 12–14.

Sayre, Anne (2000[original 1975]), *Rosalind Franklin and DNA: A Vivid View of What It Is Like to Be a Gifted Women in an Especially Male Profession*, New York, Norton.

Schwartz, Michael and Thompson, Michael (1990), *Divided We Stand: Redefining Politics, Technology and Social Choice*, Hemel Hempstead, Harvester Wheatsheaf.

Sedgwick, E. K. (1994), *Epistemology of the Closet*, London, Penguin.

Shakespeare, Tom (1995), 'Back to the Future? New Genetics and Disabled People', *Critical Social Policy*, 44/5, 22–35.

Shakespeare, Tom (1998), 'Choices and Rights? Eugenics, Genetics and Disability Equality', *Disability and Society*, 13 (5), 665–81.

Shakespeare, Tom (1999), '"Losing the Plot"? Medical and Activist Discourses of Contemporary Genetics and Disability', in Conrad, Peter and Gabe, Jonathan (eds), *Sociological Perspectives on the New Genetics*, Oxford, Blackwell, 171–90.

Shaw, Alison (1999), '"What Are 'They' Doing to Our Food?": Public Concerns about Food in the UK', *Sociological Research Online*, 4, 3, http://www.socresonline.org.uk/socresonline/4/3/shaw.html accessed 10 April 2003.

Shiva, Vandana (1998), *Biopiracy: The Plunder of Nature and Knowledge*, Dartington, Green Books.

Shuttleworth, Sally (1990), 'Female Circulation: Medical Discourse and Popular Advertising in the Mid-Victorian Era', in Jacobus *et al.*, 47–68.

Silver, Lee (1998), *Remaking Eden: Cloning and Beyond in a Brave New World*, London, Weidenfeld & Nicholson.

Smith, David Norman (2001), 'The Stigma of Reason: Irrationalism as a Problem for Social Theory', in Ashman and Baringer, 151–182.

Sokal, Alan (1996), 'Transgressing the Boundaries: Towards a Transformative Hermeneutics of Quantum Gravity', *Social Text*, 46–7 (Spring/Summer), 217–52.

Sokal, Alan (1997), 'Alan Sokal Replies [to Stanley Aronowitz]', *Dissent*, Winter, 110–11.

Sokal, Alan (2001), 'What the Social Text Affair Does and Does Not Prove: A Critical Look at Science Studies', in Ashman and Baringer, 14–29.

Sokal, Alan and Bricmont, Jean (1998), *Intellectual Impostures: Postmodern Philosophers' Abuse of Science*, London, Profile.

Spengler, Oswald (1926), *The Decline of the West, Volume 1: Form and Actuality*, New York, Knopf.

Steinberg, Deborah Lynn (1997), *Bodies in Glass: Genetics, Eugenics, Embryo Ethics*, Manchester University Press.

Stepan, Nancy L. (1991), *In the Hour of Eugenics: Race, Gender and Nation in Latin America*, Ithaca, NY, Cornell University Press.

Stolte-Heiskanen, Victoria (ed.) (1991), *Women in Science – Token Women or Gender Equality?*, Oxford, Berg.

Stoppard, Janet M. (2000), *Understanding Depression: Feminist Social Constructionist Approaches*, London, Routledge.

Swann, Brenda (1999), 'Introduction', in Swann and Aprahamian, xxi–xxv.

Swann, Brenda and Aprahamian, Francis (eds) (1999) *J. D. Bernal: A Life in Science and Politics*, London, Verso.

Thompson, Lana (1999), *The Wandering Womb: A Cultural History of Outrageous Beliefs about Women*, New York, Prometheus.

Thomson, Matthew (1998), *The Problem of Mental Deficiency: Eugenics, Democracy and Social Policy in Britain 1870–1959*, Oxford, Clarendon.

Touraine, Alain (1971[original 1968]), *The Post-Industrial Society*, New York, Random House.

Treichler, Paula, A. (1990), 'Feminism, Medicine and the Meaning of Childbirth', in Jacobus *et al.*, 113–38.

Treichler, Paula A., Cartwright, Lisa and Penley, Constance (1998), *The Visible Woman: Imaging Technologies, Gender and Science*, New York University Press.

Tucker, William H. (1994), *The Science and Politics of Racial Research*, Champaign, University of Illinois Press.

Turner, Bryan (1987), *Medical Power and Social Knowledge*, London, Sage.

Turney, Jon (1998a), 'Curse of Frankenstein', *Times Higher Educational Supplement*, 3 April, 17.

Turney, Jon (1998b), *Frankenstein's Footsteps: Science, Genetics and Popular Culture*, New Haven, CT, Yale University Press.

Velikovsky, Immanuel (1950), *Worlds in Collision*, London, Macmillan.

Wajcman, Judy (1991), *Feminism Confronts Technology*, Cambridge, Polity.

Weber, Max (1930[original 1905]), *The Protestant Ethic and the Spirit of Capitalism*, London, George Allen & Unwin.

Weber, Max (1991a), 'Politics as a Vocation', in Gerth, H. H. and Mills, C. Wright (eds), 77–128.

Weber, Max (1991b), 'Science as a Vocation', in Gerth, H. H. and Mills, C. Wright (eds), 129–56.

Webster, Andrew (1991), *Science, Technology and Society*, London, Macmillan.

Weingart, Peter (1978), 'The Relation Between Science and Technology – A Sociological Explanation', in Krohn *et al.*, 251–86.

Wieder, D. Lawrence (1974), *Language and Social Reality: The Telling of the Convict Code*, The Hague, Mouton.

Wilkinson, Iain (2001), *Anxiety in a Risk Society*, London, Routledge.

Wolpert, Lewis (1992), *The Unnatural Nature of Science*, London, Faber.

Woods, Alan and Grant, Ted (1995), *Marxist Philosophy and Modern Science*, London, Wellred.

Woolgar, Steve (1981), 'Interests and Explanation in the Social Study of Science', *Social Studies of Science*, 11, 365–94.

Woolgar, Steve (1988), *Science: The Very Idea*, London, Tavistock.

Woolgar, Steve (ed.) (2002), *Virtual Reality? Technology, Cyberbole, Reality*, Oxford University Press.

Wynne, Brian (1996a), 'May the Sheep Safely Graze? A Reflexive View of the Expert-Lay Knowledge Divide', in Lash, Scott, Szerszynski, Bronislaw and Wynne, Brian (eds), *Risk, Environment and Modernity: Towards a New Ecology*, London, Sage, 44–83.

Wynne, Brian (1996b), 'Misunderstood Misunderstandings: Social Identities and Public Uptake of Science', in Irwin, Alan and Wynne, Brian (eds), *Misunderstanding Science?: The Public Reconstruction of Science and Technology*, Cambridge University Press, 19–44.

Wynne, Brian (2003), 'Seasick on the Third Wave? Subverting the Hegemony of Propositionalism', *Social Studies of Science*, 33 (3), 401–17.

Yearley, Steven (1991), *The Green Case: A Sociology of Environmental Arguments, Issues and Politics*, London, HarperCollins.

Yearley, Steven (1996), *Sociology, Environmentalism, Globalization*, London, Sage.

Young, Robert (1969), 'Malthus and the Evolutionists', *Past and Present*, 43, 109–45.

Young, Robert (1971), 'Darwin's Metaphor: Does Nature Select?', *Monist*, 55, 442–503.

Young, Robert (1972), 'The Historiographic and Ideological Contexts of the Nineteenth-Century Debate on Man's Place in Nature', in Tiech, M. and Young, R. M. (eds), *Changing Perspectives in the History of Science: Essays in Honour of Joseph Needham*, London, Heinemann, 344–438.

Zeitlyn, David, Bex, Jane and David, Matthew (1997), 'Cultural and Technical Networks: A Qualitative Approach', *Education for Information*, 15 (4), 351–61.

Zeitlyn, David, Bex, Jane and David, Matthew (1998), 'Access Denied: The Politics of New Communications Media', *Telematics and Informatics*, 15 (3), 219–30.

Zeitlyn, David, David, Matthew and Bex, Jane (1999), *Knowledge Lost in Information*, London, British Humanities Press.

Zucherman, Harriet and Cole, Jonathan (1975), 'Women in American Science', *Minerva*, 13 (Spring), 82–102.

# Author Index

# Subject Index